T0320863

Deploying Feminism

BRIDGING THE GAP

Series Editors
James Goldgeier
Bruce Jentleson
Steven Weber

Deploying Feminism

The Role of Gender in NATO Military Operations

STÉFANIE VON HLATKY

OXFORD
UNIVERSITY PRESS

OXFORD
UNIVERSITY PRESS

Oxford University Press is a department of the University of Oxford. It furthers
the University's objective of excellence in research, scholarship, and education
by publishing worldwide. Oxford is a registered trade mark of Oxford University
Press in the UK and certain other countries.

Published in the United States of America by Oxford University Press
198 Madison Avenue, New York, NY 10016, United States of America.

Library of Congress Cataloging-in-Publication Data
Names: von Hlatky, Stéfanie, 1982- author.
Title: Deploying feminism : the role of gender in NATO military operations / Stéfanie von Hlatky.
Other titles: Role of gender in NATO military operations
Description: New York, NY : Oxford University Press, [2023] |
Series: Bridging the gap series | Includes bibliographical references and index.
Identifiers: LCCN 2022027297 (print) | LCCN 2022027298 (ebook) |
ISBN 9780197653524 (hardback) | ISBN 9780197653548 (epub) |
ISBN 9780197653531 | ISBN 9780197653555
Subjects: LCSH: North Atlantic Treaty Organization—Armed Forces—Women. |
Western countries—Armed Forces—Women. | Iraq War, 2003-2011—Women. |
Kosovo War, 1998–1999—Women. | Women and the military—Western countries. |
Gender mainstreaming—Western countries.
Classification: LCC UA646.3 .V64 2022 (print) | LCC UA646.3 (ebook) |
DDC 355/.031091821—dc23/eng/20220706
LC record available at https://lccn.loc.gov/2022027297
LC ebook record available at https://lccn.loc.gov/2022027298

DOI: 10.1093/oso/9780197653524.001.0001

1 3 5 7 9 8 6 4 2

Printed by Sheridan Books, Inc., United States of America

To my mother,
Kristina

Contents

Figures

Tables

Preface

I encountered the topic of gender in military operations while doing research on alliance politics, during a visit to the NATO headquarters in Brussels, back in 2009. It is during that visit that I first noticed that the Women, Peace and Security (WPS) agenda was gaining traction at NATO. I paused to ask myself if a military alliance could have feminist inclinations. The military's version of feminism is admittedly different from the feminism of scholars or civil society. NATO's policies and action plans on WPS have focused on integrating a gender perspective in its core tasks, namely collective defense, crisis management, and cooperative security, in addition to increasing the representation and participation of women in NATO's structures and operations. It more recently ushered in new policy guidance on sexual exploitation and abuse and conflict-related sexual violence. As part of this process, the narrative was about promoting gender equality, but the practical consideration became operational effectiveness. To illustrate, I was struck in particular by a commander's handbook about female engagement teams, which specified that women soldiers would have an easier time talking to male adolescents, who would be eager to chat women up, revealing valuable intelligence in the process. To get closer to a feminist interpretation, one would instead need to ask how prioritizing gender equality outcomes might lead to adaptations in operational planning.

NATO did not initiate this gender turn in international security. The United Nations (UN) spearheaded these changes by adopting Security Council Resolution 1325 in 2000. It institutionalized the principle that, in order to achieve lasting peace, women's needs and experiences should be better accounted for in both conflict resolution and peace processes. These norms questioned why women have not been represented and heard in matters of international security when they are half of the population. Feminists have been asking *where are the women* for decades, but the UN took a real step forward in 2000, following sustained activism and pressure from civil society. There is still a long way to go, but I hope this book can contribute to our collective understanding of WPS and why it is important to scrutinize its implementation.

This book was a labor of love, and it was a marathon, not a sprint. I could not have completed the journey without my students, colleagues, friends, and family. They cheered me on at every milestone. I would like to thank all of the wonderful people who contributed to this project, starting with Meaghan Shoemaker, Sara Greco, Jeffrey Rice, Lindsay Coombs, Thomas Hughes, Claire Gummo, Jacob Townsend, Andréanne Lacoursière, Marianne Bouchard, Charlotte Duval-Lantoine, Bibi Imre-Milei, Morgan Fox, Heni Pupco, Hannah Hollander, Naomie Healey-Greene, and Charlie Blatt. I would also like to thank Heidi Hardt, a close friend and colleague. It is with her that I first tried to make sense of NATO's gender policies, with a grant from the NATO Science for Peace and Security Programme. Heidi, along with Meaghan Shoemaker, Steve Saideman, Chad Pillai, Trevor Teller and Colin Farrelly, provided valuable comments on drafts of the manuscript. The anonymous peer reviewers were extremely generous with their feedback too, even as these reviewer reports had to be submitted during the pandemic. I am also grateful for the support of Kerry Buck, Mary Pierre-Wade, Greg Smith, Jean-Marc Lanthier, Christine Whitecross, Lise Bourgon, Magda Dvorakova, Alan Okros, Darlene Quinn, Bradley Orchard, Stephen Hanson, and Jan van der Felsen. While writing this book, I have benefited tremendously from the insights and advice of Gaëlle Rivard-Piché, Marie-Joëlle Zahar, Sarah-Myriam Martin-Brûlé, and Maya Eichler. I want to thank everyone at the Centre for International and Defence Policy (especially Maureen Bartram and Christian Breede) for ongoing support, as well as the Centre for International Peace and Security Studies at McGill University for welcoming me during my sabbatical, which is when I did the bulk of the fieldwork and writing. Finally, I received considerable financial support from my Canada Research Chair (Tier 2) in Gender, Security, and the Armed Forces; NATO; Queen's University; the Social Sciences and Humanities Research Council; the Government of Ontario; and the Canadian Department of National Defence for my fieldwork and student training activities. I am very proud that this book is part of the Bridging the Gap series at Oxford University Press. I firmly believe that a commitment to academic scholarship can inform policy innovation but only if we are mindful in connecting the two, a commitment I know I share with the co-editors of this series.

As with my previous projects, I leaned on my family quite a bit to see this through. I am grateful most of all to my husband Philippe Lacoursière, who was strong on the home front with our sons Ian and Zac while I flew around the world to complete the research for this book. We have fantastic friends and family we can always count on to keep us in good spirits. I am dedicating this book to my mother, Kristina von Hlatky, who has always been an exceptional role model.

Acronyms

ACO	Allied Command Operations
ACT	Allied Command Transformation
AOR	area of responsibility
CAF	Canadian Armed Forces
CIG	Commander's Initiative Group
CIMIC	civil–military cooperation
CJTF-OIR	Combined Joint Task Force–Operation Inherent Resolve
CONOPS	Concept of Operations
CMX	Crisis Management Exercise
CST	Cultural Support Team
eFP	enhanced forward presence
EOD	explosive ordnance disposal
ETAT	embedded training and advisory team
EULEX	European Union Rule of Law Mission in Kosovo
FET	female engagement team
FOM	freedom of movement
FPU	force protection unit
GENAD	gender advisor
GFP	gender focal point
HQ	Headquarters
IR	international relations
ISAF	International Security and Assistance Force
JFC	Joint Forces Command
KFOR	Kosovo Force
KLA	Kosovo Liberation Army
KLE	key leader engagement
KSF	Kosovo Security Forces
KTRBN	KFOR Tactical Reserve Battalion
LEGAD	legal advisor
LMT	liaison and monitoring team
MNBG	multinational battlegroup
MOD	Ministry of Defense
MSU	multinational specialized unit
MTT	mobile training team
NAC	North Atlantic Council

NAP	national action plan
NATO	North Atlantic Treaty Organization
NCGP	NATO Committee on Gender Perspectives
NCO	non-commissioned officer
NFIU	NATO Force Integration Unit
NGO	non-governmental organization
NMI	NATO Mission in Iraq
OSCE	Organization for Security and Co-operation in Europe
PAO	public affairs officer
PDD	Public Diplomacy Division
POLAD	political advisor
SACEUR	supreme Allied commander Europe
SASE	secure and safe environment
SHAPE	Supreme Headquarters Allied Powers Europe
SR	special representative
SSR	security sector reform
UN	United Nations
UNESCO	UN Educational, Scientific and Cultural Organization
UNMIK	United Nations Mission in Kosovo
UNSCR	United Nations Security Council Resolution
WPS	Women, Peace and Security

1

Introduction

The Role of Gender in NATO Military Operations

In the US Army *Commander's Guide to Female Engagement Teams* (FETs), the military makes the case for how the presence of women on operations can enhance operational effectiveness: "Using female Soldiers to interact with local Afghan civilians may be the best kept secret weapon available to the brigade combat team . . . to gain acceptance and information from the local civilian population."[1] The guide was developed to support American and NATO efforts in Afghanistan. The underlying assumption in the guide is that Afghan men will not find women in uniform as intimidating to talk to when compared to their male counterparts, that local men (and adolescent boys especially) may even want to impress female soldiers through these interactions, and that female soldiers ask different questions, which may benefit information gathering.[2]

On the dusty battlefields of Afghanistan and Iraq, paying attention to gender roles both within the armed forces and across theaters of operation became a military asset for NATO and coalition forces, shedding light on a persistent capability gap: women.[3] In those missions, cultural norms precluded male troops from kicking down the door of a hostile compound without also having women as part of the unit to search and interrogate the female inhabitants. Female soldiers, then, were performing to the same standard as men but also taking on a particular gender role when an operation called for it. In Western democracies, military leaders have been trained to highlight stories about how women in the armed forces improve operational effectiveness. Military public affairs showcase pictures of women soldiers interacting with local women and children, imagery which was on full display during the 2021 evacuation of Kabul and that NATO leveraged for public diplomacy purposes throughout its engagement. Yet, military organizations only think through a gendered lens when they have to; it is not part of their DNA.[4]

Deploying Feminism. Stéfanie von Hlatky, Oxford University Press. © Oxford University Press 2023.
DOI: 10.1093/oso/9780197653524.003.0001

Militaries have turned to women when they needed more people (i.e., *manpower* shortages), when their legitimacy as national institutions was called into question because of court cases, and/or when deploying women in operations served specific mission tasks, such as searching other women at checkpoints. Even in the 1990s, before 9/11 and the beginning of operations in Afghanistan, United Nations (UN) and NATO peacekeeping operations in the Balkans called for the use of a gendered lens to make more accurate assessments of the battlespace. The prevalence of wartime sexual violence and a greater focus on human security after the end of the Cold War redefined the parameters of conflict resolution. This book updates the discussion on the role of gender in military operations by asking why and how it matters in the NATO context. Drawing from original fieldwork across NATO missions in Kosovo, Iraq, and the Baltic region, the book's line of inquiry questions the progressive facade that paying attention to gender has garnered in the military.

Deploying Feminism might seem like a deliberately provocative title, but it draws attention to the militarization of global norms that were originally intended to advance gender equality.[5] In the military domain, these norms find their endorsement in the Women, Peace and Security (WPS) agenda, a series of UN resolutions that were adopted to account for the gendered nature of conflict. I argue that, in the process of implementation, armed forces have interpreted this agenda with a predominant focus on the gender composition of the armed forces and on the principles that guide operational performance. Indeed, there are two main mechanisms by which these norms are militarized when armed forces are tasked with making their operational plans a reality. The first mechanism employed by military forces consists of presenting women as force multipliers on the basis of gender considerations, as per the previous example from Afghanistan where women are referred to as a "secret weapon." The second mechanism consists of leveraging gender-based analysis to improve mission outcomes, which can be done by men or women. There are other ways by which WPS principles are affecting military operations, like placing a greater focus on conflict-related sexual violence or preventing sexual exploitation and abuse; but they are secondary as areas of operational focus, especially for NATO. While more and more military institutions are adopting WPS norms and ostensibly subscribing to the feminist ideas that propelled the creation of these norms, the process of translating them into military practice distorts their original intent, what I refer to as *norm distortion*. I define norm distortion as a mechanism by which a norm's original meaning is transformed in the process of its implementation. In practice, then, the military rationale and narrative underpinning the WPS agenda are profoundly rooted in a single, overarching concern: operational effectiveness.

The practices described in this book are consistent with a particular type of feminism that has flourished in security and defense institutions; it is a type of feminism that is not anti-military but instead open to the idea that military institutions can act as agents of progressive change.[6] British academic and feminist activist Cynthia Cockburn has deplored this shift, commenting on how WPS norms, once recognized as a global feminist victory, have been diverted:

> It was "our" achievement. It was "our" project and "our" success. Yet the more energetically we push for its implementation, the more we see its limitations. Worse, we realize how it can be used for ends quite contrary to those we intended. In this respect, NATO is a thought-provoking case. No. . . . more than that, it's an enraging example of how good feminist work can be manipulated by a patriarchal and militarist institution.[7]

While the adoption of Resolution 1325 and the launch of the WPS agenda were initially seen as feminist achievements, the agenda was subsequently implemented in ways that fueled cynicism.[8] NATO's adoption of the WPS agenda was not done in consultation with civil society; it was packaged by NATO for NATO and tailored to the pursuit of its own goals.[9] As Shepherd has perhaps best put it, feminists criticize the WPS agenda for making war "safe for women" rather than challenging military entrenchment in the way the international community approaches conflict resolution.[10]

Deploying Feminism, with its oxymoronic undertones, illustrates the major shift that has occurred in military institutions. Most prevalent within Western armed forces, but certainly visible elsewhere, the objections about including women in the military on the basis that it would undermine operational effectiveness have been replaced by the opposite argument: that women improve operational effectiveness because of the gendered dynamics of war. If you have seen the movie *Whiskey Tango Foxtrot*, you may recall that Tina Fey's character, a journalist reporting from Afghanistan, gained valuable information about the destruction of a well after talking to Afghan women in a village, information that was not accessible to male soldiers patrolling the area.[11] In this instance, although the soldiers are learning a valuable lesson about their operating environment, the local women are no better off. Yet, this is an example of the kind of gender-based epiphany that is being embedded into military training.

One of the key historical reference points within those trainings is invariably UN Security Council Resolution 1325, the resolution that launched the WPS agenda. A core message of the agenda is to increase the participation of women during all phases of conflict so that women have a greater voice in conflict prevention, conflict resolution, and post-conflict reconstruction. In terms of military considerations, the resolution also stressed the importance of recognizing that women, men, boys, and girls all experience conflict differently, which has implications for operational planning and the conduct of missions.[12] Finally, gender-based violence is recognized as a reality of war, leading the UN and national governments to formulate guidelines about how sexual violence should be addressed in conflict and how armed forces can better train to respond to such situations. The adoption of the WPS agenda facilitated the national and global institutionalization of terminology in support of norms on gender and conflict. Indeed, since the adoption of Resolution 1325, many member states have adopted their own national action plans (NAPs) to improve the gender balance within their security organizations, including the armed forces, as well as to include gender-aware programming as part of their domestic or international policies.[13]

Governments and international organizations have even been adopting the language of feminism overtly, through the pursuit of feminist foreign policies, drawing a link between more inclusive societies and international stability.[14] Since civilian bodies often task the armed forces with implementing these policies on the ground, especially when aid agencies and diplomats have limited access due to deteriorating security conditions, commanders have had to interpret how this fits into their military lines of effort. The military is often seen as designed to "kill people and break things," but increasingly, its tasks have demanded a more rigorous analysis of the human terrain, meaning the communities within which soldiers operate.[15] *Deploying Feminism* examines this normative revolution in military affairs, which posits that gender awareness has become crucial to all missions. This is how feminist ideas have been militarized.

This book thus analyzes military activities that reference WPS norms, with a focus on NATO military operations. If the military seems like an unlikely candidate to be at the forefront of this normative shift, it has nonetheless been one of the primary agents of change, in the context of operational deployments. Ultimately, troops are trained to follow orders. But what happens when these orders clash with the way they have been indoctrinated in the military? Learning gender-based analysis, for example, is not yet part of basic training. Moreover, a common thread across the armed forces of Western democracies is the problematic ways in which women have been integrated into militaries. If gender integration is still a work in progress within the military, how can the armed forces be asked to promote greater gender equality when they are deployed in other countries? Although women may now face fewer professional barriers when contemplating military service, gender dynamics within armed forces are still fraught.[16]

In parallel to the gender integration debate, there are greater calls for armed forces to perform gender mainstreaming as part of strategic planning and to put more women on the front lines based on an operational rationale. These ideas have even been formalized in allied doctrine. Specifically, NATO's Bi-Strategic Command Directive 040-001 urges the military to engage in gender mainstreaming, defined as "a strategy used to achieve gender equality by assessing the implications for women and men of any planned action, in all areas and at all levels, in order to assure that the concerns and experiences of both sexes are taken into account."[17] This directive is to be achieved, in part, by having more female personnel deployed as part of NATO operations: "internal aspects including measures to remove barriers for the active participation of women in relation to the execution of operations and missions must be emphasized."[18] Through detailed case studies of NATO missions in the Baltics, Iraq, and Kosovo, this book shows that women's near absence in those missions has inhibited gender mainstreaming efforts. Bluntly put, it is hard for an organization that displays so little diversity to consider a diversity of views when carrying out its work abroad.

The International Policy Context: Gender on the World Stage

The UN, through the 1995 Beijing conference and the adoption of UN Security Council Resolution (UNSCR) 1325, recognized that women's greater participation and gender mainstreaming could enhance our understanding of contemporary conflicts and improve international responses. Feminist engagement through the UN World Conferences on Women and Human Rights and in the lead-up to the adoption of UNSCR 1325 created space for non-governmental organizations (NGOs) and women's groups to shape these emerging international standards.[19] A major achievement of transnational feminist activism was to make the topic of women and armed conflict more visible as part of the Beijing platform in 1995. This was an important milestone in terms of engaging members of the UN Security Council, whereby women from conflict zones were invited to provide testimony, influencing the proceedings tied to UNSCR 1325.[20] Beyond the activism of feminist advocates and NGOs, celebrity diplomacy also bolstered the case for WPS. At the UN, actor Emma Watson has been advocating on behalf of the #HeForShe campaign, designed to make men stakeholders on the road to gender equality and to pitch gender equality as a human rights issue, rather than a women's issue.[21] Celebrity diplomacy built on this momentum, including Angelina Jolie teaming up with NATO's secretary-general, Jens Stoltenberg, to pen an op-ed in 2017 titled "Why NATO Must Defend Women's Rights."[22]

Governments have also taken up the call by adopting WPS NAPs of their own, reappropriating the language set out in UNSCR 1325 and sister resolutions. In these plans, governments introduce policies meant to increase the representation of women in the foreign service, defense, intelligence, and law enforcement and assess general compliance with WPS resolutions through various performance indicators, like how much aid money goes to programs supporting women and girls or how many people are trained in gender analysis. Some states have gone further and have placed these international commitments at the center of their foreign policy.[23] Sweden was the first to declare it would pursue a feminist foreign policy, followed by Canada, France, Mexico, and Luxembourg. Released in 2015, Sweden's foreign policy statement's primary message was unequivocal:

Equality between women and men is a fundamental aim of Swedish foreign policy. Ensuring that women and girls can enjoy their fundamental human rights is both a duty within the framework of our international commitments, and a prerequisite for reaching Sweden's broader foreign policy goals on peace, and security and sustainable development.[24]

In sum, international security organizations like the UN and NATO, along with governments and NGOs, have contributed to a global dialogue that has redefined norms about gender and conflict. These norms are codified in successive UN Security Council resolutions that highlight (1) the need to include more women in peace processes, (2) the perpetration of gender-based violence during war, (3) the underrepresentation of women as peacekeepers, and (4) the need for greater diversity at all levels of governance to respond to international security challenges.[25] Measuring success at both the domestic and international levels has been decisively output-driven. The NGO community, which performs an important external monitoring function, has decried the slow pace of progress, which signals that conventional metrics are insufficient to assess how the WPS agenda is improving gender equality. Efforts have been heavily concentrated on increasing the representation of women in the security realm and increasing gender awareness more broadly, indicators that are easy to track and measure but do not fully capture the pace of progress in terms of improving gender equality and sustainable security outcomes.

Norms and Military Practices

The preceding sections outlined the policy trajectory of WPS norms in military contexts, which have in practice focused more narrowly on women's participation and including gender analysis in military thinking. After their adoption by organizations like the UN and NATO, these norms have influenced military practices and have been influenced by them to the point of distortion. Norm distortion, as alluded to previously, is the mechanism by which armed forces interpret WPS norms through the prism of their own military culture, which then changes the originally intended meaning of those norms. The main idea is that international norms are diffused through communities of practice (i.e., governments, international organizations, armed forces, civil society organizations, and scholars) that share the same policy space despite their distinct professional backgrounds.[26] While the actors participate in ascribing meaning to these norms, the process by which these norms are implemented and who is in the lead when these norms are put into action are just as influential. Thinking back to the adoption of UNSCR 1325, which helped institutionalize norms of gender equality at the UN, we can understand that in conflict settings the most visible manifestations of these commitments are troops which carry out broad mandates of conflict resolution, capacity building, and peace support operations. In this context, military actors have taken WPS norms in stride, with perhaps some mild grumbling, and carried on with their day-to-day business.

When comparing different countries' development assistance budgets with defense budgets, one can easily understand how the WPS agenda can become militarized. The power asymmetries between military organizations, the foreign service and development agencies, contribute to how gender equality principles, the original impetus behind the WPS agenda, become subsumed by the practice of using gender analysis to improve operational effectiveness. While the claim that militaries instrumentalize WPS norms in support of warfighting and other militaristic tasks is well established in the feminist international relations (IR) literature, the mechanism presented in this book is novel in that it views the process of norm distortion as being entrenched in a principal–agent problem.[27] Militaries have been delegated authority to implement the WPS agenda, and, as such, much gets lost in translation when these strategic directives are converted into operational guidance and then tactical action.[28]

My argument on the distortion of WPS norms helps explain prevailing narratives surrounding the role of women in military operations, whereby mission outcomes are said to be improved by their very presence. While there has been a strong focus on the participation of women in the military, the incorporation of gender considerations within doctrine, military training, operational planning, and missions has evolved in parallel. In other words, predominantly male organizations are experimenting with gender mainstreaming, integrating a gendered lens to their strategic, operational, and tactical tasks in the pursuit of greater operational effectiveness.

To recap, norm distortion is thus a process by which institutionalized norms adopted by a principal (like NATO) are redefined by one of its agents (the military) in a way that is in tension with its original purpose or, more forcefully, that changes the original purpose of the introduced norm. This phenomenon happens when certain actors are overrepresented in given spaces. In the present analysis, deployed military forces are the dominant actors in volatile security environments (compared to civilians) since they deploy with more personnel, money, and resources. Moreover, governments and international organizations (the principals) enable norm distortion by implicitly or explicitly accepting the norm's misinterpretation, or redefinition, instead of tightening their oversight or providing the military with incentives to do things differently. In fact, presenting WPS through the lens of operational effectiveness is often portrayed as a way to get military buy-in. This can certainly be seen as co-optation, but it is not necessarily nefarious.

This process happens directly and indirectly. Given well-ingrained operational planning processes, implementation of any new guideline happens almost by default because military planning is routinized. Militaries have their orders and get on with it, but it does not mean there is automatic organizational buy-in. In fact, the way gender concepts have been introduced in the NATO context demonstrates that the argument on operational effectiveness was explicitly favored over the promotion of gender equality principles to avoid resistance from NATO officials.[29] These coping mechanisms contribute to norm distortion, but these dynamics also become self-perpetuating the further away one gets from NATO headquarters: from the strategic level down to the tactical-level interactions because there are principals and agents all the way down. Armed forces are hierarchical and institutionalized organizations; they are part of the government bureaucracy and must translate political and strategic directives into military action. It is during this implementation process that the initial intent of policies gets distorted and further militarized.

This problem is compounded by the lack of military training and education on gender at critical career milestones, the appointment of gender focal points and gender advisors who have a wealth of operational experience but no prior exposure to the role, and gender analysis that is outwardly focused and that does not scrutinize professional practices within the military (e.g., the different experiences of women and men throughout their military careers). The outcome is the overall militarization of gender to serve operational effectiveness, rather than gender equality goals, because global norms on gender ultimately leave military culture untouched. The scholarly literature has picked up on some of these themes and is fairly vocal in its criticism of the WPS agenda and its implementation.

Scholarly Debates and the WPS Agenda

Scholarly debates on the WPS agenda, norms, and civil–military relations have all influenced the core argument of this book, namely that when WPS norms are implemented by military organizations, they are distorted from their intended purpose and made to serve operational effectiveness above all else. Because feminism has multiple and contested meanings, the pursuit of gender equality on a global scale is not clear-cut. Similarly, as WPS norms travel and are diffused, they do not have a fixed meaning upon which we can measure the extent of norm distortion. Definitional clarity is thus key to establish the scope conditions of this endeavor: the norms in question here refer to norms on gender in the context of peace and security, which are primarily, but not exclusively, being promoted under the banner of the WPS agenda. To understand the militarization of gender equality principles by national armed forces and international organizations, I draw from feminist IR and civil–military relations scholarship, as well as liberal and constructivist work on norm diffusion.[30]

WPS scholarship is mostly anchored within the feminist IR literature and accommodates eclectic perspectives and methodological approaches.[31] Beyond the academic literature, there are many reports from the policy community and civil society organizations that monitor the implementation of the WPS agenda at the UN, within regional organizations, and across member states that have adopted NAPs. The literature on the WPS agenda is a reflection of an ongoing conversation between the world of academic research and more policy-oriented discussions on gender and security.

This literature allows for a general examination of WPS discourses, resolutions, and institutional implementation. It comments on the evolution of the WPS agenda, the transnational advocacy involved, and the tensions that have emerged as gender equality ideals have been molded to fit the existing goals of international organizations.[32] In other words, efforts to "mainstream" gender equality principles within international policymaking have been met with much criticism from academia and civil society. The literature surveys the different issue areas embodied by the WPS agenda, which at times examines its more formal four pillars of participation, protection, prevention, as well as relief and recovery. In terms of more traditional areas of international policy, the literature intersects with discussions on diplomacy, development, peacekeeping, and other types of military intervention.[33]

On the topic of WPS implementation, Laura Shepherd's work has been particularly influential. She has concluded that certain themes, like conflict resolution, peace processes, and sexual violence, have received more attention than others, which may ultimately mirror the priorities of influential UNSC members.[34] The literature features national-level WPS implementation processes, with a heavy focus on the role of NAPs. NAPs vary greatly based on geographical location. For many authors, the militarization of gender relates to colonialism because it reinforces hierarchies between the Global North and Global South.[35] To illustrate, Global North countries tend to have NAPs that are externally focused, meaning that they center around gender inequality outside of their borders, in conflict-affected areas where militarized solutions are often privileged.[36] In this manner, countries such as Canada, the United States, and the United Kingdom establish themselves as global champions of gender equality without problematizing their own position within global relations of power that go on to reproduce patterns of gender inequality.[37] In the NATO context, Matthew Hurley has noted that NATO reproduces essentializing conceptions of gender when showcasing how applying a "gender perspective" occurred in Afghanistan.[38] By contrast, countries in the Global South tend to have more internally focused NAPs, introducing initiatives that focus on promoting gender equality at home rather than abroad.

Using the term *feminism* in the title of the book invokes the way it is used in government and military contexts. In scholarly debates, there are visible tensions between different strands of feminism, and this translates into challenges when it comes to seeking engagement with organizations like NATO, a military alliance.[39] But these academic debates in the literature have practical ramifications.[40] Indeed, the feminist undercurrents that are present in the WPS agenda are closest to the standpoint feminist approach, which assumes that differences in gender translate into different lived experiences in conflict settings.[41] Standpoint feminism, therefore, allows for a brand of feminism which *could* work with or within the military establishment in adapting their operational assessments to take into account those lived experiences, even if these fall short of recognizing intersectional manifestations of oppression.[42]

A standpoint feminist view, applied to female representation in national armed forces, would emphasize different models of recruitment, pushing for gender-based reforms that focus on *equivalency* instead of strict *equality*. Equivalency "acknowledges without prejudice the differences of physical biology and socially constructed gender in sentient individuals enacting personal agency and . . . emphasizing maximization of the contributing qualities an individual brings to the exchange."[43] Some authors have leveraged women soldiers' own lived experience and standpoint, arguing that the military can empower women's voices by offering them a unique platform for action.[44]

The idea of encouraging greater women's participation by demonstrating their military effectiveness or comparative advantages on the battlefield is an extension of this logic.[45] These types of arguments in support of gender integration are pitched as a win–win whereby diversity is an antidote to discriminatory practices but also brings benefits to the military by broadening the perspectives available to it.[46] This kind of narrative has been picked up at NATO too, with the secretary-general recently professing that "diverse armed forces are strong armed forces."[47] This argument is used in the context of UN peacekeeping, where women are seen as playing a positive role engaging with citizens of local communities, even if they make up less than 5% of military personnel.[48] The UN showcases the positive role female peacekeepers have on the ground, based on four core arguments: 1) by their very presence, women reduce conflict and confrontation; 2) female peacekeepers provide reassurance for women and children in conflict-affected communities; 3) this translates into greater attention paid to local women's needs; 4) the presence of women among a peacekeeping force makes peacekeepers more approachable in general.[49]

Some scholars, like Claire Duncanson, have also focused on the role of male peacekeepers in challenging "traditional gender dichotomies" by tempering the warrior model of soldiering.[50] Similarly, Paul Higate and Marsha Henry acknowledge that "peacekeeping can also give rise to 'positive' militarized masculinities, when constructed on notions of faith, restraint and discipline."[51] This is further nuanced in Sandra Whitworth's work, which shows the tensions between the peacekeeping model, which promotes the idea of a "benign soldier," and the hypermasculinity and violence that prevail in the way soldiers are socialized and trained.[52]

Official feminist discourses, meaning the narratives driven by government and military organizations, are also influenced by liberal feminist ideas. The liberal feminist approach focuses on gender representation goals as a priority and does not necessarily problematize the process of gender identity construction and patriarchal structures of power. Liberal feminist ideas are compatible with the drive for transformation and change through diversity strategies that are pursued by international organizations, governments, and armed forces. For example, Duncanson points out how the liberal feminist movement pushed for the institutionalization of women's empowerment in international forums, including the WPS agenda.[53] Similarly Sjoberg refers to "feminist liberalism" as "interested in including women in the legal and social structures of the international arena."[54] This advocacy work pulls from instrumentalist arguments that claim "women are the untapped resource."[55] Liberal feminism has been criticized for "being too focused on women becoming like men . . . [and overlooking] such differences as a person's race, socioeconomic status, and sexual orientation, therefore not embodying intersectionality."[56] A policy prescription from liberal feminists would therefore be that "an increase in the number of women in militaries will change the institution's fundamentally masculine dynamics," despite the lack of evidence that proves this.[57] Women gaining "the right to fight," then, is very much in line with liberal feminism, which pushes for greater women's participation in traditionally male spheres.[58]

By contrast, more critical approaches to feminist scholarship, which includes radical and Marxist feminist thinking, tend to reject the notion of transformation from within by highlighting the fundamental incompatibility of the armed forces with the feminist project.[59] Militarized masculinity, in other words, is at odds with the pursuit of gender equality.[60] For example, as long as the military enterprise is characterized by hegemonic or toxic masculinities that exclude and/or harm women and other marginalized groups on the basis of gender, race, or ethnicity, this approach does not view the integration of women in the armed forces as desirable at all.[61] To the contrary, this logic takes us in the opposite direction and envisions eliminating national armed forces based on the belief that, at best, their very presence incites conflict and, at worst, militaries are institutions of exclusion and oppression. Here, feminist solutions in support of conflict resolution require a fundamental rethinking of how foreign and defense policy decisions are made.[62] By extension, then, these feminist approaches have been skeptical of gender mainstreaming efforts advanced by the UN and have viewed the WPS agenda as the co-optation of advocacy efforts to advance women's rights.[63]

With these contributions from the literature in mind, this book pays close attention to the prevailing narratives tied to the promotion of the WPS agenda. The literature indicates that more nuance is needed in how the gendered roles of women and men play out in conflict and post-conflict situations.[64] Also, gender is often emphasized in WPS narratives at the expense of other markers of identity, such as race, nationality, religion, and sexuality, among others, which can often form the basis of discriminatory and violent behavior.[65] The topic of gender equality cannot be separated from other sources of inequality and insecurity tied to class, race, and sexuality.[66] At present, a large part of WPS research has been carried out by authors in the United States, Canada, Australia, and western Europe, with more intersectional perspectives becoming increasingly prevalent.[67] There is also a smaller subset of literature that looks more explicitly at the military dimension through NATO. Adopting a military perspective immediately yields important insights in terms of how the global norms embodied by the WPS agenda are then diffused through the prism of a distinct professional culture.

Who is implementing the agenda ultimately influences what is implemented and how.

The second source of theoretical inspiration for the norm distortion argument is principal–agent theory, from the literature on civil–military relations. True to principal–agent theory, a person or group (principal) delegates authority to others (agents), who act on their behalf but not always as the principal intends. The extent to which agents carry out their delegated responsibilities in a way that is consistent with the expectations of the principal is at the heart of research puzzles inspired by the principal–agent framework.[68] This framework can accommodate different theoretical traditions, which my argument on norm distortion seeks to do.[69] In the NATO context, it means that the member states of the alliance are co-principals, represented by their NATO ambassadors within the North Atlantic Council (NAC).[70] Following consensus-based decision-making, the NAC adopts the priorities, policies, and directives that will guide the alliance's activities, many of which are implemented by the armed forces of NATO member states and partners. There are also civilian agents at NATO, who are part of the International Staff and other NATO organizations. In the context of NATO's military operations, NATO delegates significant authority to its military commanders, and civilian representatives' presence and involvement vary from mission to mission. For instance, there was greater civilian involvement in Afghanistan's Resolute Support mission, given the presence of a senior civilian representative, than there is in the Kosovo Force (KFOR), where there is no civilian counterpart to the military commander. The civil–military balance influences how oversight is exercised.

In the field, military commanders interpret the strategic and operational directives they are given and translate these into action. Controlling what military commanders do under a NATO umbrella is easier than in many other militarized principal–agent relationships, given the institutionalized nature of the operational planning process. Still, there are significant differences in terms of how political and strategic-level directives are implemented in the context of multinational operations.[71] Using the principal–agent framework serves to highlight that the amount of discretion commanders have in a NATO context varies by issue. Commanders will be highly constrained when it comes to targeting decisions, for example, but have much looser constraints and oversight when it comes to integrating a gender perspective within their operational orders because WPS considerations are not yet as familiar as, say, the Laws of Armed Conflict.[72] Because norms on WPS and their resulting NATO directives are rather new, they might not have the knowledge to properly oversee the work of their subordinates and may have few incentives to prioritize a gender advisor in their command group as opposed to other special advisors, like legal or political advisors, who are better socialized within military institutions and whose role is better understood. The same can be said of civilians overseeing the work of the military: the rewards and penalties associated with implementing WPS are rather weak, even if the accountability mechanisms are improving.

The third scholarly debate which is central to the book relates to norm adoption and diffusion, popularized by scholars like Finnemore and Sikkink, who break down the life cycle of international norms.[73] Here, the key process is how WPS norms were adapted to the military's norms on operational effectiveness, rather than changing the military's conception of operational effectiveness so that gender equality and human rights become central considerations of military action. Though speaking about norms in the context of Asian regionalism, Amitav Acharya identifies a similar process that he calls *grafting*. He defines it as a "tactic norm entrepreneurs employ to institutionalize a new norm by associating it with a pre-existing norm in the same issue area."[74]

In the NATO case, there are important dynamics at play between the international/regional level and the national level, as norm adoption by NATO has an impact on its member states. The militarization of WPS norms results from military actors interpreting guidance from civilian decision makers when implementing those norms on the ground. The idea that institutionalization of a new norm leads to its reinterpretation is one I build on to introduce the book's central argument about norm distortion. Jeffrey T. Checkel's concept of normative suasion is also instructive here as it illustrates agents attempting to redefine their interests and preferences in light of new norms as a way to internalize "new understandings of appropriateness."[75] What my argument on norm distortion brings to the table is that the way norms are redefined might bring about a reinterpretation of the norm that is in tension with its original meaning or intent, a type of norm contestation that operates through the prism of military culture.[76] The meaning of WPS norms in the NATO context, therefore, is very much influenced by the military's own understanding and reinterpretation of those norms.[77]

There are more scholarly contributions that speak to the socialization process by which norms are adopted and repurposed, but they do not quite get at the different interpretations that can emerge in a single context, as is the case between civilian and military actors, for instance.[78] In an article that I co-authored with Heidi Hardt, we interviewed seventy-one NATO officials and analyzed ninety-seven of NATO's gender guidelines to explain why and how WPS norm implementation differs when comparing the behavior of those working in civilian versus military posts.[79] We argue that the military has a better record of implementation because of its hierarchical organizational culture, its corresponding standard operating procedures, and the connection that previously deployed military officials made between the emerging WPS norms and operational effectiveness.[80] We also demonstrate that NATO prioritizes two objectives in its implementation of WPS norms and corresponding directives: gender balancing (i.e., increasing women's representation) and integrating a gender perspective in operational planning (but not as much in civilian planning). This book builds on this earlier work and proposes the first comprehensive study on gender norms in NATO missions, explaining why norm distortion occurs in the process of translating high-level commitments into tactical actions.

To summarize, this book provides a detailed account of how WPS norms have changed military practices. Governments and international organizations are transforming their practices to recognize the gendered nature of conflict, but missing from existing accounts is how this has affected the military and the tasks it is asked to carry out, from disaster assistance to warfighting. Insights from IR and civil–military relations are helpful to make sense of policy innovation and to understand how military culture shapes routine practices, which may sometimes stall change.[81] The book aims to bridge the scholarly conversations of feminist IR and strategic studies, answering the call of scholars like Laura Sjoberg and Ann Tickner, who have lamented the absence of such a dialogue.[82] While feminist IR uncovers the gendered nature of conflict and war, as well as their depiction in historical accounts and the media, the field of strategic studies tends to focus on a genderless examination of how military force is used to achieve political ends.[83] Recognizing that military culture has remained constant, despite changing demographics, this book brings gender considerations to the fore by comparing NATO operations and how they adapt to new norms of warfare enshrined in allied doctrine to "integrate a gender perspective" (in NATO parlance).

Plan of the Book

I apply my theoretical argument on norm distortion and the militarization of WPS norms to the NATO context, but it applies to other international security organizations that oversee military operations and where civil–military dynamics are present. Nevertheless, although the theory has broader applicability, NATO is still an important test case because civilian–military linkages are dense and there is an integrated military structure for operational coordination. Therefore, it can be assumed that if WPS policies are not well coordinated within NATO, such coordination would prove more difficult in international organizations that have either a broader mandate (like the African Union or European Union) or a more diverse membership (like the UN).[84] As such, NATO is a good place to start to identify the mechanisms of WPS implementation. That being said, findings from this NATO context might be quite different if this theory were to be applied in a UN context. Already in the EU context, scholars have found a greater focus on the equality narrative, as opposed to gender mainstreaming.[85] At the UN, the origins of gender mainstreaming for peace operations are distinct from NATO's, and the composition of the armed forces that carry out UN peacekeeping mandates are from the Global South rather than Western countries. A distinct project comparing different international security organizations' implementation of WPS norms would be a fruitful avenue for future research.

If we look at NATO operations or missions exclusively though, we need to refine the case selection criteria further. NATO runs a range of missions and activities listed on the website and the secretary-general's annual report. While the mission in Afghanistan was NATO's biggest operation, I could not secure approvals to conduct fieldwork there safely. For this reason, I exclude Afghanistan as an operational setting for this study, but I have included all other core missions and activities where there is a land component, given that interacting with local women is such a big part of the military's WPS rationale.[86]

After Afghanistan, the second most important NATO mission is its KFOR with 4,500 military personnel. NATO deployed to Kosovo in 1999 and, following the end of the airstrikes, established a stabilizing presence with KFOR.[87] NATO renewed its commitment when Kosovo became independent in 2008. UN Resolution 1244 governs KFOR's activities, which revolve primarily around tasks ranging from providing security during elections to training and capacity building with national security forces. KFOR is best described as a peace operation and includes four primary objectives: "contribute to a safe and secure environment; support and coordinate the international humanitarian effort and civil presence; support the development of a stable, democratic, multi-ethnic and peaceful Kosovo; support the development of the Kosovo Security Force."[88] This translates into a broad range of military tasks, from crowd and riot control to infantry tasks, training, and liaising with local and international partners. KFOR troops are meant to secure the environment and ensure the freedom of movement of all communities. The communications element of the mission is also very important, to maintain support for the NATO presence. I conducted fifteen interviews with KFOR personnel and toured the bases, facilities, and areas where mission tasks are carried out.

Further, the case study analysis includes the battlegroups in the Baltics and Poland, prior to Russia's invasion of Ukraine, on February 24, 2022. While these battlegroups were not run by NATO's integrated military command, like KFOR and the NATO Mission in Iraq (NMI), they were still under the NATO banner of enhanced forward presence.[89] The original four battlegroups are led by Canada in Latvia, the United Kingdom in Estonia, Germany in Lithuania, and the United States in Poland. These battlegroups are multinational and, at the time of my visit, had a total of seventeen participating NATO countries contributing close to five thousand troops, including the lead nations, or *framework nations*, in NATO parlance.[90] I conducted thirty interviews in Latvia and Lithuania with battlegroup commanders and their personnel. I conducted additional interviews in the capitals, with civilian and military personnel who support the mission but are not working on the bases out of which the battlegroups operate.

The third mission that was selected for comparison is NMI. NATO became a member of the Global Coalition to Defeat ISIS in 2017 and launched NMI in 2018. Under the banner of training and capacity building, NATO performs a number of diverse military tasks. For example, the NATO secretary-general's annual report describes the priorities of the Iraq mission as "countering improvised explosive devices; explosive ordnance disposal and demining; civil–military planning support to operations; reform of the Iraqi security institutions; technical training on Soviet-era equipment maintenance; and military medicine."[91] I conducted fifteen interviews at NMI's Baghdad headquarters and the Operation Inherent Resolve headquarters.

In terms of methods and techniques, I am using comparative case study analysis, where the command structure, civil–military balance, mission tasks, and gender composition vary across the cases. I relied primarily on interviews, using Lee Ann Fujii's relational approach, as well as the analysis of primary documents.[92] Relational interviewing "requires the researcher to become familiar with the interviewee's language or lexicon" and calls on active listening.[93] In relational interviewing, the researcher is focused on learning more about how the participants "make sense of the world by engaging them in dialogue" and "the data emerge from interaction, rather than interrogation. It is particularly well-suited for those that investigate how people construct meaning."[94] I supplemented the fieldwork with interviews at NATO headquarters and Supreme Headquarters Allied Powers Europe, as well as operational-level headquarters in Mons, Belgium, and Naples, Italy. In total, over one hundred interviews were conducted with civilian and military staff during the 2019–2021 period. Additional off-the-record meetings informed my background knowledge on the topic and helped identify the key stakeholders I needed to interview. In choosing participants from this study, I strived for balance in terms of civil–military and gender representation. At the tactical level, I sought out participants from different rank levels and positions.[95]

This book aims to carefully scrutinize the implementation of WPS norms by military organizations, by focusing on the conduct of NATO missions. Chapter 2 delves deeper into the topic of gender and the military, examining both issues of gender representation within armed forces and the integration of gender analysis within military operations. The chapter also addresses the tension between the two goals and concludes that greater participation of women is necessary but not sufficient for gender-aware operations. It also problematizes the claim that women might be better at performing certain military tasks than men, which is one of the arguments made in the debate on gender integration. Chapter 3 provides a thorough description of NATO's processes for operational planning and analyzes the execution of its missions and operations in light of its WPS policies and directives. This chapter breaks down this process from the strategic level to the tactical level and explains how political decisions are translated into military tasks.

Chapters 4, 5, and 6 present the case studies. They focus on NATO's missions in Kosovo, the Baltics, and Iraq respectively, to show how gender considerations are addressed on the ground. The analysis presented in those chapters is based on a mix of fieldwork in those countries as well as interviews in NATO's strategic and operational-level headquarters. They will demonstrate that because gender directives are new and broad, military commanders enjoy considerable latitude in their application. And since gender equality does not fit neatly into how militaries assess mission success, gender directives are put at the service of operational effectiveness. Nevertheless, NATO reporting and accountability mechanisms translate into fairly consistent application by member states, with the caveat that some issue areas remain completely gender-blind. For certain military tasks, like in-mission tactical infantry training, gender policies and directives simply get sidelined as inapplicable. The concluding chapter revisits the argument and findings to engage in a discussion on the practical implications for Western democratic governments and their militaries. It offers recommendations on how to make national armed forces more responsive to important normative shifts about the role of gender in military operations.

Conclusion

Militaries around the world are paying closer attention to gender, both internally, and in terms of the missions they carry out. The central argument of the book proposes that global norms about gender and security have been militarized because the armed forces have been delegated considerable authority in the implementation of WPS norms. The book thus picks up on insights from feminist IR that have focused on the militarization of the WPS agenda.[96] The theoretical story also lines up with principal–agent theory in that the book scrutinizes the process by which militaries have been delegated authority in this space. As I have argued with Heidi Hardt elsewhere, the military very often has first mover advantage when it comes to implementing WPS directives, and this gives it broad discretion when it comes to interpreting gender norms and how they matter within the context of military operations.[97] While our argument zoned in on the interactions of civilian and military officers at NATO headquarters, this book takes a decidedly operational approach to examine how militaries carry out their tasks in mission settings.

The introduction surveyed recent policy developments relative to the inclusion of women in traditionally male spheres and of the growing recognition of the gendered implications of warfare. Describing those changes makes apparent that a normative shift is happening but that there are enduring tensions underlying the gender-based assumptions about military power and the liberal values espoused by some democratic governments and international organizations. Indeed, ideas on gender equality and female leadership have been around for decades, but the military is an organization that has been quite insular when it comes to adapting its culture to the reality of having more women within the ranks. In other words, even with greater diversity, the core of military culture has remained relatively intact. This has implications for other changes, including the process of gender mainstreaming, whereby gender analysis is included in policymaking, operational planning, and missions. The result has been a distortion of the WPS agenda's true purpose. Instead of focusing on promoting greater gender equality, gender considerations have become militarized. This book aims to contribute to our understanding of why the WPS agenda has not yet been transformative in its pursuit of greater gender equality.[98]

The book's contribution is to expand the scope of previous research around NATO's integration of gender in military operations, which tilts heavily toward the mission in Afghanistan and the period prior to 2014 when NATO was less focused on Russia and more focused on promoting its commitment to WPS. Theoretically, while existing scholarship does touch on the militarization of WPS norms, no other work replicates the causal mechanism here, which combines insights from feminist IR, the literature on norms, and civil–military relations.[99] This offers a way to connect previous work that has been published on gender and NATO within the broader literature about how gender equality norms are institutionalized within international security organizations.

2

Gender Wars and Gender in War

In the 1990s, human security emerged as the new lens for understanding contemporary conflict, heavily influencing how states and international organizations responded to conflicts in the Balkans and Africa in particular. The recognition that sexual and gender-based violence is routinely used as a tactic of war and that existing conflict resolution and peacebuilding approaches failed to include women emerged as lessons learned during this initial post–Cold War period. This set the stage for the emergence of Women, Peace and Security (WPS) norms at the United Nations (UN).[1] In the year 2000, a more gender-responsive agenda was tabled with the adoption of UN Security Council Resolution 1325. Women's organizations and feminist scholars participated in the civil society advocacy efforts which led the UN to inaugurate the WPS agenda.[2] More than ever before, the international community made an explicit link between armed conflict and gender equality considerations.

The implementation of WPS norms, however, tells a more complicated story. While feminist ideas inspired this significant normative shift at the UN, deploying these ideas in conflict and post-conflict settings has been delegated, in part, to military organizations that have one goal in mind: operational effectiveness. Armed forces are trained to stay focused on mission objectives and set military tasks, making implementation of new norms almost a given.[3] But what this book argues is that delegating authority to the military means that these norms are interpreted through the prism of military culture. As alluded to in the introductory chapter, I refer to this process as norm distortion, whereby norms adopted by international organizations are repurposed by the agents tasked to carry out the groundwork, in this case, the military. The result is that the pursuit of gender equality goals gets deprioritized in the process, even if a gendered lens is applied in support of military tasks.

This chapter starts with a discussion on the militarization of feminist ideas and explains how this came to be through policy debates and the experiences of two war-intensive decades after 9/11. While WPS norms have influenced

Deploying Feminism. Stéfanie von Hlatky, Oxford University Press. © Oxford University Press 2023.
DOI: 10.1093/oso/9780197653524.003.0002

military organizations, there are palpable tensions we can observe between those norms and traditional military culture, tensions which are most visible in the push to diversify the armed forces and adopt more gender-responsive practices, from training to operations.

The Militarization of Feminism

Feminism is still a controversial, highly charged term. Even in the era of #MeToo and the mass commercialization of feminist ideas, debates about equity, diversity, and inclusion, spanning from gender to race, remain inherently political. Norms about gender are embedded within institutions and culture, making them difficult to change. The most hardened target is perhaps the military, an institution that has evolved by glorifying stereotypical interpretations of masculinity, promoting toughness, aggressiveness, and brazenness. However, the military, as an organization, is not alien to change, even if it does not adapt particularly swiftly. In many democratic countries, including most NATO countries, we are asking militaries to adopt "a feminist vision of peace and security," as Megan Bastick and Claire Duncanson have put it, leading to concerns of militarizing the WPS agenda (and feminism more broadly).[4] If militarization is the process by which these norms become "controlled by, dependent on, or [derive their] value from the military," how does this process manifest itself?[5] Concretely, the militarization of WPS norms leads to two major changes for armed forces. The first is that it diversifies the ranks to make room for more women and underrepresented groups, eliminating harmful behaviors in the process, from sexual misconduct to unconscious biases in recruitment and promotion processes. This is a tall order in the civilian realm, where members of large organizations are not necessarily indoctrinated within a particular culture, but the military is a special case, even if not as unique as it is often made out to be.

The second thing we are asking armed forces to do is to change the way they think. From traditional campaign planning with fairly static depictions of the enemy, there is now an expectation that service members will analyze the contemporary battlespace using a variety of social indicators to understand, for example, an oftentimes deterritorialized, transnational adversary. This includes perfecting one's skills to perform gender analysis as women and men occupy different roles in contemporary conflict situations, with implications for operational planning and mission execution. For example, the rise in female suicide bombers defied previous assumptions about women's roles in conflict, largely relegated to the civilian bystander or victim.[6] Women's ability to avoid detection has increased their lethality in certain cases and has led to more scholars studying this phenomenon and greater attention being paid to the gendered dynamics of terrorism by governments worldwide.[7]

Examples like these have made their way into training packages for the armed forces. In NATO's training about gender in military operations, for example, troops are taught that

> Seeing women exclusively as victims and not as agents of violence can also risk the safety of the civilian population and NATO or NATO-led forces. Female suicide bombers, for example, are now used by multiple non-state actors who exploit the gendered assumptions regarding women's connection to non-violence; using them as suicide bombers who can move more freely on the streets and get through checkpoints easier.[8]

Gender analysis, then, becomes one of the tools through which governments and armed forces mainstream WPS norms into their day-to-day activities, whether those activities happen to be policymaking or warfighting. In a sense, the military is a good candidate to undertake this kind of profound, normative shift precisely because it has doctrine and standard operating procedures to guide its practices. Change the doctrine, change the behavior. On the other hand, military culture has been heavily criticized for condoning toxic manifestations of masculinity and the institutional resistance to external scrutiny of the traditional warfighter ethos.[9] This external pressure has led to removing the professional barriers to women in the military and to acknowledging that contemporary warfare requires skills that amount to more than fighting the enemy.[10] While it might not be realistic to expect the military to do it all—to be humanitarian first responders *and* a highly lethal fighting force—the reality is that the armed forces are being asked to do more, not less, in a security environment plagued by natural disasters and pandemics, as well as non-state and near-peer threats. This certainly contrasts with the role of the armed forces during the Cold War.[11]

Just like in other professional sectors, some argue that more diverse forces will lead to a greater diversity of views, which strengthens the military's ability to respond to a more complex security environment. Others push back on the idea that greater female representation is needed, arguing that everyone (both male and female) can participate in implementing WPS norms or perform gender analysis as part of the professional skill set and that this is a more realistic pathway to change.[12] This book addresses this tension head on by keeping the focus on both diversity within the armed forces and the influence of WPS norms, as embodied by UN Security Council Resolution (UNSCR) 1325, over military practices. Ultimately, the two considerations are intrinsically linked. The implementation of WPS norms implies an awakening to gender analysis, overcoming certain conscious and unconscious biases about gender roles; but this is difficult to do in a professional environment which lacks diversity. People with similar backgrounds tend to have similar biases and blind spots, which is why the conversation on gender awareness and operational outcomes is difficult to separate from the composition of the force and its overall lack of diversity.

In the subsequent sections, it will become all the more obvious that cultures do not emerge in a vacuum. The military has a warrior culture that evolved in an all-male environment. People who have been successful (professionally speaking) in that culture are unlikely to break or reshape that dominant warfighting model, and as such, the WPS agenda very often is made to fit that model. Any discussion of change, therefore, is incomplete without asking the question of who perpetuates that culture and who disrupts it.

A Military Culture of Exclusion

Is the military a unique institution? Few employers today require unlimited liability from their employees. Unlimited liability means that there is an expectation that service members might put their life on the line in the service of their country, but it also has more routine implications, like exposure to physical and mental risks, unparalleled in other professions.[13] The military's uniqueness is often brought up in debates over gender integration in the armed forces. In the United States, excluding women from combat was held up for as long as it was because top general and flag officers were able to make the argument that the armed services are different from the rest of society and that gender integration risked undermining military effectiveness.

Women's uniqueness has also been evoked to support the view that they do not belong in the military. Two arguments have been especially prevalent. The first is that the general population would not be able to stomach women coming home in body bags, while they would be more tolerant of men sacrificing their life for their country. The second argument has to do with women's abilities, especially their physical fitness compared to men, an issue which flares up every time changes are made to the requirements of military physical fitness tests. Megan MacKenzie singles out these types of arguments as enduring tropes in debates over gender integration in the military and the inclusion of women in combat roles.[14]

To be fair, military organizations were not explicitly designed to disadvantage or persecute women. National armed forces have been known to exclude by race, gender, and sexual orientation; and such restrictions, whether we refer to don't ask, don't tell policies or combat exclusion rules, "were designed to perpetuate an all-male preserve and career advantage."[15] Even for White men, the hypermasculine roots of military culture have established, as Christina Jarvis argues, "the dominant model of American masculinity as white and able-bodied [and] also helped create a range of alternate, marginalized masculinities that departed from this norm."[16] The institutionalization of this norm was set through a variety of procedures and practices and was particularly forceful in periods of conscription since compulsory enlistment led to the mass military management of young men. During World War II, the American army issued *Soldiering for Uncle Sam*, a notebook meant to track the measurements of men's chests, biceps, and calves, among other things.[17]

Feminist scholarship captures this reality with the concept of militarized masculinities, demonstrating how the "fusion of men, masculinity and soldiering within militaries has been facilitated by the exclusion of the feminine."[18] Of course, the military's exclusionary practices did not stop there. These practices also had clear implications for marginalized groups, like Black Americans, who were subjected to quotas so that their numbers in the Army would not go over 6%.[19] Units were segregated, and Black servicemen could not command White soldiers until Roosevelt's 1942 Executive Order 9279 to eliminate restrictions on participation and Truman's 1948 Executive Order 9981 to end the practice of segregation in the armed forces.[20] Questions raised about the competence of Black soldiers at the time were repurposed in the debate on women's participation in the armed forces. Though many of the formal barriers to service imposed on women, members of the LGBTQ communities, and people of color were lifted, the hypermasculine ideal has survived; and the remnants of exclusionary policies endure through stereotypes about merit and performance.[21]

Lawmakers and courts have pushed back on the tropes used to keep women out of certain roles, especially the combat arms. To illustrate, the Canadian Armed Forces (CAF) were so resistant to fully integrating women within their ranks that they introduced the Servicewomen in Non-Traditional Environments and Roles project, from 1979 to 1984, to evaluate women's suitability for combat and other occupations from which they were excluded. Even after these trials, when there was no evidence to show that the presence of women undermined operational effectiveness, the CAF maintained that there was "a bona fide occupational requirement" to exclude them.[22] With pressure mounting from the Canadian Human Rights Tribunal and previous developments surrounding the Royal Commission on the Status of Women and then the adoption of the Canadian Charter on Human Rights and Freedoms, the CAF moved on to new trials in 1987, this time specifically to examine the suitability of women in combat roles. The Combat Related Employment of Women trials were short-lived as the chief of the Defence Staff opened up combat roles later that year, finally succumbing to external pressure.

On the road to removing professional barriers to women wanting to serve, we see other tactics to restrict their access emerge, like the imposition of ceilings or caps on servicewomen. In the United States, there was a 2% ceiling on women in the military, and they could not be promoted beyond the rank of lieutenant colonel, policies which were struck down in 1967, thanks to the advocacy of the Defense Advisory Committee on Women in the Services.[23] Other notable discriminatory practices included prohibiting married women from joining the armed forces and terminating the employment of women expecting a child. Military academies in the United States, access to which is important to progress in the leadership track, only became coeducational in 1976.[24] These barriers help explain why there are few female leaders at the top, even in militaries where women make up between 15% and 20% of the force; barriers and discriminatory practices inhibited their professional development and advancement.

Making the Pitch for Diversity: From Boardrooms to the Military

Most Western democracies have all-volunteer, professional armed forces, which means that the military has evolved into a large bureaucracy. Typically, about half of the defense budget goes to pay and support military personnel. As militaries grow, they must recruit and retain personnel and compete with other large organizations to attract talent. One of the arguments most often used by military leaders to promote diversity within their organization is access to a broader talent pool. In other words, why would an organization deny itself the entire pool of available talent by excluding whole categories of people? The distortion of WPS norms occurs when diversity is instrumentalized and used to make the business case for gender integration, rather than to focus on striking down discriminatory practices because they harm people and corrupt the professional culture. As formal processes to diversify the ranks of the military took their course, the need to foster buy-in from military leaders solidified these instrumental narratives about women.

Within that mindset, assessing the comparative merits of men and women began (as shown in a US Defense Department report from the 1970s) weighing in the recruitment needs of the military as a gendered trade-off: "if today's recruiting market is between a high quality female and a low quality male. . . . The average woman available to be recruited is smaller, weighs less, and is physically weaker than the vast majority of male recruits. She is also much brighter, better educated, scores much higher on the aptitude tests and is much less likely to become a disciplinary problem."[25] Instrumentalizing women's participation thus has a long history. While those ideas remained peripheral to the debates on gender integration within the military until much more recently, women's participation is often framed in reference to its utility rather than appealing to rights-based or moral arguments. The argument that women might have unique attributes or qualities when compared to their male peers has also been made in an operational context.[26] The argument about excluding women because it would undermine operational effectiveness was flipped on its head: greater diversity, and the employment of women more specifically, could, in certain cases, enhance operational effectiveness.

Discussions on the comparative advantages of men and women have proliferated in the civilian world too. When scientists review the top traits (referred to as the *Big Five* traits) associated with leadership, such as extraversion and conscientiousness, women perform just as well as men. For other qualities that are increasingly valued for managing staff, such as emotional intelligence and empathy, women tend to perform better.[27] Men have a comparative advantage when it comes to physical aggressiveness, but that is rarely an asset on the job except, some might argue, for the military. Even in the armed forces, the skill set is widening, and any use of physical violence must be carefully calibrated and controlled. The use of unbridled violence runs counter to the laws of armed conflict and has resulted in major stains on the military's reputation. One can think of the 1968 My Lai massacre perpetrated by US troops in South Vietnam; the Somalia affair, which involved Canadian Airborne Regiment soldiers murdering a Somali youth in 1993 during United Taskforce operations; or, more recently, accounts of war crimes being perpetrated by Australian soldiers in Afghanistan, where prisoners, farmers, and civilians were unlawfully killed.[28] These incidents are often explained away as isolated events and the work of a few "bad apples" rather than seen as an extension of militarized masculinity.[29]

Militarized masculinity has more explicitly been addressed in the context of sexual harassment and assault within the armed forces and of sexual exploitation and abuse conducted by deployed troops. This discussion on women's comparative advantages should not obscure the many comparative disadvantages that women in the military may face. Women's presence in organizations where they will represent a token minority can place them at higher risk of sexual harassment. While men also suffer from sexual violence, US studies consistently show that women make 80%–90% of the sexual harassment complaints.[30] In the military, US data shows that close to 70% of women experience sexual harassment on the job, while in civilian organizations, like academia and government, that percentage is 40%–60%.[31] Considering that most women do not disclose or report incidents of sexual harassment, despite suffering the associated costs like stress and depression, these numbers are alarming.[32] In the military, scandals such as Tailhook in the United States resulted in greater scrutiny being placed on the armed forces and the formation of special task forces, surveys on sexual harassment, and external investigations. Sexual misconduct scandals in Australia and Canada have led to calls for cultural change within the armed forces.[33] Toxic and hypermasculine workplace cultures can explain how some environments become permissive of sexual violence, but the underrepresentation of women is also a significant factor.[34] In fact, boosting the presence of women in peace operations, an explicit goal of UNSCR 1325, has been raised as a solution to curtail sexual violence perpetrated by male peacekeepers in theater, based on the assumption that "the discipline of male peacekeepers improves when they work with female colleagues."[35] As the norm distortion logic would suggest, the action of increasing women's representation is consistent with WPS norms; but its militarized manifestation, which entails having uniformed women police their male counterparts' behavior, does nothing to advance women's place in the military, nor is there evidence that this protects host populations from sexual exploitation and abuse.[36]

The studies and evidence surveyed above boil down to a sobering account of how the experiences of men and women might differ within the military. The military presents an interesting challenge because it is one of the last publicly funded institutions that has removed formal professional barriers to women's participation. Are there truly differences between men and women when it comes to doing their military jobs if they meet the same admission and performance standards? The idea that women and men might have comparative advantages in operational settings has been conveyed in military training materials and in narratives to solicit buy-in for WPS norms, most often expressed as how the presence of women can improve operational effectiveness. The next section thus expands on the idea of making the pitch for diversity, focusing more explicitly on the operational context.

Women and Operational Effectiveness

While international organizations like the UN and NATO have been championing the inclusion of more women in operations by using the argument of operational effectiveness, some academic and gray literature has been more critical. Within this literature, two objections in particular have been raised. The first has to do with the unintended consequences of sudden demographic changes within the armed forces. For example, sexual harassment and assault against female military personnel continue to be enduring problems, even within their own units. Other unintended consequences include increased exposure that can lead to social stigma, backlash, or even threats. An extreme example is the case of Niloofar Rahmani. As the first female fixed-wing pilot in Afghanistan, she received so many threats that it prompted her to seek asylum in the United States.[37] Asking women to carry the burden of change and bear such risks, as in Rahmani's case, is unfair, according to this line of argument. A Special Inspector General for Afghanistan Reconstruction report published in 2016 highlighted this challenge: "Nearly every woman felt the international community made a mistake by not providing more training and public-awareness campaigns about women's rights in Islam, to men as well as to women."[38]

The second argument is also about fairness, but it relates to performance standards. By trumpeting the idea that increasing the number of women might increase operational effectiveness and mission success, organizations and governments are placing expectations on women's performance in the field that their male counterparts do not have to meet.[39] Moreover, given the low numbers of women deployed on operations, even doubling their numbers, as the UN proposes to do, means only a marginal increase of female troops. An alternate viewpoint is that determining the gender composition of deployed troops is the purview of national governments but that all personnel can be more gender-responsive through better training.

In *Teaching Gender in the Military: A Handbook*, a publication of the Geneva Centre for Security Governance, also known as DCAF, the benefits of gender training are presented as both an operational necessity and a legal obligation. The legal case is usually pretty straightforward as many governments and most international bodies have long enshrined the principle of gender equality into national law and international standards. As for the operational case, gender training is presented as increasing troops' understanding of their operating environment. The argument that is advanced is that if you ignore 50% of the population when conducting military activities in host communities, namely women, then it can impair situational awareness, especially when the mission tasks call for patrols and engagement with locals. Similarly, cultivating local support for the presence of foreign troops, which contributes to force protection, depends on fostering good community relations with both local women and men. As such, integrating a gendered lens in the context of military operations can have a clear operational rationale.[40] In Afghanistan and Iraq, the practical implication of this was a need to deploy more women, given the cultural realities that soldiers encountered when patrolling communities: male troops were struggling to find female interlocutors. It was through experiences like these, in Afghanistan and Iraq, that WPS norms really gained traction because they resonated with commanders on the ground.[41]

What we have seen, therefore, is that after decades of trying to exclude women from combat on the basis that they might impair operational effectiveness, the script has been flipped. The reality is that even if their contribution was not recognized formally before, women had long participated in combat. The hypocrisy was perhaps at its highest points during the US military involvement in Panama, Kuwait, and Iraq; women who deployed faced no less risk than their male counterparts but were not recognized for

their contributions or eligible for combat medals because they were technically barred from combat roles. Moreover, in these conflicts and those that
followed, the line between combat and non-combat became increasingly
blurred. As Francke notes, "The complicated coding formulas that suppos-
edly kept women out of the most dangerous, front-line combat and combat
support jobs would not shield them from the fluidity of the modern battlefield or sophisticated long-range weapons."[42] As women became visibly active participants in war, there was more media coverage of female soldiers,
content that was curated to satisfy the public's curiosity about women in the
military. Though this provoked resentment and backlash in military circles,
given that women were given privileged airtime, it also became obvious that
public support for women's participation did not waver, even after some
women were made prisoners of war or killed in action. This contradicted
some of the earlier claims made by defenders of combat exclusion rules, who
argued that public support would break if there were female casualties.[43]

Putting the mediatization of women in war aside, the number of women
deployed on military operations was still quite low and, in fact, remains
low today. Across NATO, there is significant variation between allies when
it comes to the total percentage of women in their armed forces, given different military personnel policies and domestic civil society activism; but
initiatives such as WPS can create some peer pressure.[44] NATO estimates
that women represent about 7% of deployed military personnel, while the
UN has outpaced the Alliance by introducing targets for the deployment of
women on its operations.[45] Work in feminist international relations and military sociology also highlights the absence of women in historical accounts of
war.[46] Even if historically there were far more male combatants, scholars are
addressing this silence.[47]

More recent literature has started to investigate how female service
members are utilized for tasks where gender can make a difference, like
the protection of civilians (especially of women and girls) and responding
to sexual and gender-based violence in conflict. While resorting to gender
analysis in an operational context is by no means the exclusive purview of
women, this task is often relegated to women, who are more frequently appointed to these roles than men. We should therefore exercise caution in
treating women's participation in operations and gender mainstreaming
as analytically distinct. Robert Egnell's work, for example, emphasizes the
need for both: "Women in combat units, as well as the implementation of a
gender perspective in operations, clearly have the potential to increase the

information gathering and analysis capability of units."[48] In other words, women's presence in military operations as well as the implementation of a gender perspective, which can be performed by both women and men, together contribute to the same outcome, namely improving information gathering and analysis activities at the unit level. Let us consider the implications of this operational rationale.

Focusing on women's and men's comparative advantages on the battlefield can lead to pigeonholing women and men into performing certain roles or, worse, mischaracterizing the diverse roles played by service members who deploy. Megan MacKenzie talks about this in the context of the wars in Afghanistan and Iraq:

> As the services prepare for female integration, a new myth has come to dominate the debate around the subject: that women who have already served in combat situations—including those who were part of frontline, female-only teams in Afghanistan and Iraq—were in fact deployed primarily to build relationships with local communities and to add a "soft touch" to counterinsurgency operations. Women in the U.S. military, this line of thinking holds, serve as "lady soldiers," not as true combatants.[49]

Other scholars have brought forth evidence of women being assigned certain tasks or roles based on their gender. Female soldiers in peacekeeping missions, for instance, tend to be sent on operations that are deemed "less risky," meaning they are deemed more suitable to be sent to traditional peacekeeping operations like in Cyprus, rather than more volatile environments like Mali.[50] The corollary of this kind of logic, which is even more troubling, is that men are more expendable.

Much of the gray literature on WPS underscores women's comparative advantages on the battlefield or in operational settings due to their gender. However, servicewomen have not uniformly embraced those ideas, nor are they naturally predisposed to "get it." Both men and women are indoctrinated into the same military culture.[51] Women display traits of military masculinity because it is embedded in their military experience, from basic training to operational experience. As Aaron Belkin notes, "the military manipulates ideas about gender as it teaches men and women how to kill."[52] There is ample evidence to suggest that women, in certain contexts, gain an operational edge because they are women and can play certain gendered roles and that these have been integrated into orders that women service members follow. For example, a woman is "sent" to speak to women in the community; it becomes part of her mission tasks. Otherwise, her mission tasks would be no different than those of her male counterparts.[53]

The next section introduces one of the models set in place to increase the number of women in operations: female engagement teams (FETs), which serve to illustrate how the link between women and operational effectiveness is routinely held up as an example of WPS norms in action. In practice, commanders exercised much discretion with little civilian oversight in developing this program that was experimental in nature and designed to gather intelligence from women rather than to support them, illustrating the logic behind norm distortion.

Introducing FETs

The FET model was introduced in Iraq with Lioness Teams in the 2003–2004 time frame and later in Afghanistan.[54] As the International Security Assistance Force and Operation Enduring Freedom pursued a counterinsurgency mindset, military commanders began to appreciate the need to engage with Afghan women on the ground in support of their efforts to win hearts and minds. Women were seen as influential members of their family unit, and whether they favored NATO forces or the insurgents mattered. FETs were therefore set up as small teams of female soldiers whose primary task was to engage Afghan women and to get them to view the presence of foreign troops favorably. Foreign women were thought to have a special status in Afghan society, often referred to as the "third gender," meaning that they were perceived as different from Afghan women and different from male soldiers. In other words, female soldiers could talk to the men on the street but also access the homes and talk to the women. The benefits of engaging with local women are perhaps best described by those who participated in creating the FET model with US Marines:

> The tactical benefits of speaking with women have already been well established. Pashtun women have on numerous occasions given FETs important information about local personalities, economics, and grievances, as well as about the enemy. The longer-term benefits of earning the confidence and support of Afghan women are more difficult to quantify but, on balance, are likely to be even more profound.[55]

The range of roles and responsibilities that were conferred onto the FETs were varied. On the one hand, the FETs had military tasks that were fairly straightforward: engaging with women and key leaders to improve the situational awareness of commanders by addressing 50% of the population that had been hitherto ignored in assessments of the human terrain (Table 2.1 summarizes the core tasks of the FET, as the model was getting off the ground).

In parallel, the FETs were also tasked with supporting women's rights through the development of training, engagement with the government of Afghanistan, and the provision of medical services for women, a task which more directly supported gender equality goals. Other tasks were tied to the protection of civilians, like special patrols tailored to women's patterns of life to improve the delivery of humanitarian aid. There was a clear tension between the tactical gains (e.g., intelligence gathering) that the FETs were supposed to deliver, while presenting themselves as helping Afghan women and women's rights more broadly in the country. In terms of operational effects, there are reports that the presence of female military members in certain situations had a de-escalating effect. This means that sometimes the presence of male US soldiers in Afghan communities would foster distrust and suspicion, while the presence of their female counterparts would not elicit the same reaction from locals. At the community level, people just seemed more comfortable engaging with the FETs. Another more intangible dimension of the FETs is their public relations value. The FET model was instrumentalized and romanticized both in Afghan society and with the NATO headquarters

Table 2.1 US Marines' Female Engagement Teams: Core Tasks within the International Security Assistance Force

Core tasks
• Facilitating female engagements and key leader engagements
• Facilitating civil–military operations
• Gathering and reporting information
• Disseminating messages
• Conducting female searches
• Supporting combat patrols as required

Source: Azarbaijani-Moghaddam (2014).

as an example of the mission's success, getting plenty of visibility in the media and in NATO's public diplomacy efforts.

There were a number of shortcomings with the FET model, chief of which was that their role was largely unknown or misunderstood by the rest of the deployed force. Another difficulty was in assessing their performance because the program was not rolled out with a defined set of performance indicators or metrics.[56] Furthermore, despite rigorous training, in the form of four months of pre-deployment training (which was not initially available), the FETs were often poorly equipped to fulfill a very broad range of tasks. FETs were composed of volunteers, but knowledge of Afghan culture was not a requirement, which probably made for a steep learning curve once deployed. Yet, because the model had received the endorsement of top commanders like General Stanley McChrystal and General David Petraeus, failure was not an option, despite the limited resources.

In Pottinger et al., we still find an overall positive assessment of having the FETs take part in short dismounted patrols in Afghan villages or even longer reconnaissance patrols, provided that they were given an opportunity for repeat visits and engagement in an area where the US forces intended to stay.[57] Under the right conditions, these patrols could then have contributed to improving situational awareness and certainly advance the success of influence activities, which were a challenge under the best of circumstances, given the language and cultural barriers. Other tasks like hosting medical clinics or door-to-door delivery of humanitarian aid were also often successful and provided additional opportunities for close encounters with local women. To be sure, the primary goal of the FET was population engagement, but the role evolved as commanders found other ways to utilize this asset, like for special forces raids in the middle of the night, where the FETs were used to gather the women and children in households after the door was kicked down by assaulters.

Since women were not allowed in combat roles at the time, the FETs had to be composed of women who were already in the military but coming from other trades, like logisticians. Once selected, their training was beefed up for their FET role. The bulk of the four-month pre-deployment training focused on a number of kinetic tasks, signaling that the employment of the FET was meant to support infantry efforts: "infantry tactics, tactical site exploration, combat tracking, night/day marksmanship, physical training, martial arts, and other skills necessary for survival in a war zone. The classroom instruction concentrate[d] on cultural training, language skills, and role playing scenarios."[58] As the FET program was evaluated both within the military and externally by experts, there were growing calls for more systematized training and institutionalization of the model. It was noted that additional training at the tactical level was necessary, especially for "tactical questioning, pulling security, and additional weapons training," as the FET could and did operate in hostile areas.[59] Women from the FET had to demonstrate leadership at the tactical level, meaning abilities in patrolling, drafting operational orders, and fighting in case of contact with the enemy.[60] Having these competencies would be essential to first gain acceptance from the infantry formations to which the FETs were attached, whether in the US Army, the Marines, or special operations forces like the Green Berets. Strong task-based unit cohesion being a determining ingredient of operational effectiveness, the training and employment of the FET adapted accordingly. FET members had to gain the acceptance of their peers before they could gain the acceptance of Afghan women.

By 2013, the FET model took hold within the US Army. As the first official FET deployment was underway out of Fort Bliss, Texas, the training was described as including "Pashto language qualification, seven-mile rucksack marches, night weapons qualification, tactical combat casualty care, combat training and other mission-essential courses to prepare the women who will be attached to infantry battalions."[61] The fifty-five-member FET underwent twenty-four weeks of training, where the combat training included "basic patrolling and reacting to contact and improvised explosive devices."[62] Those who volunteered for these positions were motivated by the idea of working in combat support at a time when combat roles were not open to women. Similar motivations seemed to have animated the women of the cultural support teams (CSTs).

The CSTs, a distinct model that increased the deployment of female soldiers, were given even more combat training. Women participating in CSTs were attached to special operations forces, providing support to Rangers or Green Berets as they were conducting night raids in Afghanistan.[63] The experience of the CSTs revealed that even among the most battle-hardened trades, the absence of women operatives was identified as a capability gap. More specifically, in the context of the Afghanistan war, special operations forces encountered important obstacles during their night raids. They were not able to interrogate or search the women and the children without compromising the mission since culturally it was not acceptable for these foreign males to barge into compounds and interact directly with them. Given restrictions on women in combat, however, when the women of the CSTs came home, their experience on the front line was not properly recognized.[64] For many, this was a demoralizing transition because combat experience is very important for professional advancement in the military.

The experience of men and women differed in other ways too. Women took issue with ill-fitting equipment since personal protective equipment issued to soldiers, like helmets, body armor, and tactical vests, was designed for men and not adapted to female frames. Another point of difference relates to how women soldiers' gender was made more salient when they were explicitly deployed on that basis, as part of CSTs or FETs.[65] They were needed *because* they were women who could engage with local Afghan women and children. Again, the argument at the time was that female soldiers had a comparative advantage in this context. This kind of logic has endured in how organizations like the UN and NATO interpret WPS norms, drawing an explicit link between gender and operational effectiveness and using these early experiences in Iraq and Afghanistan as training and policy points of reference.

Gender in Operational Planning and Missions

Over time, these lessons on gender and operational effectiveness have been formalized in WPS policies and directives adopted by governments, national armed forces, and international organizations. The literature indicates that the presence of women improves information gathering, enhances the credibility of foreign forces, and increases force protection and force acceptance.[66] When it comes to sexual violence, Bridges and Horsfall note that victims and survivors of sexual and gender-based violence are more likely to confide in or report to female peacekeepers and that women in peace operations have a civilizing effect on their own forces, by deterring the perpetration of sexual exploitation and abuse by their male counterparts.[67] Increasing the representation of women as a strategy to prevent sexual exploitation and abuse by their male peers is an absurd proposition to feminist observers and, as mentioned earlier, exemplifies the full extent of norm distortion.

As international security organizations like the UN and NATO provide command authority for multinational troops in conflict areas, they have developed their own training packages addressing gender in military operations, which further institutionalizes this mindset. The Nordic Center for

Gender in Military Operations in Sweden, for example, offers both NATO- and UN-certified courses designed for gender advisors, military trainers, and commanding officers (see Table 2.2). Upon completion of these courses, participants are expected to display gender awareness in how they carry their day-to-day work, whether in headquarters or in the field.

Gender advisors provide gender analysis in support of command groups, while gender focal points are dual-hatted personnel (civilian or military) who are tasked with bringing up gender considerations within their divisions. This provides what NATO refers to as a gender structure, to steer the implementation of WPS policies and directives. Gender training and the deployment of gender advisors and focal points are pitched as evidence of the commitments made through UNSCR 1325 and the WPS agenda, but have these strategies been successful at promoting gender equality?[68] Scholars such as Jody Prescott have argued that instead of furthering gender equality, Resolution 1325 and national action plans on WPS have "bureaucratized" and "diluted" the pursuit of gender equality goals.[69] Other feminist scholars echo Prescott's concerns by criticizing these global norms for essentializing conceptions of gender.[70] Further criticism points out that gender mainstreaming is inadequate precisely because it is mainstream and, thus, not profoundly transformative.[71] There is thus healthy skepticism with regard to agendas promoting gender equality that are designed and implemented by military organizations.[72] When new norms on WPS are introduced but the organizational culture of the armed forces remains unchanged, we see implementation but on the military's terms. To illustrate further, we can turn to how NATO made the WPS agenda fit with its raison d'être as a military alliance.

Table 2.2 Gender Advisor Course Learning Objectives

- Provide advice to commanders and staff on integrating a gender perspective in planning, execution, and evaluation for NATO's core tasks: peace enforcement, security force assistance, collective defense, crisis management, and cooperative security
- Provide advice on how to integrate international frameworks and guidelines concerning gender in military processes, procedures, and products
- Establish relationships and liaise with all elements of the staff as well as with relevant external actors
- Analyze the different security risks of men and women in a gender analysis
- Assess risks and occurrence of conflict-related sexual and gender-based violence and recommend actions

Source: Swedish Armed Forces (2016, 24).

WPS at NATO

As the rest of the book is dedicated to NATO's experience implementing WPS norms, it is worth stating that the idea of incorporating a gendered lens as part of all NATO policies and operations is relatively new in historical terms, given that the alliance was founded in 1949. NATO's first response to Resolution 1325 was a policy document drafted in 2007 with the Euro-Atlantic Partnership Council, which outlined the alliance's commitment to the WPS agenda. During its 2010 Lisbon summit, NATO adopted an action plan on the implementation of Resolution 1325 to develop a systemic approach to integrate the gender perspective in NATO-led operations and missions.[73] Finally, in June 2014, NATO updated its WPS strategy and increased its visibility with the help of the secretary general's then special representative for WPS, Mari Skåre. This commitment was also included in the 2014 Wales summit declaration, as well as subsequent declarations, with corresponding updates being made to key WPS policies and military directives.

In the world of academic research, there are few detailed accounts of NATO's journey with regard to WPS norms. One notable exception is a book by Katharine Wright, Matthew Hurley, and Jesus Ignacio Gil Ruiz, which provides a historical overview of the NATO Committee on Gender Perspectives, previously the Committee on Women in NATO Forces.[74] Rooted in historical analysis, the authors describe the institutional commitment to promoting women's advancement and integrating a gender perspective but also institutional resistance to these ideas. While their book is not about WPS specifically, it grapples with a number of related themes, such as military women, "teasing out the tensions between advancing women's status within the military and the instrumentalization of women and later gender concerns to support militarism."[75] Therein lies the major gap in the literature, according to them, namely that "feminist scholars have remained blind to the way NATO functions and upholds militarism" through member states' socialization when joining the organization, which acts as a "teaching machine."[76]

The research featured in the next chapter delves deeper into how NATO functions and showcases recent accounts of institutional resistance to WPS norms, echoing the work done by Wright, Hurley, and Ruiz. In the interviews I conducted at the NATO headquarters in Brussels, for example, a few respondents referred to NATO "dinosaurs" who continue to lurk the hallways, snarling at the idea of the alliance embracing a WPS agenda. Other people might use a more flattering term and call those individuals NATO "purists." These are national representatives and NATO personnel who want to enforce a narrow military reading of the core tasks of collective defense, crisis management, and cooperative security. However, with time, the NATO Women, Peace and Security Office, as well as gender advisors and focal points, have made the case for how gender intersects with those tasks. This much is reflected in the latest updates to NATO's WPS policies and directives. As this chapter makes clear, NATO's experience in Afghanistan has further cemented a common understanding of how gender matters in the context of military operations. From early experiments with the FETs to the development of training packages, NATO's interpretation of WPS norms finds its meaning and organizational buy-in through the concept of operational effectiveness.

Conclusion

Before detailing how NATO has integrated norms on gender and conflict within its operational template, this chapter laid the groundwork by summarizing the debates and events that influenced how the armed forces have leveraged WPS norms. These norms, promulgated by the UN, have led to a renewed focus on the lack of female representation within military organizations and the failure to take into account a diversity of perspectives when designing responses to conflict resolution. Now that states and international organizations have attempted to *deploy feminism* along with their soldiers, it is time to examine how the evidence stacks up to the lofty principles brought about by the UN's introduction of WPS norms. Military organizational cultures tend to be rigid, hierarchical, and bureaucratic; attitudes have admittedly proven difficult to change. The single-minded pursuit of operational effectiveness can best explain the militarization of WPS norms.

My book offers the first account of how this occurs in the context of NATO military operations. The interviews and fieldwork I conducted take the reader to Belgium, from NATO's headquarters to Supreme Headquarters Allied Powers Europe and all the way down to the tactical level, as soldiers implement guidance on gender within individual missions in Iraq, the Baltics, and Kosovo. Additional interviews at the NATO Joint Forces Command in Brunssum and Joint Forces Command in Naples complete the picture as these commands ensure the operational planning links between the decision makers in Brussels and the soldiers on the ground. The next chapter details how NATO institutionalized WPS norms within its policies and across the organization, which provides the foundations for how these norms are then carried out in military operations. NATO is a crucial case insofar as its common allied doctrine and integrated military structure sustain its reputation for being a global leader on multinational military adaptation, from technical interoperability to the promotion of alliance norms and values.

3

Deploying Feminism in NATO Operations

How do you change the norms of an organization like NATO? On the one hand, NATO is a bureaucracy at the service of sovereign member states, with distinct political and military cultures. On the other hand, when these states unanimously agree on policies or on a course of action, NATO acts as a powerful socializing platform to update the security practices of allies and partners. Normative change in any organizational setting is challenging, but making things worse for NATO is the frequent turnover in personnel across its headquarters (HQ) and divisions, to say nothing of the military rotation cycles within operations.[1] In other words, a lot gets lost in translation and lost in transition. Nevertheless, NATO has changed significantly since it was founded in 1949; and the Women, Peace and Security (WPS) agenda serves to illustrate this point. First, the demographic makeup of NATO has evolved with time, with more and more women working for the organization from top to bottom.[2] Second, the alliance has broadened its portfolio, which includes everything from nuclear deterrence, cyber warfare, and climate change, to gender. NATO's Policy on Women, Peace and Security has introduced new norms to the alliance; and Supreme Headquarters Allied Powers Europe's (SHAPE's) Bi-Strategic Command Directive 040-001 provides corresponding military guidance at the strategic, operational, and tactical levels to translate NATO's political intent into tangible military action across missions and activities.

This chapter explains some of the key policies and processes that have institutionalized WPS norms at NATO. The chapter is divided into two parts: it introduces political decision-making and policymaking processes within the Alliance and then describes how these are implemented on the military side. Before concluding, this chapter also identifies some challenges linked to the implementation of NATO's WPS agenda. Understanding the machinery of NATO is essential to track organizational change and to explain why principal–agent dynamics lead to the distortion of WPS norms.

Deploying Feminism. Stéfanie von Hlatky, Oxford University Press. © Oxford University Press 2023.
DOI: 10.1093/oso/9780197653524.003.0003

Why NATO Adopted the WPS Agenda

When the United Nations (UN) adopted Resolution 1325 in 2000, other organizations took notice and endorsed the agenda. While NATO is rather unique, because it is a military alliance that behaves like an international organization, it decided to follow suit. The catalyst, according to NATO officials, was the European Union making more substantive progress on this file early on with the appointment of a gender advisor (GENAD) as early as 2006 for the EU operation in the Democratic Republic of the Congo, along with more detailed documentation on WPS for EU member states.[3] Because NATO and the European Union share a core group of members, it makes sense not to have too much dissonance when it comes to endorsing international principles and norms. While this might explain the relative timing of the decision, it only accounts for part of the motive. NATO's mandate is tied to the UN's, and this much is enshrined in its foundational treaty dating back to 1949.[4] In fact, this short treaty containing only fourteen articles stresses that NATO's actions should be consistent with the UN's principles and charter. Therefore, when the UN recognized that gender considerations should be central to the pursuit of international peace and security by adopting Resolution 1325, NATO had to pay attention. A third reason one can point to is NATO's Euro-Atlantic Partnership Council as the WPS agenda was identified as low-hanging fruit for more partnership engagement. Since NATO is constantly identifying opportunities to engage with partners, the International Military Staff came up with military directives that would provide guidance to the command structure on how to implement gender principles within operations like the International Security and Assistance Force (ISAF) and the Kosovo Force (KFOR). The changes were further institutionalized with the development of NATO-certified training packages on gender (courses on gender are offered at the NATO School Oberammergau, the Nordic Center for Gender in Military Operations, and online through Allied Command Transformation's learning platforms). Finally, the International Military Staff's Office of the Gender Advisor requested that NATO members (and later partners) report on their military's gender representation, personnel policies, and gender in operations.[5]

An additional rationale can be introduced to explain why WPS norms took root within NATO: the operational experience acquired in Afghanistan. As one interviewee put it, "if people have been to Afghanistan, they get it."[6] Soldiers deployed to Afghanistan needed to engage with local women to get a better understanding of the communities with which troops were interacting. Not every NATO country and partner embraced this new mindset, but those operational needs undoubtedly shaped how Western armed forces interpreted the utility of WPS norms. The next section turns to how NATO proceeded to further institutionalize those changes through its policies and military procedures, elevated WPS principles as part of its public diplomacy efforts, and designed gender training for personnel and staff.

NATO Policies on Diversity and Gender Mainstreaming

NATO periodically updates its Policy and Action Plan on Women, Peace and Security, often following the timing of summits and ministerials.[7] The policy states that "gender mainstreaming and increased representation of women in NATO civilian and military structures and in Allied and partner forces improve our effectiveness and contribute to a more modern, agile, ready, and responsive Alliance."[8] The idea that gender mainstreaming could have featured in the official text of a NATO Summit Declaration would have been brushed aside as ludicrous for the better part of the alliance's existence. While the NATO officials and members of national delegations that I interviewed acknowledged that resistance and eyerolling were frequent, they now claim that "the reluctant countries have fallen in line. There are no more jokes—people are held accountable even during committee work."[9] Another official noted that nations find it "hard to withhold support at the NAC [North Atlantic Council] and the DPRC [Deputy Permanent Representatives Committee]."[10] There is also more accountability as the assistant secretary-generals have to report annually to the NAC on how their division is implementing WPS policies.

The Policy and Action Plan explicitly links gender to NATO's three core tasks, namely collective defense, crisis management, and cooperative security. Gender is also included in NATO's political guidance, an important document that sets the alliance's priorities and level of ambition for a four-year cycle.[11] The Defence Policy and Planning Committee provides this guidance to defense ministers, shaping the work that is done at NATO.

In addition to being organized around the three core tasks, the policy identifies three guiding principles, which are listed in Table 3.1.

The policy refers to the concept of integration by highlighting gender mainstreaming as a methodology (i.e., making sure that the actions NATO

Table 3.1 Guiding Principles for NATO/Euro-Atlantic Partnership Council Policy on WPS

---

1. **Integration:** Gender equality must be considered as an integral part of NATO policies, programs, and projects guided by effective gender mainstreaming practices. Achieving gender equality requires the recognition that each policy, program, and project affects women and men.
2. **Inclusiveness:** Representation of women across NATO and in national forces is necessary to enhance operational effectiveness and success. NATO will seek to increase the participation of women in all tasks throughout the International Military Staff and International Staff at all levels, including in meetings, training opportunities, and public engagement.
3. **Integrity:** Systemic inequalities are addressed to ensure fair and equal treatment of women and men in the alliance. Accountability on all efforts to increase awareness and implementation of the WPS agenda shall be made a priority in accordance with international frameworks.

Source: NATO/Euro-Atlantic Partnership Council (2018).

undertakes include both men's and women's perspectives). In this way, the intent of the policy is to embed principles of gender equality within NATO structures and programming. This can range from increasing the representation of women across divisions within the NATO HQ, reflected in the inclusiveness principle, to making sure military planners recognize that "a gender perspective" is part of operational assessments. While NATO can implement changes to improve women's representation in its *own* institutions and has policies in place that feed into its *own* diversity and inclusion reporting (led by the Executive Management Division), improving the representation of women in national forces is more aspirational as ultimately this is framed as a national decision and NATO has not explicitly directed its members to deploy more women.[12] As the Joint Force Command Naples (JFC-Naples) GENAD put it, "gender integration and representation is a national responsibility—I don't push for it. It would not go well."[13] This applies to other alliance dynamics as deployed contingents in NATO missions are most responsive to their national chain of command, and country-specific policies vary on WPS as much as they do on other matters, like military caveats and rules of engagement.[14] The third principle of integration relates to barriers, discriminatory practices, and unprofessional conduct. In addition to its own code of conduct, NATO adopted the Policy on Preventing and Responding to Sexual Exploitation and Abuse in 2020, which it defines as "any actual or attempted abuse of a position of vulnerability, differential power, or trust, for sexual purposes, including, but not limited to, profiting monetarily, socially or politically from the sexual exploitation of another."[15] In 2021, NATO also released its Policy on Preventing and Responding to Conflict-Related Sexual Violence.[16]

The WPS action plan lists the desired outcomes for each of the objectives recorded in the WPS policy, specifying planned actions, the timeline for implementation, and the leading entities, which is intended for both civilian and military officials working in a NATO context. One of the stated desired outcomes is that "NATO has a robust institutional framework that supports continued, sustainable progress *to advance gender equality* through the implementation of the WPS Policy" (emphasis added).[17] In other words, these outcomes are stated in fairly broad terms and then refined as they are adopted by different NATO institutions and commands, as well as across missions and activities.[18] This is where variation is first introduced in the way WPS norms are interpreted.

To oversee implementation, there is dedicated NATO staff on both the civilian and military sides of the house. At the top of the NATO HQ pyramid, there is the special representative (SR) for WPS, who works with different NATO divisions to tailor WPS policy implementation and provides advice to the secretary-general. GENADs, officers in NATO's integrated military command structure, present advice at Allied Command Operations (ACO), Allied Command Transformation (ACT), the International Military Staff (within the NATO HQ), JFC-Brunssum, and JFC-Naples, and on missions. GENADs are meant to

- Provide advice to commanders and staff on integrating a gender perspective in planning, execution, and evaluation for NATO tasks: peace enforcement, security force assistance, collective defense, crisis management, and cooperative security
- Provide advice on how to integrate international frameworks and guidelines concerning gender in military processes, procedures, and products
- Establish relationships and liaise with all elements of the staff as well as with relevant external actors
- Analyze the different security risks of men and women by employing a gender analysis
- Assess risks and occurrences of conflict-related sexual and gender-based violence and recommend actions[19]

GENADs are often responsible for designing or delivering gender educa-tion and training; upholding external stakeholder engagement, including with civil society groups; and coordinating with other GENADs, within their own organization or with partner organizations or countries.[20] An example of how a GENAD might contribute to NATO activities at the strategic level is through the Crisis Management Exercise, which war-games a crisis that NATO might face. The SR on WPS works with GENADs to provide "injects" into the scenario, meaning they introduce specific events that disrupt the flow of the exercise to provide participants with an opportunity to apply a gender perspective. This might take the form of devising a plan for internally displaced people, which accounts for the different needs of women, men, boys, and girls; or it might involve the perpetration of sexual and gender-based violence by the enemy, with implications for how NATO forces should respond.

The day-to-day tasks of all NATO committees are guided by decisions made at the NAC, the highest political decision-making body at NATO, with advice from the Military Committee. Within NATO's bureaucracy, the International Military Staff coordinates with the International Staff in pre-paring working documents for the political working committees. These taskings tend to follow the rhythm of ministerials, summits, or periodic mis-sion reviews. Once a working document is ready, it will be presented to the delegations via their representative on the committee. The committee rep-resentatives for each member state will have to check with their capitals and will receive national instructions on the document. Then, negotiation on the document will happen in committee, and the agreed-upon language will be a reflection of both the initial working document and the adjustments from the national instructions and committee negotiation process. Needless to say, the process of drafting and revising NATO's policy documents is a time-consuming endeavor but similar across issue areas, whether the policy focus is space, maritime security, human security, burden-sharing, readiness, or gender. Like all decisions at NATO, documents must achieve consensus across all member states in order to receive final approval from the NAC.

At the working level within the NATO HQ, there is a WPS committee whose meetings are called and chaired by the SR for WPS. The committee is composed of gender focal points (GFPs) from the delegations (whose work can be supported by GFPs from the International Staff or the International Military Staff, as well as military GENADs).[21] On the civilian side, GFPs are often (though not always) women at more junior levels of employment, which speaks to how this file is perceived as a women's issue and often deprioritized. In the best-case scenario, GFPs volunteer for these positions, rather than being "voluntold." GFPs who work for delegations may then raise the topic of gender within the working committees they participate in, such as the Defence Policy and Planning Committee, the Operations Policy Committee, Political Affairs, and the Political and Partnerships Committee.[22] Depending on the government of the day, the WPS portfolio benefits from the support of individual allies, with countries like Canada, the Netherlands, Spain, Iceland, or Norway typically leading the pack.

The NATO Committee on Gender Perspectives (NCGP), for its part, provides advice to the Military Committee; and once a year, it tables a report to the NAC on WPS policies, the action plan, and overall implementation. With representation from both allied and partner countries, which includes both civilian and military delegates, the NCGP has a broad advisory mandate and can be a conduit for sharing best practices on gender mainstreaming, both within NATO and with other international organizations.[23] Alongside the formal discussions and decision-making processes NATO undertakes re-garding WPS, there exists an informal committee called the Friends of 1325. The purpose of this informal gathering, which occasionally features a guest speaker, is for representatives to brief each other on what their delegations are doing. It is a good sounding board for brainstorming or talking about some more sensitive challenges and often a place where grievances can be aired out.[24]

NATO's Military Directives on Gender Perspectives

Once political decisions are adopted by allies, policies are actioned through NATO's integrated military command structure. This section will thus focus on NATO's operational planning process, which is led by ACO at SHAPE in Mons, Belgium. The other major command, ACT, is in Norfolk, Virginia. Together, ACO and ACT represent NATO's bi-strategic command. The way the WPS policy is interpreted on the military side is through NATO's *Bi-Strategic Command Directive 040-001 on Integrating UNSCR 1325 and Gender Perspectives.* This is the overarching document that includes a gen-dered lens in operational planning and missions. It operationalizes the twin considerations of improving gender representation, women's participation more specifically, as well as including gender analysis in military planning efforts. NATO's *Gender Functional Planning Guide*, a more detailed document, breaks down the provisions of the Bi-Strategic Command Directive into more discrete tasks at the strategic, operational, and tactical levels. Developed by ACO, this document provides key planning information for military staff and lists of tasks intended for GENADs and GFPs.[25] This document stresses the need to include a gender perspective in planning efforts and to consider women's roles as active participants in conflict and post-conflict spaces.

The *Gender Functional Planning Guide* features a quote by SHAPE's top general, the supreme Allied commander Europe (SACEUR), which illustrates this discursive shift from gender equality to operational effectiveness: "Gender equality and women's empowerment are critical to the security and success of the Alliance and its partners."[26] The title for NATO training packages further underscores the point: "Improving Operational Effectiveness by Integrating a Gender Perspective" (course code ADL169).[27] NATO's military directives frame gender equality to be in support of making the alliance more operationally successful, rather than focusing on military tasks that can contribute to gender equality goals, which are central to achieving sustainable security outcomes.

NATO documents and training products employ various arguments and examples, like focusing on how consulting local women in host countries can contribute to providing a clearer operating environment for NATO troops. The guidance also specifies (albeit in a footnote) that its principles apply to kinetic operations: "There is a commonly accepted misperception that a gender perspective is deemed less important during kinetic operations. In fact, kinetic operations often cause significant damage to the social and cultural fabric of a society and thus, gender dimensions become ever more important in the stabilization and reconstruction processes that follow."[28] Therefore, NATO makes the claim that gender considerations are relevant from kinetic to non-kinetic operations. However, the suggestion that kinetic operations can be a conduit for the pursuit of greater gender equality is at odds with the feminist ideas that paved the way for UN Security Council Resolution (UNSCR) 1325. A feminist approach would prioritize minimizing the "significant damage" that military operations cause as the best pathway for stabilization. This is NATO's paradox: looking at gender equality through ballistic eyewear. Such routines, procedures, and training support the institutionalization of WPS norms but prioritize a particular interpretation of those norms, an interpretation that is reinforced by GENADs who are motivated by the need to secure organizational buy-in.

Indeed, to fulfill its political and strategic intent of including a gender perspective at all levels, NATO has created a gender advisory structure that includes high-level representation within the NATO HQ and through the SR for WPS, as well as a network of GENADs and GFPs at all military levels, from strategic to tactical (see Figure 3.1). To this end, GENADs and GFPs support military planning tasks and operate within NATO's established, rigidly hierarchical military structure.

The *Gender Functional Planning Guide* also includes an internal focus: "force composition, engagement capacity/capability, communications, Standards of Behaviours or Codes of Conduct."[29] No further detail is provided though as this link between gender and what should be provided by NATO allies' national armed forces is rarely made in the documentation.

As the GENADs or GFPs carry out their tasks, they must work in parallel with other planning staff, such as the J2 (intelligence cell), J5 (plans), legal advisor, and civil–military cooperation (CIMIC) cell, at the very least. My research shows that, whether at NATO or at the national level, and fairly consistently across the armed forces of individual NATO member states, the role of GENADs or GFPs has not necessarily been properly socialized. As a result, their inclusion is sometimes contested or not well understood. During interviews, GENADs and GFPs routinely expressed their frustration in needing to explain what they do to superiors and subordinates, on top of performing their day-to-day tasks, though most were confident the situation was generally improving: "I don't get push back like I used to. When I got here, it was just about filling the position."[30]

Back to the operational planning process itself, the guidance of the Bi-Strategic Command Directive and the *Gender Functional Planning Guide* is more easily understood when broken down across the three levels of military activity: strategic, operational, and tactical. Evidence of this should be reflected in NATO's Concepts of Operations (CONOPS) and Operational Plans (OPLAN) and through relevant gender annexes and appendices, like Annex RR in NATO OPLANs.[31] For each of NATO's missions or operations, the GENAD is responsible for introducing a preliminary gender analysis of the conflict, specifying how the conflict and the resulting operation might impact men and women differently. Beyond mission analysis, GENADs and GFPs then work to influence the content of reports and to adapt military tasks in a way that is consistent with the Bi-Strategic

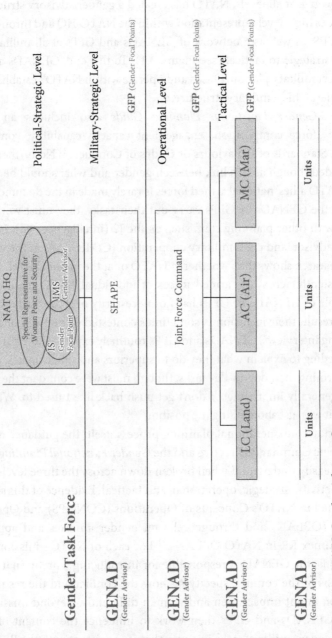

Figure 3.1 NATO Gender Advisory Structure

Source: NATO Allied Command Operations (2015).

Command Directive and the *Gender Functional Planning Guide.* The training packages developed for NATO also provide additional guidance to GENADs and the rest of the staff on how to incorporate a gender perspective as part of their work.

Gender and Operational Planning

References to UNSCR 1325, WPS, or "the gender perspective" can also be found across NATO's broader military planning apparatus, including the alliance's military planning bible, the *Comprehensive Operational Planning Directive* (COPD), perhaps most relevant for our purposes, with the next chapters focusing on NATO missions.[32] The following discussion on NATO's operational planning process is divided into three parts: strategic (political and military), operational, and tactical. The strategic level is where political guidance is adopted and translated into military mandates and objectives. The operational level then translates the strategic objectives outlined by the NATO HQ and SHAPE into actionable plans that the tactical level can execute. The tactical level is focused on execution but can also provide feedback to the operational planning processes based on what is experienced on the ground and any changes in the operating environment that might impact the OPLAN.[33] All plans and assessments are approved by states, and NATO's decision-making and planning process is incredibly iterative, going from the NAC, touching almost every nook and cranny of the HQ in Brussels, then heading to SHAPE, the JFCs in Brunssum or Naples (depending on the operations area), and then going to the theater level (see Figure 3.2).

The NATO personnel interviewed acknowledged that Afghanistan has sharpened their risk analysis skills. The J5 staff, who are in charge of plans, were quick to point out that some of the indicators used are gender-based. For example, tracking the number of girls attending school might now be considered tactical intelligence, and fluctuations in attendance could indicate changes in the security environment: "in certain districts, if we see that no women are going to school, that is a risk from the military perspective."[34] By collating the information from different districts, one might inform the operational risk analysis. Tracking the number of women who were wearing burkhas was also an indicator of societal change that could inform how the

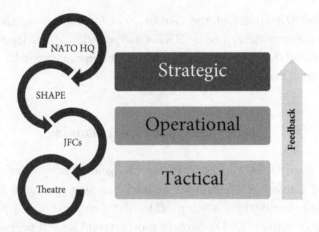

Figure 3.2 NATO's Operational Planning Process

mission was progressing. Gathering this kind of data was and is part of the risk and mission analysis that goes into operational planning.

Strategic Level

The operational planning process starts with the NAC tasking HQ staff and SHAPE to provide a comprehensive military assessment. Ultimately, the responsibility falls on the SACEUR to report to the NAC on NATO missions and activities. On the military side, the lead for planning is the J5 cell, which gathers information from the different J branches (referring to the continental staff system NATO uses) as part of this process.[35] J5 helps in translating political guidance into military plans. Assessments then scrutinize the performance of set military tasks and analyze the economic, social, and political factors that can influence the mission.[36] In other words, military personnel at SHAPE are meant to carry out a comprehensive analysis of the operating environment, drawing from a lot of external data and reports, to complement their own analysis of the NATO military experience in places where its military operations are carried out, like Afghanistan (until 2021), Iraq, or Kosovo. This kind of comprehensive planning involves looking at all factors that may have an impact on operations and then submitting this analysis to countries for approval. Naturally, J2 (intelligence) has an important role as gender assessments can be considered part of the demographic intelligence that is collected to understand the operating environment and support the commander's understanding of how the mission evolves.[37]

The COPD specifies the different phases of operational planning, starting with the initial situational awareness that is done at the strategic level. This is about getting the lay of the land and understanding the environment where forces will be deployed to carry out the mission. For this phase, the GENAD should consult with staff internally who contribute to crisis analysis (this might include, e.g., the Operations Staff within the International Military Staff) and attend key meetings such as the daily updates of the Comprehensive Crisis and Operations Management Centre at SHAPE but also reach out to other stakeholders, external to NATO, such as international organizations or non-governmental organizations (NGOs) with experience in the area. GENADs should also coordinate with their counterparts at both the operational and tactical levels.

The GENAD is also an advisor to the commander. Depending on the GENAD's personality and skill set, this staff's authority may be well established or not. What is more, depending on the commander, the GENAD may have a prominent role to play or not. Because the role is not as well understood as some of the more long-standing advisory positions and because gender can generate resistance from military stakeholders, the GENADs who seem to have traction are those who are able to demonstrate their operational relevance from the get-go.[38]

The second phase is the SACEUR Strategic Assessment. GENADs should contribute input at this stage to include "the impact of gender on the causes and potential resolution of the crisis."[39] This assessment, when completed, goes back to the Military Committee and the NAC for approval. At each stage, the GENAD is expected to participate in comprehensive consultation, contribute to meetings, and engage with external stakeholders, constantly seeking input and feedback and keeping the gender analysis dynamic and current. Then, the NAC initiating directive provides guidance for missions or operations, from objectives to end state. It is based on a comprehensive military assessment but is subject to political wrangling until all allies agree on a final version of the document that will provide guidance for future operational plans. The NAC initiating directive first included WPS as part of NATO's military strategic objectives in the lead-up to the Resolute Support Mission in Afghanistan, which "facilitated the integration of a gender perspective throughout the planning cycle."[40]

The cycle is then repeated, whereby this political language must be reinterpreted by the J5 staff to set out new plans, recommend new options, or recommend staying the course. The cyclical nature of this exercise follows periodic mission reviews, a process that happens every six months on average (except for Kosovo, which is annual), though NATO allies always have the flexibility to ask for additional assessments. This might be the case if costly mistakes have been made or if there are abrupt or unforeseen changes in the mission. An example of this occurred in 2012 and 2021 when the United States pulled out of Iraq and Afghanistan, respectively, which prompted NATO to conduct a quick assessment and to withdraw in short order.

The third phase entails developing military response options, where the GENAD can press for conflict-related sexual violence indicators to be included; raise the importance of key stakeholders in the theater of operations, such as women's groups or NGOs; and specify how each of the options is reflective of a gender perspective and contributes to the development of the Strategic Planning Directive. A GENAD's goal is that gender analysis is provided in all of the key operational planning products. There are usually three military options provided, and they are consistent with NATO's level of ambition. Usually, the three options correspond to small, medium, and large packages, meaning courses of action that are different in scope, scale, and risk. These three options are provided with specific resource requirements, contextualizing the military aspects within the broader operational picture. SACEUR then recommends one of the three options to the NAC and offers a rationale for this recommendation, with details on how the mission can be achieved successfully.

The fourth phase is the development of a strategic-level OPLAN, which includes the CONOPS based on the chosen course of action emerging from the previous phase. Sometimes a gender annex only appears in the OPLAN (if required in the CONOPS, this will be specified in the NAC initiating directive). The OPLAN is sent back to NATO for approval before it flows back down to SACEUR to generate the Combined Joint Statement of Requirements (CJSOR). SACEUR then leads a process whereby it will go to individual NATO allies to ask for contributions based on the CJSOR, with the deputy SACEUR coordinating troop contributions. SHAPE is not going into these negotiations completely blind thanks to the NATO Defence Planning Process, which culminates in a repository of agreed-upon capabilities that NATO has available for operations (in principle).[41] If SACEUR's requests are not met in the first instance, individual allies might receive additional pressure through military, and sometimes political, channels.[42]

An example of how gender perspectives might influence the statement of requirements is through a request for female personnel. The operational rationale for this type of request would be that uniformed women are needed to perform searches or to provide security around a school for girls. In Afghanistan, there were specific requests for women advisors to conduct tasks surrounding hospitals, to provide security during elections, to observe polling stations, etc. The idea that a CJSOR might specify a required percentage of female military personnel is still quite a way off, even though other institutions, like the UN, set these targets to encourage more women in operations. SHAPE personnel expressed the limitations of such an option as allies, they claimed, might not be able to fill the request given the low representation of women in combat trades. Ultimately, this is a political decision as these types of targets would have to be written into the political guidance. In this case, member states would have to provide a rationale for why they are putting this additional constraint on the CJSOR. Other examples of where there would be an operational requirement for more women would be a mission with partners such as Kurdish female fighters or Afghan female security forces.

Within this process, the GENAD can contribute to develop the CONOPS and specify gender requirements, including resources that should feed into the force generation process, develop measures of effectiveness and performance, as well as identify complementary non-military actions informed by a gender perspective to support military actions. The GENAD can also contribute to complementary annexes, such as the legal annexes in the OPLAN or the rules of engagement. This level of involvement again assumes that other branches and advisors are open to this input, which will depend on the GENAD's perceived level of authority, competence, and, one might argue, personality. This phase also entails ensuring consistency between gender annexes of the CONOPS and OPLAN at different levels (strategic and operational) and working with the J1 staff (military personnel) "to review gender-related job descriptions for the operation."[43]

The J2 (intelligence) cell might also highlight how gender can be an effective tool for lethal and non-lethal targeting. When clearing cities of insurgents, non-lethal targeting that includes gender considerations might translate into a focus on information operations tailored to female populations to derail the enemy's defensive planning. In the 2017 operations against Daesh in Mosul, getting information to the women so that they could move their children out left primarily men exposed to the fight, improving lethal targeting of coalition forces while minimizing effects on vulnerable populations, whose exposure creates greater risk of civilian casualties and more risk aversion. Using a gender perspective in this context is one of the more extreme embodiments of how WPS norms have been militarized as avoiding female civilian casualties represents a very minimal benchmark for supporting gender equality.

Phase 5, execution, entails regular monitoring and reporting. This assessment should lead to identifying gaps and adjustments. Reports are done monthly and are submitted to the Command Group. The GENAD may also report to the Military Committee based on guidance provided in the NAC directive and offer input to the periodic mission review.[44] To gather the necessary data for these efforts, the GENAD continues to work their network both internally, with NATO staff and military personnel, and externally, with subject matter experts.

The sixth and final phase is focused on transition. This phase relies on lessons learned and the compiling of data that can be useful for monitoring and reviews. This helps fulfill the reporting requirements but is also a useful repository of data and information about the operation.

Operational Level

The operational level is summarized succinctly by a former deputy commander of Allied JFC-Brunssum: "This level of warfare spans the gap between the military strategic (in our case, SHAPE, NATO HQ and Host nation governments) and the tactical."[45] While the strategic level outlines the political objectives and the military means deployed to achieve them, the operational level works to make those instructions more specific and actionable for the deployed army, air force, and navy personnel who are in theater. This work is undertaken by two operational-level HQs: JFC-Brunssum and JFC-Naples. These HQs "synchronise and coordinate lethal and non-lethal activity across a specified area to deliver an effect."[46]

When it comes to WPS, the goal is to conduct a gender-based analysis for the joint operations area. Ideally, the gender-based analysis is comprehensive and considers information about the local population, the host country's armed forces, governmental institutions, civilian organizations, etc.:

The better the gender analysis, the more possibilities we have to improve our planning process and consequently our effectiveness. For example, if we detect that in order to engage women in a determined area we need other women on our side, the inclusion in the tactical level of Female Engagement Teams (FET) will be essential to improving our efficiency. If we know that the enemy is going to use sexual violence as a tactic of war, the deployment of our forces and tasks and orders to subordinate units must include measures to prevent and respond to that situation.[47]

The GENAD provides recommendations as a special advisor within the command group regarding how gender considerations might be relevant for military exercises or operations. Additionally, the GENAD works with GFPs who are dual-hatted officers tasked with implementing the gender guidelines for their respective divisions and offices. And so, the daily routines are similar to those of the GENAD at SHAPE or the GENAD at the tactical level, when it comes to the task of advising the commander and providing gender training internally to military personnel and staff. The most important documents in this respect are the COPD and the Comprehensive Preparation of the Operational Environment (CPOE), which is an analysis of the joint operations area. This is where the GENAD reflects on what is happening in the joint operations area and across the range of ongoing or anticipated operations and exercises. The GENAD at JFC-Brunssum summarizes this task as "gender-based differences that may affect the operations. It is impossible for one person to study all of this. I would need more people in J2 and CIMIC to study the problem in depth."[48] The process runs its course from the CPOE to the factor analysis, then to the mission analysis brief, followed by the CONOPS where a paragraph on gender might be included, and finally, the OPLAN, which includes an annex on gender (Annex RR).

The GENAD at JFC-Brunssum says that he is increasingly asked to provide more tangible things, not just doctrine. Although operationalizing gender guidelines is an ongoing challenge for GENADs, another entry point to illustrate the relevance of including a gender perspective is through the development of scenarios for military exercises. At the time of my visit, planning for Trident Jupiter was well under way. A typical inject (meaning a prompt in an exercise's scenario) might be an instance of conflict-related gender-based violence: "our soldiers detect that the enemy is doing that. They have to send a message up the echelon and then take action."[49] Another example is information operations since there are gendered elements to enemy propaganda: "there was an article in *Russia Today*, Americans support Afghan point of view of sexual abuse of children. They use fake news . . . biased news, to make sure that everybody is against NATO."[50]

Finally, the GENAD at the operational level receives reports from the tactical level: there are monthly reports but also periodic mission reports twice a year (or annually for KFOR). The important points from the reports are then communicated to the Command Group and to the network of GFPs who can disseminate this information within their group or division. There is also reporting to SHAPE as information and reports circulate up and down the chain of command.

Perhaps the most important function played by these commands, in both Naples and Brunssum, is to distill the political and strategic-level intent into useful tasks for the tactical level. The other challenge is tied to NATO's strategic reorientation. Since NATO has done mostly out-of-area operations and crisis response since the end of the Cold War, getting back to drawing up advanced plans for the defense of NATO represents an adjustment. The JFC-Brunssum GENAD adds that the "COPD is a complete tool where everything is taken into account. And for Russia, we should not just look at Russian weapons . . . there is a society that is supporting all of this, so gender should be taken into account."[51] The thorny question then involves whether this analysis should also feature NATO countries. For example, within the context of NATO's enhanced forward presence (eFP), Latvia has controversial citizenship laws that impact Russian-speaking minorities in unique ways. This might be a societal consideration worth embedding into operational planning, but it might also be pushed aside because it would be viewed as criticizing the domestic policies of an ally and as too politically sensitive to include in an assessment. It is an important operational consideration because it contributes to the anti-NATO Russian narrative but is a blind spot for how allies plan their activities due to intra-alliance political sensitivity.

Moving from the strategic to the operational level, the phases are similar but more action-oriented. Phase 1 starts with the Initial Situational Awareness but is narrower in focus than at the strategic level. At this stage, it is important to provide a thorough assessment of the national and regional governance system and to include a socioeconomic analysis to identify priorities from a gender perspective.[52] Phase 2 is the Operational Appreciation of the Strategic Environment; the advice feeds into the processes that were previously described (SACEUR's strategic assessment and the military response options). This is done by providing information to the ACO GENAD, who adds this operational advice into the consultation and drafting process.

Phase 3 is the Operations Estimate and includes the mission analysis and the development of courses of action (COAs). Because gender is a cross-cutting issue, GENADs have a lot of reporting lines and can rely on their GFP network to support these efforts at all levels. The gender analysis conducted is also tweaked and updated based on conversations and briefings with other planners. This is an ongoing consultative process. Similarly, as the GENAD at the operational level interacts with the GENAD at ACO or with the GENAD or GFPs at the tactical level, information can be updated and/or synchronized. The key to this phase is making sure the gender perspective is present in the commander's planning guidance (where a paragraph on gender is required) and in the Operational Liaison and Reconnaissance Team as they are important for translating advice and guidance into action. Part of this work involves contributing to the CIMIC team on one day and offering advice on the initial force estimate the next, further demonstrating how cross-cutting the GENAD's role is.

For COA development, it is interesting to note that the *Gender Functional Planning Guide* specifies that "even the most kinetic of COAs need to consider gender."[53] This means including a gender perspective in all effects and actions, anticipating potential impact, identifying complementary non-military actions, and weighing in on the pros and cons of each COA. In assessing COAs, war games might help further examine how the gender perspective intersects with planned actions. Contributing to the commander's critical information requirements is possibly the most important entry point for the GENAD at this stage, in order for the gender perspective not to be buried in an annex and ignored.

Phase 4, the Operational Plan Development, includes the CONOPs development and the OPLAN. Gender considerations should be mainstreamed into these documents, where relevant, again, to avoid having gender relegated to the RR annex only. For example, the GENAD might provide advice on rules of engagement and might draft a separate paragraph on gender within the CONOPS in addition to the annex. GENADs' contribution to the CJSOR process, but also the theater capability statement of requirements and manpower statement of requirement, assures that the gender element of missions is properly resourced.[54] The CJSOR, as previously mentioned, is how NATO approaches the participating countries to solicit equipment, military assets, and personnel, so it is critical that the GENAD influences those requests.

Based on the fieldwork I conducted, this was an area where GENADs struggled to have those requests addressed at higher levels; requests for deploying more women in theater, based on clear operational rationales, are most often ignored.

There will also be a gender paragraph and annex for the OPLAN, ensuring that there is consistency with the language included in the CONOPS. GENADs should also contribute to planning efforts surrounding the employment of forces. Namely, input into strategic communications is key as language should be communicated about how NATO operations fulfill gender objectives and WPS norms more broadly. For targeting, GENADs are also considered to be specialized advisors, so their role can also inform planning of both lethal and non-lethal targeting processes and decisions. For force preparation, the GENAD will be asked to develop relevant pre-deployment training slides for the force protection plan, and existing measures taken might impact gender-related activities. For example, the requirement of wearing a helmet on patrol for force protection might be eased when female soldiers dismount to engage with women in communities.

Phases 5 and 6 are execution and transition, respectively, just like at the strategic level.[55] Here, GENADs should be given access to advise the commander and chief of staff. Ensuring that tasks are properly resourced and reporting progress on all fronts is the brunt of this effort, while the transition phase requires close coordination with the host country. This is important to guarantee that all efforts are sustainable beyond the mission's completion or beyond the arrival of follow-on forces. Lessons learned should also be captured and shared to support adaptation and improvement over time.

Tactical Level

At the tactical level, although the guidance is not as formal, the GENAD still has to be everywhere, interacting with the Command Group, on the one hand, and staying connected to all functional branches, on the other.[56] Ultimately, the GENAD works to gain the right access and be seen as a useful advisor to the commander, with the chief of staff playing a gatekeeping role in this respect. GENADs at the tactical-level face a unique situation in that they join the force once a tactical formation has been set up and is deploying. The GENAD will then participate in training efforts but can also look for deeper involvement in tactical-level planning and execution processes throughout the operation. The guidance suggests that this is not a given, and much will depend on the GENAD's own competence and persuasiveness: "When the tactical force believes that the GENAD is an enabler and a positive contributor to the achievement of the operational and tactical objectives, this will support the integration of the GENAD and gender perspective into the force."[57]

What those documents reveal is that there is more emphasis on specifying the role of GENADs and conducting sound gender analysis as part of the operational planning process than on gender balance in the force. Nevertheless, there are some areas where gender might be a consideration in force generation and employment, especially to prevent or respond to sexual and gender-based violence. Although no rationale is provided as to why, it is mentioned that women, girls, and boys are particularly vulnerable; so it is often assumed (sometimes incorrectly) they might prefer female responders. Moreover, this consideration is included in Annex RR and likely left unread by people other than the GENAD, who by all accounts is rarely empowered to weigh in on force generation. There are precedents, however, in both the UN and NATO contexts, like employing FETs in Afghanistan or instances when more female soldiers or police officers are deployed for sexual violence prevention and response tasks.

At the tactical level, much of the work done by GENADs and GFPs is mission-specific, and their roles will be detailed in the three subsequent case study chapters. Aside from the reporting requirements, which are expected by the chain of command, the GENADs deployed in theater will have to make an individual assessment of how gender considerations may or may not support the mission's core military tasks. The GENAD can also be called upon to provide gender training internally (to NATO forces) and externally (to host country forces) and set training requirements for troops with the commander. Finally, the GENAD should also be connecting with stakeholders, such as GENADs in other international organizations that have a presence in the host nation (e.g., the European Union, the UN, the Organization for Security and Co-operation in Europe), and networking with domestic or international civil society organizations, especially women's groups.

In sum, the existing NATO guidance offers concrete steps to make sure that WPS norms are reflected in plans, mission execution, and assessments. Emphasis is placed on the necessity to perform a gender analysis, or incorporating a gender perspective (in NATO terminology), to better understand the operating environment. The guidance is vague, however, when it

comes to tying this analysis to the pursuit of gender equality goals in operational settings. Furthermore, although NATO underscores the operational value of a diverse force in theater, and this is explicitly mentioned in
NATO documents and in interviews, there is no mechanism at present to
incentivize allies to deploy more women, even when there is an operational
rationale to do so. What NATO has done is to provide greater visibility to
its women leaders via its public diplomacy efforts. For example, when the
positions of NATO Defense College commandant and NATO Mission in
Iraq (NMI) commander were held by women, this was publicized as evidence of success on the WPS front. The former commandant at the NATO
Defense College, commenting on the low representation of women, took
this in stride: "this is good socialization, if they [staff and personnel] can be
exposed to women who are senior ranking officers."[58] As for the female two-
star general who commanded NMI, military officials at JFC-Naples confided
that "some don't know how to deal with her. NMI has women on staff but it
is merit, NATO is not in the business of positive discrimination."[59] From the
interviews I conducted, it became clear to me that the integration of a gender
perspective is much less controversial than increasing the participation of
women in operations.

Another striking aspect of the preceding discussion is the sheer scope and
depth of the responsibility that ultimately falls to GENADs, from developing
and delivering training to providing advice to the commander. It is striking
especially given the lack of understanding about what GENADs do, which
is a precondition for gaining the access and airtime needed to carry out
WPS-related tasks. Moreover, many of these GENADs and GFPs have only
begun to cultivate their expertise on gender upon their assignment to such
positions. While NATO offers and mandates gender training for GENADs
and GFPs, much learning happens on the job, with the corresponding
burden of educating one's professional environment about what gender is
and why it matters for NATO. This and other challenges are discussed in the
next section.

Resistance and Challenges

A general concern expressed by the NATO officials I interviewed at the
Brussels HQ relates to encroachment. Certain states, and probably the United
States most strongly, are reluctant to increase NATO's influence or control

over their policies. Control is probably overstating things because the alliance could never dictate the pace of change and is always subject to the rules of consensus decision-making by its member states. Nevertheless, the policymaking process and committee structure of NATO set a momentum for the alliance's day-to-day work that can pressure capitals into making quick decisions. For example, the adoption of the policy and action plan on WPS followed a rushed timeline to get the right language accepted so that it would be ready by the 2018 NATO Summit in Brussels. Enthusiasm across states varied depending on whether WPS was seen as a national priority or not. As such, stalling is a tactic that has been used to passively resist progress on gender issues. More active resistance—citing concerns over encroachment—is another tactic.

On the military side, one of the persistent sources of resistance to including gender analysis in operations is tied to the perception that this increases the burden on commanders in the field. There are more implicit signs of resistance, like staff officers or deployed troops simply not acknowledging that paying attention to gender is now part of the policies and directives they must follow.[60] At the same time, these same detractors also request more metrics and evidence on how including gender as a consideration can improve operational outcomes. This is a conundrum for GENADs because without the commander's full involvement and buy-in, implementing any kind of monitoring and evaluation framework is extremely difficult. Relatedly, the gender-based indicators included within the comprehensive assessments will not necessarily deliver the quick wins that military personnel who come in on say a six-month rotation want. Social change can take time. The quick wins, then, are more about how gender analysis can improve operational effectiveness, rather than how furthering gender equality can translate into more sustainable security outcomes.

Another point of contention relates to resources, which can entail both personnel and money. On both fronts, the primary body tasked with implementing the policy and action plan on WPS is the WPS Office within the NATO HQ in Brussels. Every division will claim that it is underresourced and understaffed, but perhaps the WPS Office's claim has merit. There is only one, now well-established, permanent position, the SR; but there is also high turnover of staff who work based on unpredictable timelines (called *voluntary national contributions*), as well as interns. While the SR has made a push for obtaining common funding to grow the WPS budget, it is unlikely that countries will agree to that on principle.

Another challenge with the implementation of gender policies and directives is the unintended consequences that emerge in theater from certain initiatives within host countries. An example of this was the push to increase the number of female security forces in Afghanistan. One of the mission objectives during ISAF (and its follow-on Resolute Support) was to have more women in the Afghan forces. However, despite the training they were provided and their formal inclusion within the security forces, they were often given marginal roles, like getting coffee. It took years to convince the Afghan Special Forces that they needed women: "we had to show them our own system for this model to be adopted in Afghanistan. And even then, it took three years for this to be implemented."[61] While it is acknowledged that these types of changes do not happen overnight, there must be better planning to make sure that women will be employed in roles commensurate with their training. Another unintended consequence relates to sexual harassment and assault in the workplace. There was a staggering level of sexual violence experienced by Afghan women working in the security forces. To mitigate this, the suggestion (eventually implemented) was that women should work in teams so that they could better protect themselves during their shifts.

A final challenge worth noting is the shortage of trained GENADs. This was already identified as a problem in 2013 (following a NATO-commissioned review) as GENAD positions were left vacant for considerable amounts of time, and it remains a problem today.[62] During my fieldwork, I too noticed at least one vacant posting. While there can be a short gap in filling positions, given the timeline of various countries' rotation schedules, long vacancies are damaging in the case of GENADs as it is just one person operating as a special advisor, so no one really picks up the slack. The next three chapters will delve deeper into more mission-specific challenges as the three case studies are introduced. The analysis will focus on NATO's missions in Kosovo, the Baltics, and Iraq.

To explain the variation across cases, I focus on the command structure of the mission and its composition, in terms of both its civil–military balance and gender balance, examining the work of key advisors and mission tasks. NMI, a mission that was planned and carried out through NATO's command structure and that has more balanced and integrated civil–military leadership, delivered the best results on integrating WPS policies and directives. By contrast, eFP is run through the Framework Nation concept; it initially was not part of NATO's command structure and displayed no consistency across battlegroups. There is almost no civilian representation when looking at the mission's leadership, and WPS considerations are almost entirely absent, save the collection of sex-disaggregated data to inform pattern-of-life assessments or the imposition of internal training requirements. NATO's mission in Kosovo, for its part, is in the middle of the two. While it is part of NATO's integrated command structure, the civilian footprint of the mission is very light, and female representation is low or entirely absent from the command team. WPS does not have a dedicated line of effort, and it is then up to the mission's own gender structure (GENADs and GFPs) to mobilize personnel's time and attention to raise NATO's directives on integrating a gender perspective, with mixed results.

Conclusion

Chapter 3 has introduced NATO's common policies and directives in support of the WPS agenda, with the twin focus of women's representation and including gender analysis in operational planning and mission execution. NATO has also taken steps to prevent and respond to sexual exploitation and abuse, as well as conflict-related sexual violence; but these are more recent developments and are not as central to the way civilian and military officials conveyed their understanding and experiences with WPS. The institutionalization of WPS norms has been significant to date: NATO has put written guidance in place, staffed new positions to boost gender expertise across its HQ, and offered training for NATO staff and military personnel. Another important test is in theater as troops on the ground have some latitude when it comes to translating strategic-level directives into action. NATO exercises its influence through the operational planning process as its procedures inform the execution of missions. On this front, gender-based analysis and what NATO calls incorporating a "gender perspective" are carried out at every stage of the operational planning process, as mandated by Bi-Strategic Command Directive 040-001 and supported by NATO's gender structure.

For the civilian staff and military personnel I interviewed, ISAF in Afghanistan represented a key reference point. The counterinsurgency and reconstruction tasks lent themselves quite well to gender-based analysis. The quintessential example that came up during interviews was that men in uniform simply could not access 50% of the population (the women) and, therefore, could not get an accurate reading of their operating environment. Not only was this NATO's longest mission but it transitioned into a training mission, Resolute Support, which ran from 2015 to 2021. Accordingly, most of the senior officers and members of command groups in the Baltics, Kosovo, and Iraq had operational experience in Afghanistan and drew parallels across the different operating environments. A lot of the examples they provided on integrating a gender perspective into operations reflected their deployment experience in Afghanistan.

Some of these "lessons learned" can be carried over to the training mission in Iraq. The training that NATO offers to the Iraqi Security Forces is not that different (though certainly narrower in scope) from the training and advising tasks that were conducted in Afghanistan. In the training packages and defense capacity-building, the entry points for a gender analysis seem fairly straightforward: introduce the WPS agenda as part of the curriculum, and tailor certain training approaches and strategies to the women students. On the deterrence front, however, things are much less clear. There are many reasons for that. The first is that the strategic picture keeps changing, and NATO has had to adapt rapidly when it comes to its relationship with Russia, following its annexation of Crimea in 2014 and then when it invaded Ukraine in 2022. The other reason is that the eFP battlegroups are on allied soil. Therefore, there are limits on what can be imposed, and there are some politically sensitive areas, like how to engage the Baltic States' Russian-speaking minorities. The third difficulty is the eFP Framework Nation concept, which initially cut SHAPE out of the loop when it came to mission design, though this was revised in 2022. More concretely, this means that NATO's common doctrine was not used systematically when eFP was launched and that NATO countries instead just looked to their own chains of command for guidance.

All of this makes the emphasis on the WPS policy and action plan more difficult to implement and helps explain the variation we can see when comparing eFP with the other two NATO missions featured in the book. The presence of the common NATO doctrine is important and narrows that variation. As one officer put it, "There is the doctrine, the [standard operating procedures], the bi-strategic command directives. . . . You don't have that fight. If you have an order, signed off by the commander, it just gets done. You get on with it. Orders are what we live and die by."[63] The adaptation of WPS norms to suit NATO's purpose has been consistent with how the military works: if it helps the mission, great; but if there is no clear link between gender and operational effectiveness, the file gets dropped or resistance builds. The case study evidence lends support to my argument that the militarization of WPS norms within the NATO context has surrendered gender equality considerations to operational effectiveness. The "business case" for the WPS agenda, in other words, has overtaken its true purpose of gender equality promotion. To be fair, NATO identifies obstacles to gender equality, urging its member states to better address conflict-related sexual and gender-based violence and to consider how conflict affects gender roles within society; it further emphasizes the delivery of programs that support gender equality goals, and the need to consult women during peace processes. That being said, when it comes to practice, the fieldwork I conducted across missions in Kosovo, Iraq, and the Baltics shows that the preferred approach is task-based, meaning that gender is linked to a narrower operational focus rather than being an important consideration in itself.

4

Securing the Environment in Kosovo

NATO's mandate in Kosovo has been the same since inception. Defined by United Nations Security Council Resolution (UNSCR) 1244, the mandate has remained somewhat frozen in time because Russia has been unwilling to revise it. "It's SASE and FOM" (pronounced "Saysse" and "Fome"), from Priština to Mitrovica.[1] "SASE" and "FOM" stand for secure and safe environment and freedom of movement, respectively, which are what NATO's Kosovo Force (KFOR) is providing Kosovar Albanians and Serbs. With over two decades of practice, NATO troops and contributing partners have fine-tuned their activities, ranging from training to patrolling. I visited the KFOR headquarters (HQ) as people were taking part in various twenty-year commemoration events. Even though the KFOR mission benefits from high levels of public approval, the anniversary was still somber given the deep wounds of the war (1998–1999).

KFOR is an important case study for gender analysis, given the high prevalence of sexual and gender-based violence witnessed throughout the 1990s in the Balkans, when Yugoslavia's dissolution turned into a horrific war right on Europe's doorstep. Because KFOR is NATO's longest-running mission, it has long-term experience in applying the NATO Women, Peace and Security (WPS) policy and Bi-Strategic Command Directive 040-001, first adopted in 2007 and 2009, respectively. Along with NATO operations in Afghanistan, there is more than a decade's worth of evidence to assess how WPS norms have been integrated into mission tasks. This chapter focuses on more recent developments, drawn from fieldwork evidence in Kosovo, complemented by interviews at Joint Forces Command Naples (JFC-Naples), the NATO HQ, and the Supreme Headquarters Allied Powers Europe (SHAPE). The chapter first provides a brief history of the conflict, then discusses the mandate of the mission and assesses how gender considerations are weaved into the execution of mission tasks. Special attention is paid to the role of the gender advisor (GENAD) as the person chiefly responsible for overseeing the implementation of a gender perspective. The gender composition of the deployed force and the overall civil–military

Deploying Feminism. Stéfanie von Hlatky, Oxford University Press. © Oxford University Press 2023.
DOI: 10.1093/oso/9780197653524.003.0004

balance are also important factors as they help explain why and how WPS norms are militarized across NATO missions. Because the number of deployed women is low, sometimes entirely absent from certain units, NATO cannot always showcase mixed teams, which places limitations on population engagement activities. Moreover, having few civilians on the ground means that the task of reaching out to local women's groups and non-governmental organizations (NGOs) falls primarily on the GENAD or women who happen to be deployed as part of KFOR units. This is not optimal, according to operational-level HQ, because "when the military steps into that humanitarian domain, there is friction between NATO and other organizations."[2]

Mission Background and Historical Context

NATO's involvement in Kosovo was a culminating moment of the war in the former Yugoslavia, with the NATO aerial campaign in 1999 serving the decisive blow. The campaign was meant to force Slobodan Milošević to the bargaining table, after evidence of indiscriminate killings of Albanians by Serbs. The campaign was relatively short-lived even if it seemed like a long time, lasting eleven weeks; and it was the only NATO operation to ever proceed without UN authorization. While the NATO campaign was successful in achieving its political objective of forcing Milošević to negotiate, it did not stop the killings. KFOR would eventually swell up to 50,000 troops to oversee the withdrawal of Serbs from Kosovo and the disbanding of the Kosovo Liberation Army (KLA), along with other groups that needed to be demilitarized under the brokered deal. The NATO presence was meant to establish military control over the country to set the conditions for a stable post-conflict transition.[3] The KLA had grown into a guerilla movement in the 1990s, in response to Serbians imposing their dominance in Kosovo, in defiance of the autonomous status it had enjoyed for decades when Tito was president of Yugoslavia.

Kosovo declared independence from Serbia in 2008 but did so unilaterally, *not* because ethnic tensions between Kosovar Albanian and Serbs had all of a sudden disappeared. In fact, as KFOR marked its twenty-year anniversary in 2019, the conditions were still not ripe for NATO's withdrawal. Even though the security situation was and remains generally stable, political tensions endure. Events in 2018 served as a recent example of this, when Serbian

Kosovar politician Oliver Ivanovic—a critic of Serbian president Aleksandar Vučić—was gunned down in front of his office.

In establishing and maintaining a "safe environment for all people in Kosovo," KFOR can be argued to be one of the rare multinational missions which has established a relatively stable security outcome in the post–Cold War environment.[4] However, there have been several instances of violence since the establishment of KFOR. The year 2004 stands out, as UN and NATO forces came under attack when responding to violent clashes between Kosovar Albanians and Serbs.[5] The 2008 declaration of independence, which is still viewed as illegal by Serbia and not recognized by several NATO allies and KFOR troop contributing countries, has further stalled political dialogue between Kosovo and Serbia. The European Union also joined the UN and NATO in 2008, as a partner organization in Kosovo, establishing the European Union Rule of Law Mission in Kosovo (EULEX) to work with the Kosovo police.

Since its peak strength of 40,000–50,000 troops, KFOR has downsized significantly to 3,000–4,000. Partly, this is due to the security conditions improving, but it is also because a lot of security management has been taken up by Kosovo's own security forces. Yet foreign troops and police forces are likely to remain in Kosovo, to assist local forces in security management tasks, so long as a sustainable political compromise is not struck with Serbia. External mediation efforts, like those brokered by the European Union or the United States, have been arduous. Under the Trump administration, for example, the United States briefly renewed its interest in Kosovo, perhaps viewing the resolution of this conflict as a foreign policy legacy worthy of flaunting during the 2020 presidential elections; but those efforts fizzled out too.[6] NATO and EU allies viewed these attempts as too heavy-handed, given that the United States threatened to freeze aid to Kosovo or to withdraw its troops to force peace talks between Kosovo and Serbia.

Kosovo has made controversial political moves of its own, provoking the concern of outside patrons, the declaration of independence in 2008 being one such example. More recently, draft laws were adopted to militarize the Kosovo Security Forces (KSF), which would "defend [the] sovereignty and territorial integrity, citizens, property and interests of the Republic of Kosovo" and could also be deployed abroad in support of international humanitarian operations.[7] Several people I interviewed within KFOR mentioned that this was a worrying development and expressed concern about the security situation deteriorating. Both NATO and the European Union preferred the status quo with the KSF to the proposed alternative, the creation of a 5,000-strong professional army.

Disinformation is also top of mind for KFOR personnel, and there is a lot of it coming from Serbia and Russia concerning the KSF: "with more and more attempts by Russia to engage in destabilizing activities in the country, there is a need to adjust."[8] According to KFOR's former public affairs officer (PAO), this fake news is "the real fight," and both Serbian and Russian media deliberately try to stir up anxiety. Full disclosure, the PAO saw this as personal since he was singled out by President Vučić, who accused him of lying on behalf of KFOR. The PAO described his approach to these disinformation campaigns as responsive: "It is important to answer more systematically, not to let them have their version uncontested."[9] Meanwhile, politicians on both sides are instrumentalizing the uncertainty over Kosovo's north, which is more heavily populated by Serbian Kosovars. Serbians in the south of Kosovo, by contrast, are surrounded by Albanian municipalities and are perhaps more poised toward reconciliation.

The list of grievances is long on both sides: it involves where the KSF is and is not allowed to go in Kosovo's territory, visa liberalization and normalization for Kosovars, potential EU membership on both sides (Kosovo and Serbia), INTERPOL membership for Kosovo, tariffs imposed on Serbia, and, of course, the controversial draft laws over the creation of a Kosovo army and a ministry of defense. The United States has traditionally been on Kosovo's side and Russia on Serbia's, though the Trump administration's diplomatic efforts temporarily muddied the waters. These allegiances are on display when traveling through Kosovo as US flags are present in areas where the majority of the population is Albanian, while Russia's backing of Serbia is fully visible in Mitrovica, where you can see Russian and Serbian flags side by side, making for an interesting sight given their similar design and shades of red, blue, and white.

While the region is aching for lasting peace, the leaders of both Serbia and Kosovo have a dodgy past. President Vučić was Milošević's information minister, while President Thaçi in Kosovo has been embroiled in organized crime (he resigned in 2020 after being indicted for war crimes). Under this old guard, the younger generation, keen on displacing the entrenched leadership, has faced many challenges, with ongoing concerns about Kosovo becoming a frozen conflict. But with rampant unemployment and high rates of domestic violence, Kosovars still want a better life.

The normalization of relations between Kosovo and Serbia is a pathway to engage with the rest of Europe and to achieve greater prosperity, and KFOR is meant to provide a stable and predictable security environment for this to happen.[10] It is a military mission, with seemingly few formal levers to exercise political influence; however, NATO has developed "a conditions-based framework tied to institutions and their development. This deviates from traditional operations."[11] In the meantime, KFOR continues its day-to-day operations and has increasingly embedded more social analysis in terms of how it approaches its core security tasks. As one former GENAD put it, "to do gender right and to have a gender perspective is a part of situational awareness. It increases force protection and is a kind of early warning system."[12] This adaptation in the way KFOR conducts its business has been brought about by experience but also by the introduction of WPS policies and directives, which have introduced new principles of intervention to a seasoned mission.

Gender, Mission Tasks, and KFOR's Mandate

Following this brief introduction to KFOR and the broader political context in Kosovo, this section now turns to the application of WPS norms within the mission. Providing evidence for this assessment requires analyzing the civil–military balance and command structure, the types of military tasks that are carried out to fulfill KFOR's mandate, the role of the GENAD, and the presence of women in NATO forces as these are the key factors that influence how norms are interpreted on the ground.

Within the KFOR HQ, in the heart of Priština, the Italian commander understands that there are expectations coming from Brussels about integrating a gender perspective across military tasks. In a sense, the mission seems well suited to do this as it involves different types of patrolling activities that provide many opportunities to interact with the local population, with a low risk of violence. These types of interactions benefit from a solid understanding of the communities' social makeup, including its gender dynamics. Although the fieldwork and interview data reveal that the mostly male Carabinieri and military forces are limited in what they can achieve in terms of fulfilling this objective, there are notable exceptions. The liaison and monitoring teams (LMTs), which are embedded within local communities across Kosovo, understand the gendered implications of their work better than, say, the infantry units in charge of riot control. The narrower the military task, the more quickly gender considerations are ignored. In other words, the case for adopting a "gender perspective" has to be made through the lens of operational effectiveness to gain any traction with the commander, or he shuts it down. These are not just the musings of a single commander. A NATO interview with another KFOR commander (2019–2020), Major-General Michele Risi, reveals that this is a more broadly shared view: "a gender perspective [is] a force multiplier and tool to better achieve our mandate."[13] The command group I met pointed out that the very fact of getting the commander to pay attention to gender or WPS is remarkable progress.

Of course, NATO is not the only game in town; Kosovo is a rather busy ecosystem of international players. Since UNSCR 1244 came into being, the UN, the Organization for Security Cooperation in Europe (OSCE), and the European Union have also established a strong foothold in the area; and all work side by side, according to different logics, resource packages, and priorities. KFOR also interacts and coordinates with the embassies of the KFOR troop contributors. International organizations operating alongside NATO have their own GENADs, which act as points of contact for NATO's GENAD. Coordination meetings or joint events can then result from this kind of interagency cooperation, which serves to increase KFOR's reach with civilian institutions and civil society organizations. The purpose of this kind of coordination is to compare notes, exchange information, and avoid duplication.[14] Some of this cooperation is routinized, there are fixed weekly or monthly meetings (the UN Mission in Kosovo [UNMIK] plays host to many of these meetings), and cooperation can also be more spontaneous, in instances of special events or unforeseen changes in the security environment.

NATO is primarily active on the security side, with tasks ranging from patrolling to riot control for the more unstable areas, primarily Serb-dominated Mitrovica in the north of Kosovo, along with other more generic tasks, such as public affairs and communications, medical evacuation, civil–military cooperation (CIMIC), etc. KFOR's mandate is articulated around the implementation of UNSCR 1244.[15] The resolution describes the contours of the Chapter VII mission, as set out in 1999, including the deployment of civilian and military personnel to enforce the ceasefire, demilitarize armed groups after the hostilities, and deter future hostilities. The mission also calls for enduring tasks such as ensuring SASE and FOM for the population and the international civilian and military actors who are operating within Kosovo, supporting public safety efforts, assisting with demining and monitoring the border, as well as working in cooperation with other international actors.[16] NATO identifies two other priorities in how it defines its missions based on UNSCR 1244, namely to "support the development of a stable, democratic, multi-ethnic and peaceful Kosovo" and to "support the development of the Kosovo Security Force."[17] True to NATO form, not all countries engage in all types of security and military tasks as national caveats come into play and leadership for certain tasks is delegated to particular NATO countries or partners, based on the assets they have committed to the mission. Certain countries, for example, do not allow their troops to engage in crowd control. The GENAD function, for its part (and for the time being), is Austrian-led.[18]

At the time of my fieldwork, the top troop contributors were the United States, Italy, Austria, Hungary, and Turkey (though Slovenia and Poland were not far behind); and the total strength was 3,526, with 28 troop-contributing countries in total. The units operating across Kosovo's territory were responsible for a mix of public safety and military tasks, which are inherent to the mandate but they were not consistently employed, despite ongoing training and high readiness (Table 4.1).

The fact that there are no riots to respond to at the moment is, of course, welcome; and while this is the case, the troops still coordinate training and

Table 4.1 KFOR Units and Core Military Tasks

Units	Description
Multinational specialized unit	Italian Carabinieri: patrolling and security operations
Multinational battlegroups (MNBGs)	MNBG-East (main US base) and MNBG-West (main Italian base): conduct peace support operations
Joint logistics support group	Support to KFOR forces
Joint regional detachments (JRDs)	Divided between three areas of responsibility: JRD-North/JRD-South provide communication and situational awareness, liaison monitoring teams (JRD-Center is the KFOR HQ)

During the time of my visit, there were three joint regional detachments, each responsible for teams of liaison monitoring teams. This has since changed: all kinetic and non-kinetic activities are now joint and operating under two regional commands (east and west). Each command has responsibility for both kinetic and non-kinetic activities, which simplifies the command and control structure since all of the elements are within the assigned area of responsibility (description provided by the deputy commander of KFOR). The command structure and latest information are available on NATO's website.

military exercises with local partners to build capacity in this area. For example, in the realm of crowd control, the Hungarian infantry and Italian Carabinieri train the KSF and frequently engage in capacity-building exercises. Even if KFOR's assets are not mobilized much in response to security incidents, its continued presence contributes to the overall security picture by providing reassurance to the population in addition to a sense of stability and predictability. The KFOR commander summarized it this way: "Often, they say that Kosovo is a political mission, I speak to politicians often, but it is a military mission. Our core business is to provide security. Security is a necessary condition for dialogue."[19] The civil–military balance of the mission is heavily tilted toward its military component. The responsibility for the inclusion of a gender perspective, therefore, lies squarely on the commander's shoulders and must be activated at different levels within the chain of command, from the GENAD down to the LMTs patrolling communities across the country. While the commander's progress is monitored at the highest level, through periodic or annual mission reviews, the political guidance on how WPS norms should specifically apply in the KFOR context is sufficiently broad that a fairly narrow military interpretation tends to prevail, as predicted by the norm distortion logic.

Entry Points for Gender Considerations

To assess how WPS norms are actualized within KFOR, the civil–military balance is a good place to start because having more civilian representation helps broaden the range of gender-based considerations that are taken into account as part of the mission's activities. Unlike operations in Afghanistan and Iraq, there are no senior civilian representatives within KFOR; but there are civilians within the military chain of command. For example, the political advisor (POLAD) is a civilian advisor to the commander, and there are locally engaged staff, like the K4 radio manager who has an important role within the mission: operating the station which disseminates messages about KFOR goals and NATO's day-to-day activities to maintain public awareness and support. Throughout this section, I will assess how military and civilian personnel perform their tasks with gender and WPS principles in mind, but I should note from the outset that the civilian footprint is small. Previous academic work has also commented on the lack of civilian control or influence.[20] The clear predominance of military stakeholders within KFOR can be explained by the fact that KFOR is the third line of defense, after the Kosovo police and EULEX, the EU mission which has deployed a police contingent. In the past, when security risks were higher, KFOR's vast footprint across the country often meant that it was the first responder, mostly because it could just get on site faster when the situation was urgent.[21] Additionally, many of the commander's political interlocutors have a military background as they are former KLA members. Therefore, there is a certain ease with which they engage with KFOR and its military leaders. Nevertheless, the KFOR commander has inroads on all fronts, from government and security institutions in Kosovo to other international organizations working in the same space. The EU special representative and the chief of EULEX are the commander's main interlocutors, along with the heads of mission for the OSCE, UNMIK, the UN Development Programme, and other organizations.

The Italian KFOR commander I interviewed was on his third tour in Kosovo. He commented on the extent to which the situation had matured, that he now had institutions and infrastructure to facilitate the work, and that he felt less desperation from the population.[22] To understand what goes on across Kosovo's communities, he relies heavily on the information and analysis garnered by the LMTs.

LMTs

To illustrate the types of tasks that are carried out on the ground and how there might be entry points for the application of WPS directives, we can use the example of Multinational Battlegroup West (MNBG-West). Its commander, who was a Turkish colonel at the time of my visit to Kosovo, oversees non-kinetic tasks across fifteen municipalities, which are carried out by twelve LMTs from six different countries (Turkey, Italy, Slovenia, Switzerland, Poland, and Austria). The commander takes part in some of those activities, like engaging with community leaders, the chief of the Kosovo police, representatives from international organizations, and leaders from religious communities. In our interview, he stressed that his primary goal is to establish relationships with the people. The LMTs do not carry pistols for personal protection; they are just in uniform, trying to demonstrate a "friendly disposition."[23] In one week, there will typically be two or three key leader engagements, which are all reported to the HQ. The working relationship with the KFOR commander, who is located at the HQ in Priština, is a close one. Protests are constantly on the radar and several soldiers specifically mentioned the protests surrounding the building of a hydro dam as communities were sounding the alarm about the environmental impacts of the construction project. Another more enduring concern is the security of the Dečani monastery, a Serbian orthodox monastery, which is protected by KFOR.

In the interview, the MNBG-West commander emphasized culture more than gender, saying that he could leverage his Turkish nationality based on mutual understanding: "we share the same history in this country."[24] I heard similar comments from military personnel from the Balkans, like Slovenia and Croatia. They mentioned that KFOR soldiers coming from certain countries are better able to understand local dynamics compared to others. There is a regular pattern of key leader engagements (KLEs) and daily activities from the LMTs, and if something appears off, then they would inform MNBG-West to arrange a patrol in close coordination with the LMT field houses and field offices.[25] This is why a good social understanding of the community is important: it enables the LMTs to assess security conditions on the ground with a fairly high level of granularity to update risk and threat assessments.

The LMT tasks might look like patrolling on the surface, but they are different from those performed by the kinetic forces deployed in Kosovo. It is less about showing a security presence and more about interacting with the population and organizing meetings with community representatives. Through their field houses and field offices, which are located within the communities rather than on base, the LMTs also have a more integrated presence across the municipalities in their area of responsibility (AOR). The LMT concept emerged after the civil unrest of 2004 that caught KFOR by surprise. The LMT soldiers I interviewed were confident that, because they have a constant and daily presence within communities and their finger is on the pulse of what is going on, they would be able to detect and warn KFOR HQ about the risk of any potential civil unrest swiftly. The LMTs are teams of eight to twelve soldiers who are assigned to specific municipalities (each municipality will have one or two teams). They are the eyes and ears and pick up on information that can help prevent the escalation of a security situation. LMTs can also be used to disseminate messages through face-to-face contacts.

LMT commanders manage small teams and start their days with short briefings on the news and what is happening in Kosovo and in their AOR.

They then brief on the scheduled activities for the day, which usually involve meetings with village leaders, religious authorities, or Kosovo police officers. In the afternoon, there are pulse patrols, meaning that the LMTs walk the streets and talk to people, though sometimes this is conducted in the evenings, when people are free after work. Toward the end of the day, there is a debrief. There is some flexibility in terms of reporting activities as LMTs do not necessarily want to be seen with forms, taking notes as they talk to people. There is a standard reporting template for NATO, which they will usually fill out in the car away from where people can see them: "we have to be likeable and open," one of the soldiers told me.[26] Sometimes LMTs are asked for things, like providing books or chairs to schools. When that is the case, they will try to arrange an activity with CIMIC teams.[27]

To inform their assessment of the local situation and to be aware of what is going on, the LMTs will also read a lot of open-source material, which is information supplemented by what they gather on patrols, with additional context provided by their interpreters. While LMTs do not work directly with international organizations, they do engage with NGOs that are active within their assigned municipalities: "usually an NGO that deals with women's rights, disabled children, or gender equality, they have good knowledge of the area."[28] The LMT leader added that

we have to complete a monthly report on gender perspectives. I have two women [military personnel] on my team and one female interpreter. In the majority of cases, it means we interview women, ask them what their job is [and] if they are comfortable with their position. I can say that the female situation in Kosovo is developing, slowly, but improving day by day. Women are increasingly knowledgeable about their rights. I can see it from the increasing number of reports that come through. They report more domestic violence.[29]

In fact, an all-female LMT has been established to specifically engage with women's shelters.[30] In the conversations I had with several KFOR troops and members of the Carabinieri, the topic of domestic violence was brought up as a top gender consideration. Rates of domestic violence are included as an indicator in political and social assessments of Kosovo, in reports done by the LMTs, or in the analyses of the POLAD, within the Command Group. My interviews offer further validation of the prevailing view found in NATO training materials, namely that having mixed LMTs delivers more useful information for the mission.[31]

The KFOR commander receives daily reports from LMTs, then special reports if there are noteworthy events, either because they represent a security concern or because they are politically sensitive. An example I was given invoked a specific scenario: LMTs might get the request to hold a meeting or assist in a certain area, and there is always a process of evaluation to see if it is a good idea or not in the context of KFOR's broader objectives and mandate. Any activity that could compromise the perceived impartiality of KFOR is scrutinized. Whom you meet and where you meet them can translate into counterproductive political signaling. This has been learned the hard way, as relayed by the LMT leader in a few stories from previous rotations.

Patrols and Exercises

In the interviews, military personnel take great pains to distinguish between kinetic and non-kinetic tasks, but most of what is done is non-kinetic: "it is a low intensity mission, especially for KFOR's kinetic forces. There is no direct threat."[32] The kinetic assets, like riot control, are not really needed, given the fairly stable situation; but there are contingency plans. For example, exercises appear to be a useful device to pre-deploy troops when there is a perceived risk and when one does not want to sound any alarms. Riots like those that happened in 2004 and 2008 could happen again, in which case the kinetic assets are prepared and ready. Prior to 2004, the troops were trained for combat, but the protests underscored the need for riot control capabilities. Because shooting at mobs was not the appropriate solution, the mission adapted accordingly; and riot control was integrated into NATO's approach to training.

Since KFOR has not recently resorted to the use of force, the non-kinetic aspect is more predominant and visible. Activities include surveillance patrols, the protection of one religious site (the Dečani monastery), and other activities linked to exercises and training, which help with further integration and coordination with other forces. The Dečani monastery is an important Serbian Orthodox Christian symbol. Built in the fifteenth century and incredibly well preserved, it is a UNESCO Heritage Site that hosts many international visitors and, therefore, is of concern to KFOR. It took a long conversation with the Italian non-commissioned officer (NCO) tasked with its protection to really understand why there was a KFOR presence there because, at first glance, it just looks like a lone Italian soldier hanging out with monks.[33] And to be fair, it is a fairly meditative military tasking, based on his description. During our conversation, he described his battle rhythm, military parlance to describe one's routine, as spending most of his day sitting alone at a sturdy wooden table, admiring the beauty of the Dečani monastery. When KFOR started, the majority of sites throughout Kosovo were protected by KFOR, whether Albanian or Serbian, Muslim or Catholic; and now, it is down to a single site.

As we chatted, the soldier, wearing his *Esercito* (Italian army) uniform, saluted one of the monks who walked by us. He turned back to me and reflected on just how different his KFOR experience is from the last time he was deployed, in Herat, Afghanistan. By talking to the monks and listening to the local visitors who come to the monastery, he can get a good picture of what is going on and can describe the patterns of life in and around the monastery. Understanding these patterns of life is one of the entry points for gender-based analysis as it requires talking to people from a variety of backgrounds, ages, and gender roles to gain an accurate picture of what is going on. The soldier noted that there are also more traditional security tasks, like monitoring the environment, investigating any incident that seems out of the ordinary, and overseeing the security of the grounds, along with a handful of guards at two checkpoints.

Toward the end of our conversation, I had to ask, "Do you think NATO's presence is necessary here?" He answered immediately and without flinching: "Absolutely necessary and fundamental."[34] An Italian colonel sitting to my left looked skeptical. He clearly disagreed. But in discussing this further, they both ultimately came around to a similar viewpoint, namely that KFOR's presence deters any disturbances and that, at least for now, removing the soldiers might not be prudent. It is, after all, a politically tumultuous time. The Italian NCO also expressed hope for the future as he has seen both Serbian and Albanian kids visit the monastery: "Kids don't know about the conflict the way the older generations do. You can see it in their eyes."[35] While the protection of religious sites is a task that now comes down to a single monastery, it still has quite a bit of symbolic significance for KFOR, as well as for the population.

Another important mission task is patrolling along the administrative boundary line, the boundary that separates Kosovo's territory from Serbia, Montenegro, and North Macedonia. Patrols in Kosovo Serb communities are especially complex because not every NATO or partner troop contributor has rules of engagement that lets it operate in those areas—again, NATO has become accustomed to managing national caveats.[36] Some NATO countries, like Greece and Spain, do not recognize Kosovo, so this naturally adds to the complexity of NATO's involvement there.

In addition to the patrols and exercises conducted by the armed forces of NATO allies and partners, there is the presence of the Italian Carabinieri. They conduct patrols as police work is their core business, but they also have military training and deploy in most of Italy's missions abroad. That means that they primarily work to maintain public order but are the tactical reserve of KFOR for military tasks.[37] In the past, the Carabinieri were frequently called upon for crowd control (they are equipped with batons, shields, non-lethal grenade launchers); but when I visited, the bulk of the activities seemed to be around CIMIC activities: "we help poor families: Kosovo Albanians and Kosovo Serbs. After the war until now, many villages there are very poor. We try to help them with food, clothes, shoes and other things."[38] There are also daily patrols, which are conducted according to a weekly patrol plan: "Our targets for patrols are the Serb enclaves. Normally, the approach with Serbian and Albanian people is different. Serbian people can get angry, they do not want to see KFOR."[39]

When I asked whether their engagement efforts reach both men and women, I was told that they mostly target men: "we approach only men because we don't know the local culture. It's quite different from Italy. The man decides everything, except for maybe women teachers. Or parents sometimes. We try to enter very gently and very slowly in this context to respect their traditional culture."[40] Finally, like most other units in Kosovo, the Carabinieri conduct daily training and organize military exercises: "Every day we have a group of people that train for riot control, to use the weapons, to communicate [by] radio. Just yesterday we did a joint exercise with other troops, with the Hungarians and Poles. We did an exercise to try to manage a situation of riot control."[41] Sometimes these exercises will be with EULEX and the Kosovo police, to practice the three lines of response, as KFOR is meant to be the third responder, behind the Kosovo police (first responder) and EULEX (second responder). In the event the Kosovo police or EULEX cannot respond or are overwhelmed, KFOR steps in and can provide riot control assets or remove roadblocks with their FOM detachment. Based on past experience, dealing with roadblocks yielded important lessons for KFOR in terms of integrating a gender perspective, in that roadblocks disrupt patterns of life; and these are different for men, women, and children. Children, for example, might not be able to go to school, while women might not access the supplies they need to support their family. In 2011, with civil unrest on the rise, Kosovo Serbians in the north of Kosovo set up roadblocks that KFOR had to respond to, given that they restricted the freedom of movement that the NATO presence is meant to ensure. The mostly unemployed men who maintained the roadblocks were not affected in the same way as women and children. The men had a financial incentive to keep the roadblocks up and had established new resupply routes, while the women and children felt the immediate disruptions more acutely. Understanding this dynamic ultimately determined the course of action chosen by the KFOR commander:

> This realization—that the situation would get worse for the local population but at different speeds for men, women, boys and girls—led COM KFOR [KFOR commander] to accelerate the process and perform a complete en-circlement of the communities to further reduce supplies. Cutting off the new resupply routes as well as the official roads would put more pressure on the leaders and push them to the tipping point more quickly. It would also shorten the crisis and thus lessen its impact on women and children. Force would only be used at a few critical roadblocks.[42]

When it comes to training activities with the Kosovo police, the com-mander of MSU said the Carabinieri had trained eighty people in four dif-ferent branches: investigation, crowd and riot control, SWAT capabilities, and negotiation.[43] Looking at the gender perspective, the Carabinieri organ-ized a self-defense class for women, given that they identified domestic vi-olence as a big social problem in Kosovo. However, the Carabinieri officers I spoke to highlighted that they had no women among their ranks in this rotation, so they had to proceed with caution. I should add that there are studies that describe the experiences of women deployed as part of KFOR, and they identify specific barriers female soldiers face when tasked with "light infantry missions" like being reoriented toward administrative tasks or being scapegoated for fraternization.[44] Then there are more tactical tasks, where the gender element might seem less salient. One example is explosive ordnance disposal (EOD). Even for EOD though, there is contact with the local population as they are often the ones who identify and report explosive hazards. The question to ask is, who is most likely to run into this potential threat within communities? This is the guidance we find in strategic-level documents developed at the NATO HQ, but it does not necessarily trickle down. Procedurally, the EOD response is straightforward: "once they get a call about a potential hazard, they'll do a reconnaissance trip to assess the situation and then they will dispose of the hazard, usually on site, while protecting people and structures in the area. We're talking primarily about exploded or unexploded ordnance, from World War I to the 1990s."[45] As such, there is exposure to the population, and the reception is enthusiastic and favorable in that context, "not like on other deployments"; and the EOD officer adds that, "a lot of people are initially shocked to meet our Taskforce Commander who is female but once she starts talking, they understand."[46] The gender composition of the force was raised in my brief conversation with the EOD officer, in the American-run Bondsteel camp, as something that is not explicitly taken into account in terms of who does what but that has effects when interacting with the local population.

Generic Military Tasks

This section delves into military tasks that are not mission-specific but that are still important to how WPS norms might play out in practice. Managing public affairs was cited by many of my interviewees as one of the most important KFOR tasks, so it is a good starting point for the discussion. Since the political discourse is seen as toxic and divisive in Kosovo, KFOR is constantly trying to push messages of diversity, unity, and reconciliation through traditional and social media outlets. One thing that is closely tracked is what the population thinks about politics and about KFOR specifically. The GENAD works with PAOs to assess whether different groups within the population perceive KFOR as improving security or not.

KFOR also has its own radio station, called K4. It broadcasts one K4 channel in Albanian and one in Serbian. The radio staff is mixed, they work together, and it is pitched as a model of interethnic cooperation; this much was stressed during my interview with the radio manager, who has been working there since the very beginning of the mission.[47] K4 broadcasts messages with approval from the KFOR commander: "we are a bridge between the commander and the general population," she said.[48] Those messages are meant to avoid politics and to instead promote positive messages or stories about multiethnicity, the peacekeeping mission, and planned KFOR military exercises. This ability to communicate all the time and anywhere across Kosovo is definitely an asset for KFOR, both for the commander and for the public affairs team. Included under the banner of public affairs are KFOR's communication efforts via K4 radio as well as the activities which are planned and overseen by the PAO and their military staff. Then, there is everyone else wearing a KFOR badge. As one medical officer suggested, this mission is different from other operational deployments: "we can take pictures with babies."[49] Still, all KFOR soldiers have to be careful when taking pictures as KFOR's image as an impartial actor needs to be protected. There are certain hand gestures that Kosovar Albanians sometimes make, like the double eagle, which involves crossing the hands to evoke the image of a double headed eagle from the Albanian flag. This symbol could play badly online if seen with KFOR soldiers in the picture. Avoiding politically charged imagery or messaging is therefore advised to KFOR personnel.

Then, there are information operations (info ops). This cell is called the effects cell, but the functional area is info ops, which boils down to sending messages to target audiences using assets such as intelligence, CIMIC (military personnel who interact with civilians), PAOs (who produce content for public consumption and disseminate information about the mission), or civil affairs (personnel who interact with institutions, like school boards or members of government).[50] At Camp Bondsteel within MNBG-East, there is no artillery or fixed wing aircraft that delivers munitions, so the work of the effects cell is focused on non-lethal targeting. Some of these activities are coordinated and carried out with the Kosovo police, like when KFOR organized a toy drive for Serbian children in Kosovo. Ultimately, the goal is to legitimize the Kosovo police in the eyes of the entire population (which means both Albanian- and Serbian-speaking populations), and working with children is often seen as a way to avoid politics while gaining good exposure within communities. The effects cell meets to discuss its targets, and then everything gets approved by the commander.

When asked about how they take gender into account, based on NATO directives, the American officer from the effects cell cites the first CIMIC event they did: the goal was to give soccer gear to a local female soccer team. This was a good news story that Public Affairs could run with. More generally speaking, their goal is to support both men and women in the security forces. They do this, for example, by trying to get more applicants and finding recruits for the Kosovo police, who currently have a force that is 14% women. In the KSF, there are between 8% and 9%. They did a recruitment campaign recently where more than 6,000 applied, but the applicants were 93% male.

Though still low, these numbers outperform female representation within KFOR, which always translates into a bit of a credibility gap.

From the effects cell perspective, the officer told me, "We have certain objectives: inform, educate, or influence certain audiences. You don't just want to focus everything on males."[51] This plays into KFOR's efforts to be seen as capable, credible, and impartial. In terms of performance metrics, doing one key leader engagement per week is what they aim for; and, of course, here too, gender balance for these KLEs would be ideal but is non-existent. The MNBG-East commander will do most of the KLE with local politicians and mayors. Otherwise, KLEs are deployed to maintain good working relationships and lines of communication with contacts within the Kosovo police and/or other institutions important to KFOR's work, just in case something goes wrong. In a nutshell, "through info ops, you shape the environment so that we don't have to respond with force."[52]

Important messages for KFOR are reassurance and deterrence:

> it is important to integrate info ops into regular ops. Everything we do sends a message: all the exercises that we do. Exercises that involve aviation, troop movements. We're training, but we're also sending a message. That shows [to the] local population that we have all these assets and equipment. We're prepared to use it, we're trained on it, we're working together. If something were to happen, [the] adversary knows there are consequences to their actions.[53]

With regard to NATO's WPS directive, the officer mentioned the importance of role models:

> when they see females in uniform, they can see little girls look up. You change their aspirations if they can see a role model like that.[54] We have a taskforce working with Women for Women, an NGO. They will not be comfortable with males. And in this part of the world, it is not like in the United States or other countries: women don't have opportunities. We got briefed before we even got here. We were told Albanians are Muslim, they have more rigid gender roles.[55]

My interview data therefore lends additional support to what is identified in the literature regarding ad hoc duties female soldiers take on while on deployment: in addition to their regular military tasks, they must perform gender-specific role modeling when connecting with local populations. The women who deploy as part of KFOR expect to do the job that they were trained to do, not to be role models for the local population; but they seem to take this new role in stride. Moreover, this aspect of the mission depends on the actual number of women who are deployed as part of KFOR (not many). When I visited, there were 3,401 troops, 219 of whom were women. Of course, these numbers shift a little from rotation to rotation, from troop contributor to troop contributor; but that is still just above 6%. In the non-kinetic elements, the GENAD says, "more women would be good as teams are complaining that they have no women on their team."[56]

Yet through the NATO chain of command, there is no tangible force generation mechanism by which missions can push member states to deploy more women on each rotation; this is a national responsibility. Some units have no women at all. For example, the MSU which is composed of Italian Carabinieri did not have a single woman (though it has had one in the past, and she was "very tough" according to the MSU commander). Logistical problems and accommodation issues were cited as the chief reason for having so few women, but it seems more complicated than that. If NATO does not force-generate positions for women, even when there is a clear operational rationale to do so, the numbers will remain low.

In terms of tactical tasks, I talked to members of the KFOR Tactical Reserve Battalion (KTRBN), which is composed of Hungarian troops trained and ready to perform a range of infantry tasks, like surveillance, reconnaissance, and crowd and riot control. I traveled to Novo Selo, Camp Marechal De Lattre De Tassigny, and first talked to the deputy commander of the battalion, who is responsible for operations and training. He had been deployed to Kosovo before, including when the battalion responded to mass protests across the country in 2004.[57] The deputy commander had visibly been briefed on the topic of my project before I really had a chance to dive into my standard introduction. During the interview, he offered that there were twenty-four women in his battalion (roughly 10%). The tactical reserve unit trains to have a high level of readiness and works with other units to know their tactics, techniques, and procedures. They conduct military exercises to put the training into practice. Alongside the training activities, they do presence patrols, working with the joint regional detachments to see what the needs are. The aim remains the same: show a presence to various communities in Kosovo to reassure them and build trust with the population.

In addition to the deputy commander, I spoke with one of the company commanders and one of the platoon leaders. The two young officers stressed the multinational training environment as the highlight of their deployment because they could learn about other countries' tactics and knowledge. The battle rhythm varies depending on whether they are doing a duty week or a training week. During duty weeks, they conduct patrols all over Kosovo, which include both presence patrols and reconnaissance patrols. They also engage with the population with the help of both Albanian-speaking and Serbian-speaking interpreters, to get a sense of what people think of KFOR. They use light Jeeps and Humvees for these types of patrols, keeping their infantry fighting vehicles parked, to be more open and more approachable. Most of the presence patrols are dismounted, which means that they will walk around a town, grab coffee, and act casual to maximize interactions with locals. Nonetheless, their role is distinct from that of the LMTs discussed earlier. They are not there to build relationships; they just collect information based on what they hear and see, and they do not have assigned municipalities, like the LMTs.

On training weeks, they will have different types of activities planned. When I visited, the first company was training with EULEX personnel (Polish police unit) who can teach urban warfare and the MNBGs (American infantry company) who can teach counterterrorism. The Hungarians bring their crowd and riot control expertise, so there are interesting opportunities for knowledge exchanges between different organizations or KFOR units. While the KTRBN does the crowd and riot control training, this is not what it does back home, which is train for regular warfare. This means that upon arrival in KFOR, they have to learn crowd and riot control and then train on it, to become specialists. The deployment is definitely seen as a professional stepping stone: "It's a good opportunity to learn leading a coy [company]. I lead one hundred and eight guys. I can prepare for my future at home. At home I am a platoon leader now, maybe I can be a deputy company commander when I go home."[58] There is also an allusion to a long-term socialization process; since Hungary's accession to NATO, it has updated its infantry tactics by working with allies, especially the Americans: "compared to the Soviet era, we had to learn how to fight."[59] Still, to them, the gender perspective is about the number of women in their unit and does not apply to their understanding of the mission tasks they carry out. And so, I asked a final question about women in the infantry, following their lead. I got a sigh, a shrug, and an answer that signaled resigned acceptance: "The society is changing. Girls or women are more accepted in the army. Just think Ranger school in the US. It's the same in every army, it's not that typical. But I think in this age, it is not a problem for them."[60]

This section served to discuss the range of tasks that are central to KFOR, from the more mission-specific tasks to the more generic ones that are still part of every mission. Overall, whether the tasks involve screening the administrative boundary line, organizing patrols, performing training activities and military exercises, or interacting with the population as LMTs, everyone I spoke to had a clear grasp of how their individual task related to the overarching mandate of SASE and FOM. What varied, however, was how NATO's gender policies and directives might apply to their own activities. This, to a certain extent, should be expected in a multinational environment which includes different training backgrounds and operational experiences, but NATO directives are supposed to provide a degree of harmonization (as detailed in Chapter 3). The next section turns to the role of the GENAD, the officer on the command team whose job it is to make sure that NATO's WPS directives (but, more specifically, Bi-Strategic Directive 040-001) are implemented in major decisions by the commander and applied across mission tasks.

GENAD Roles and Constraints

The GENAD draws information from different sources, from KFOR's intelligence branch to the LMTs or reconnaissance teams, who also interact with the local population. The GENAD's office is in the Priština-based KFOR HQ, which facilitates engagement opportunities with civil society groups and international organizations (UN, EULEX, and the UN Development Programme). The commander has regular contact with the heads of the other missions, but the GENAD also has a working relationship with their counterparts, even if there are no set, regular meetings. Not unlike the other GENADs I talked to, this male GENAD from Austria found the work difficult because of the general lack of awareness about what his role as a GENAD entails. This echoes past testimony from GENADs in Kosovo who struggled to have gender taken seriously, with one report noting that "aside from a few notable accomplishments, feelings of marginalization and powerlessness seem the recurring themes among gender advisors in Kosovo."[61] He also mentioned that in terms of workload, the range of tasks he is responsible for is too long—from providing internal training (something that is necessary to socialize the GENAD concept within the KFOR HQ) to submitting comprehensive monthly reports up the NATO chain of command to organizing outreach activities with external stakeholders, like civil society organizations or academic institutions.

The internal training is designed to facilitate a common understanding of NATO policies and directives on WPS and the inclusion of a gender perspective within the mission. There is a fair amount of public outreach that goes on too. On the day of my visit, for example, the GENAD was about to participate in a conference looking at gender perspectives in the information environment and the gendered aspects of disinformation. Balancing the internal tasks, such as advising the commander, training staff, and filing paperwork, with the external tasks, such as public outreach and representing NATO at conferences, makes it difficult to find a clear focus over the course of this six-month tour. From what I could observe, having the GENAD's attention divided in this way also undermined his influence internally, which was already tenuous because not everyone deployed on the operation has worked with a GENAD before.

NATO is attempting to increase awareness of the role by holding the annual NATO Conference on Gender Perspectives, in Brussels. The NATO HQ is quite active on the WPS front and wants perspectives from the field. As I conducted the interview, the GENAD mentioned he would soon be flying out to attend this conference, sharing some insights on how gender considerations intersect with KFOR. However, he acknowledged that every trip of his takes him out of KFOR HQ and, therefore, has the potential to undermine the role he must play internally within the mission and his importance in the eyes of the commander. The message that the GENAD must constantly stress is this: gender analysis assists in better understanding the operating environment. For the GENAD, the pathway to achieve this is through the joint effects coordination team, as well as info ops and psychological operations. Using a gender perspective can help better design campaigns to influence what the population thinks about KFOR but also how patrols are conducted and who is interviewed. The KFOR commander has the final word on all of these aspects, but the GENAD chimes in and provides advice. For example, if the public affairs team posts a video clip on Facebook, the GENAD might point out the absence of women to the commander and that featuring kids and women would be a better strategy. While the GENAD can provide recommendations to everyone, he is focused solely on the non-kinetic aspects of the mission. As such, while he could in theory work with all of the branch chiefs, he deals primarily with the LMTs, given their direct contact with the population, as well as psychological and info ops, the intelligence branch, and public affairs.

This description is consistent with the commander's intent and understanding of the GENAD's role: "the GENAD is part of the command group, part of most processes. We were lacking a GENAD during the first two months because of rotations gone bad. Now I have an Austrian colonel. The idea is to inject everything 'gender' at the beginning. I read this as human terrain and what helps the mission. Here, it's all about the mission. If something helps the mission, it's important."[62] The commander appeared confident about how the GENAD fits in, even more so than the GENAD himself. "Everyone thinks I deal with women" is how the Austrian colonel described people's impressions, while tidying up his desk, looking a little deflated.

When this GENAD came to Priština to work at the KFOR HQ, the position had not been filled, so he had to build it back up, given the lack of handover. One of the main tasks he focused on was training personnel and staff. Different trainings are tailored to specific audiences, from command group training to LMT training. The GENAD is also assisted by a network of focal points, a team of military personnel from different branches, who take on this role as a secondary duty. Having the position unfilled for several months, prior to the Austrian colonel's arrival, essentially meant that little was done on this file and that all GENAD-related responsibilities were neglected. Upon arrival, the GENAD simply sent an e-mail around asking for volunteers. For such an established mission, it struck me as surprising that a process to identify gender focal points (GFPs) was not already firmly in place; that with each rotation, GENADs have to ask for GFPs and train peers on WPS to cultivate awareness.

I went through the GENAD's internal briefing slides with him, and I could see that he spends some time at the outset of his presentations making clear that his job is not about responding to sexual harassment and abuse within the HQ, which signaled to me that this is a frequent misconception. This slide clearly indicates that sexual misconduct is for the J1 (military personnel branch) and the military police. These incidents, the GENAD said, are reported to the chain of command; and as the procedure runs its course, the perpetrator is sent home or disciplined. I asked him about how his trainings are received internally, and he sighed. He noted that he can be effective within the mission because of his rank. Otherwise, he said, it would be very difficult to do the work. If he were a captain or major, he is certain that he would be dismissed. As a colonel, however, people listen. Being a male GENAD may also have helped, "as it surprised others and got folks curious."[63] In general, he does not press too hard, though, mentioning that "if I raise it [gender] at every meeting, then they would put me in the corner."[64] The GENAD also acknowledged the challenges of working in a multinational environment: "I have noticed that some nations are more open minded, and others have a lack of information. We cannot change things with a few slides. It depends on how you have been raised. For example, the Scandinavians and Canadians, they are advanced on this topic and very eager."[65] He smiled as he said that, knowing that I am Canadian, but he probably meant it.

Other challenges the GENAD faces are common in other facets of the mission, I came to realize: "Measuring the effects of our actions is difficult because we are trying to measure mindsets."[66] Those are problems that he can tackle with other teams. For example, he referred specifically to participating in working group meetings during which the gender perspective is assessed as part of the mission's broader non-lethal targeting efforts. But when I asked for an illustration of this, the only example I got once again related to domestic violence.

When it comes to the GENAD's reporting requirements to higher-level HQ, JFC-Naples and SHAPE, he emphasized the importance of analyzing different segments of the population, as well as their unique needs or vulnerabilities. The major topics of concern are rampant unemployment and domestic violence, which the GENAD said increased by 30%, including against men and boys. There are 8,000 shelters for women and girls, a factoid the colonel picked up during his attendance at a shelter opening ceremony. Though the GENAD seems like a lonely posting at times, other advisors are actively thinking about how gender impacts the operating environment; but how that then shapes mission adaptation is less clear. The next section turns to some of these other key advisors.

Other Key Advisors

During my conversation with the GENAD, I had the distinct feeling throughout the meeting that the officer was not comfortable in his role and was not at the top of the pecking order within the Command Group. By contrast, the POLAD appeared much more confident in underscoring the importance of gender analysis as part of the broader social and political assessments that are necessary for a smoothly run mission. This confidence might stem from the fact that the POLAD is a more established advisory position within the Command Group and so better understood and accepted by peers, even if it is a civilian position. The POLAD's job is to track topics that might have security implications for the NATO mission. The POLAD digests information from various sources and contacts and then makes sense of it all to the commander so that it feeds into the decision-making process. The POLAD also prepares the commander for KLEs, which is military speak for meetings with persons of interest. As the lone civilian voice (compared to the GENAD, who is a military officer), the POLAD brings a much-needed perspective within meetings. And finally, the POLAD I talked to had a longer deployment window, which necessarily contributed to a richer understanding of the political context. The POLAD had been there for a year and a half and was living in Kosovo with his family. He had deployed as a soldier in the late 1990s and, intrigued, pursued a graduate degree to better understand the region. He is what the military would call a "subject matter expert," though that is not always the case when appointing a POLAD to a command group. He painted the picture in the following terms: "many of the military tasks that they have in KFOR are easy, but the political implications of executing these tasks are huge."[67]

The POLAD was very good at anticipating my questions, and he basically just dove in: "Measuring operational effect through the J5 (Plans and Ops) is like going through a phonebook of indicators."[68] That exercise, which is performed at the mission level, then feeds into an annual review process at the strategic-level HQ (SHAPE in Mons, Belgium), which determines whether KFOR's troop level should increase or decrease. The POLAD admitted that whether those indicators truly measure progress is uncertain as the indicators are mostly focused on outputs rather than outcomes, an observation which was echoed during my visit to JFC-Naples, the operational-level HQ for KFOR. The POLAD's assessment of the gender perspective mirrored that of the GENAD: "In this mission, since we are following social issues, social discontent, and expressions of social discontent, like protests, or socioeconomic issues that could translate into security issues, the gender perspective is extremely important. This country has huge problems with domestic violence."[69] Everywhere I went, the issue of domestic violence was stressed and was the go-to example of how KFOR tracks gender considerations. Yet, the POLAD added something new: "Aside from veteran organizations and political parties, women's organizations are best at mobilizing numbers in the street, which makes them interesting politically. The ability to mobilize is of interest to us."[70] This illustrates that there are two sides to the coin of NATO's gender policies and directives. First, gender analysis is seen as necessary to make sure the mission is in line with the population's needs. Second, gender analysis can be leveraged for the benefit of the mission and its operational effectiveness. It is this latter function that seems to have the most traction in the predominantly military environment of KFOR, though, arguably, the first can feed into the second.

Confirming my earlier hunch, the POLAD also seemed sensitive to the divided attention that any GENAD must grapple with: focusing internally, dealing mostly with the mission's military personnel, or focusing externally, engaging with local stakeholders and counterparts from other international organizations. The POLAD noted that, "internally, there are varying degrees of understanding of what the GENAD position entails, including for the GENADs themselves. Some GENADs are seen as having more of an internal role, meaning they are viewed as protecting the integrity of women's rights on base, for example."[71] The POLAD, however, favored the external dimension: "I see it [the position of GENAD] as a Kosovo-wide gender expert."[72] Such comments on the fuzziness of the role is something I would encounter in every NATO environment I visited as part of my fieldwork; this was not unique to KFOR.

Beyond the KFOR environment, NATO also has civilian and military advisors to support capacity-building efforts in Kosovo. Also based in Priština, this team of fifty, about twenty-five of whom are advisors, is known as the NATO Advisory and Liaison Team. The director is a military official, the deputy director is a civilian, and they are not part of the KFOR chain of command; they are under the Operations Division of the International Staff. In providing advice to Kosovo institutions, the NATO advisors include material on the WPS agenda, though I am told this can sometimes be controversial for cultural reasons.[73] Whether on WPS or other aspects of the capacity-building efforts, sometimes the advice just is not taken up by the KSF or ministerial staff. This aspect of NATO's work in Kosovo is quite similar to some of the advisory functions that are part of the NATO Mission in Iraq (Chapter 6), as are some of the challenges experienced by the civilian advisors who are women. For example, they say that they encounter resistance from some of their host-country interlocutors, and that, being a woman and a civilian automatically lessens their credibility when compared to their peers who are men and military.[74]

Conclusion

KFOR's tasks have evolved quite a bit since its inception, even as the mandate has remained the same. Kinetic tasks have progressively faded into the background, while non-kinetic tasks are more relevant for the day-to-day KFOR presence in Kosovo. The consensus within KFOR is that kinetic assets are still needed though, given the politically uncertain environment. Even if the level of threat is low, tensions could unexpectedly flare up, especially if sudden troop drawdowns were announced. These fears are perhaps compounded by the fact that relations between Kosovo and Serbia remain tense. The situation has not changed much: there is a diplomatic stalemate despite EU- and US-led efforts, and the irritants have not been resolved, like the Kosovar tariffs on Serbia and the plans of creating a Kosovo army.

One point that is interesting to note about my fieldwork in Kosovo is that many of the people I interviewed had previous tours either in Kosovo or in Bosnia. They were familiar with the region and could comment on how things had changed since their last visit. This was not the case in Iraq or in the Baltics. I was especially struck by the comments of the LEGAD, who said "I realize now that this tour is the worst. In 2008, you had to ensure the security much more than now. Now it's a completely different tour and mission, as it is a more political environment. It is not technically an operational environment."[75] Even if I had not previously been to the region, it was obvious to me that the kinetic elements of the mission appeared superfluous. They were useful in providing training opportunities or for participating in military exercises with various stakeholders in Kosovo, but on the whole, they were ready but underutilized. This is a good thing because it means that the security situation has stabilized, but the fact that there is no drawdown of forces means that the political climate is not stable enough to permit a full transfer of security responsibilities to the Kosovo police or the KSF. And so forces find ways to stay busy and to be ready in case something happens, leveraging training, exercises, and broader engagement activities with different partners in Kosovo.

It is within these parameters that the application of NATO policies and military directives on gender has been tailored to fit the operational context. Awareness of those policies and directives appears highest in the areas where they matter most operationally: through the efforts that are deployed to influence the population, whether these are the patrols carried out by the LMTs, the K4 broadcasts, CIMIC activities, or general public affairs tasks.

This seems to be an improvement from past reviews of KFOR performance dating back to 2013, which indicated that KFOR did not account for gender perspectives in its security analysis and that KFOR staff struggled to see how gender was relevant for their work.[76]

Another important finding from this chapter is that the lack of women deployed on the mission makes certain tasks more difficult or sensitive. It is just not as easy to engage with local women, let alone finding entry points to promote greater gender equality. Moreover, KFOR GENADs have internal responsibilities that do not directly advance mission objectives through the incorporation of a gender perspective across different lines of effort. Instead, they spend a lot of time providing training to different units and teams, to better socialize the idea of how gender might matter for their work and to foster greater acceptance of the very NATO policies and directives that have created a space for having GENADs in command groups.

To the extent that military personnel are aware of these NATO objectives, it is taken seriously so long as these can be tied to mission priorities and shown to improve operational effectiveness. The topic is still sensitive, and I could sense the general unease my questions sometimes generated. Although KFOR uniformed personnel did not mind talking about gender-based analysis and how that can enhance the military's understanding of the operating environment, they are faced with a contradiction: to get to that refined understanding entails engaging with local women, but they feel ill-equipped to do so because of the lack of women within NATO contingents, in addition to perceived cultural barriers with Kosovo Albanians in particular. While the people I interviewed very often wanted to push aside the topic of women in the military entirely, we inevitably circled back to it when it became clear that, for the performance of certain military tasks, having more women on the mission would deliver clear operational benefits. This, ultimately, is a very narrow understanding of what the NATO policies and directives were originally intended to emphasize, namely that improving gender equality is an important component of achieving more sustainable security outcomes. Perhaps this should come as no surprise since these WPS policies and directives have been around for just over a decade; with time, it is reasonable to expect that greater clarity will be provided by civilian decision makers and policymakers to inform military action. For now, the military's own interpretation of how WPS norms should translate into military tasks is assessed on the merit of their operational value, consistent with the logic of norm distortion. Because the military is professionally socialized to focus on the mission and operational effectiveness, most everything it does will be brought back to this key consideration, even gender analysis. This is what drives the mechanism of norm distortion and the civilians who monitor these activities might not want to interfere with this kind of military-focused implementation because it still contributes to further institutionalizing WPS norms within NATO.

5

Deterring in the Baltics

How does gender intersect with collective defense and deterrence? NATO's inability to answer this question is plainly visible in its policy on Women, Peace and Security (WPS). It is focused on three main outcomes, ensuring that "mechanisms to encourage exchanging information and sharing best practices are strengthened; gender perspectives are addressed in efforts and strategies related to Emerging Security Challenges [like cyber, hybrid warfare, and terrorism]; gender perspectives are included in [the] defence planning process."[1] In practice, however, enhanced forward presence (eFP), the multinational battlegroups that were first established in the Baltic states and Poland, has been at the forefront of how WPS might be taken into account as part of collective defense and deterrence. The alliance formed these battlegroups in response to Russia's annexation of Crimea in 2014, and they were further bolstered in 2022, following the launch of a full-scale military invasion of Ukraine. From the German-led battlegroup in Lithuania to the troops under Canadian command in Latvia, soldiers are planning tank and infantry maneuvers to deter Russia from directly threatening the alliance and preparing to defend NATO territory, if necessary. In the heart of those training areas, how can WPS norms take hold? The civilian guidance that one might find in policy documents being scarce, it is no wonder few tangible examples are emerging from this operational context, compared to Afghanistan or Iraq. Moreover, commanders approach the management of their respective battlegroups differently because prior to Russia's 2022 invasion of Ukraine, NATO was not in charge of the operational planning process. Contributing countries therefore exercised significant discretion in how they ran each battlegroup and whether or not they integrated WPS norms as part of that process. Because WPS norms were often dismissed or ignored altogether, the mechanism of norm distortion had more discrete manifestations.

This chapter offers a discussion on the eFP battlegroups but does not describe the transformations that took place after 2022 as the implications of Russia's invasion of Ukraine continue to be in flux. At the outset then,

Deploying Feminism. Stéfanie von Hlatky, Oxford University Press. © Oxford University Press 2023.
DOI: 10.1093/oso/9780197653524.003.0005

eFP battlegroups were led by four framework nations (Canada, the United Kingdom, Germany, and the United States), each taking the lead in coordinating the efforts of the multinational contingents under its command. For the Canadian commander, the government back in Ottawa expects reports that line up with its feminist foreign policy, but in contrast, there is no such impetus behind the efforts of the British-, German-, and American-led battlegroups. Since there is no precise guidance on how WPS norms relate to collective defense scenarios, I was interested in seeing how commanders operationalize NATO gender directives at the tactical level, without the institutional umbrella that NATO provides for its operations, including its gender structure (see Chapter 3). This is a looser principal–agent arrangement, between NATO and individual allies, than the one discussed in Chapters 4 and 6 and, as such, has implications for the way WPS norms are made tangible on the ground. Here, too, the gender balance and civil–military integration matter; but because NATO did not exercise its harmonizing influence like it has in other missions, other factors shaped the implementation of WPS norms. As these operations took off, commanders had a lot more discretion, so their competence and individual commitment to WPS (or lack thereof) mattered more than for the NATO Mission in Iraq (NMI) and the Kosovo Force (KFOR), as did the political directives coming through the national chains of command.

My fieldwork started in Adazi, Latvia, where the NATO training area is located; and I was greeted by the Canadian battlegroup commander, who had a presentation ready to go on how he was integrating a gender perspective into his activities. He skimmed over his preamble on NATO's gender policies and guidelines and went right into the tactical challenges of implementation. At first, I thought this was a success story for the institutionalization of those policies and guidelines, but I quickly revised my thinking: this is just one commander. Nevertheless, the Canadian Armed Forces (CAF) is pushing for greater gender literacy across the force; but then, commanders vary in their ability and willingness to make gender mainstreaming one of their priorities. This created a sharp contrast between the Canadian-led battlegroup and the German-led battlegroup in Lithuania, where WPS norms were interpreted as the prevention of sexual harassment within the contingent, period.

This chapter will provide a discussion of eFP by focusing on two of the original battlegroups: the Canadian-led battlegroup in Latvia and the German-led battlegroup in Lithuania.[2] It will offer first some background on the security environment and why the mission was set up and then an overview of how gender considerations might factor into military tasks. In addition to fieldwork carried out in Latvia, Estonia, and Lithuania, interviews conducted at the NATO headquarters (HQ), Supreme HQ Allied Powers Europe (SHAPE), and Joint Forces Command (JFC)–Brunssum helped in identifying any discrepancies between how the mandate is articulated politically and how it is carried out by military commanders on the ground. I show that, far from being institutionalized, implementation varies significantly across battlegroups. Moreover, the idea that women enhance operational effectiveness was almost entirely rejected by the service members I interviewed, save a few community outreach examples. While gender advisors (GENADs) are not deployed as part of each battlegroup, I engage in a discussion about their roles and constraints, as well as those of other key advisors who can (or could) contribute to integrating NATO's WPS norms within eFP's activities.

Mission Background and Historical Context

The Baltic countries and Poland are on the frontlines of the NATO–Russia rivalry. This much is clear when one looks at a map or is exposed to local news. To the Baltic states and Poland, collective defense and deterrence should always be the top priority of the alliance, when compared to NATO's other two pillars of crisis management and cooperative security. Their heads of state as well as foreign or defense ministers underscore this point on every international platform. The security environment, which is characterized by one of the most vulnerable geographies of NATO's territory, has further deteriorated starting with Russia's annexation of Crimea in 2014 and worsened sharply after its broader invasion of Ukraine in 2022.

The Baltics are wedged between Russia's mainland and its enclave of Kaliningrad, in addition to neighboring Belarus, upon which Moscow has a firm grip. The initial fear was that Russia could carve out a small portion of Baltic territory in a quick fait accompli, forcing a response by NATO, whose reinforcements come through the Suwalki gap and could then be blocked by Russian anti-access/area denial capabilities. With Russia's large-scale war in Ukraine starting in 2022, all of NATO's eastern flank became more directly threatened, prompting the alliance to double the number of battlegroups and increase troop levels to reach 40,000 military personnel under direct NATO command.[3]At the 2022 Summit in Madrid, NATO member states agreed to further increase their troop presence on the alliance's eastern flank, among other commitments, signaling a pessimistic outlook for NATO-Russia relations, in line with a more acute perception of threat.

Things were not always this bad. What should have been a wake-up call was the Russo–Georgian war in 2008, but it did not galvanize NATO into action. Back then, there were different views regarding the extent to which Russia represented a threat to the alliance. Everything changed for NATO's eastward outlook in 2014 with the annexation of Crimea and then more decisively in 2022. From the Wales Summit in 2014 to the 2021 Brussels Summit, NATO heads of state have been explicit about the rising tensions with Russia. For example, the 2018 communiqué states the following:

> The Euro–Atlantic security environment has become *less stable* and predictable as a result of *Russia's illegal and illegitimate* annexation of Crimea and ongoing destabilisation of eastern Ukraine; its military posture and *provocative military activities*, including near NATO borders, such as the deployment of modern dual-capable missiles in Kaliningrad, *repeated violation* of NATO Allied airspace, and the continued military build-up in Crimea; its significant investments in the modernisation of its strategic forces; its *irresponsible and aggressive* nuclear rhetoric; its large-scale, no-notice snap exercises; and the growing number of its exercises with a nuclear dimension. (emphasis added)[4]

In the 2021 communiqué, any ambiguity about the nature of the relationship with Russia is removed, with Russia explicitly being singled out as a threat, accompanied by an even longer list of misdeeds.[5] In 2022, at the Madrid Summit, Russia was described as "the most significant and direct threat to Allied security."[6] This adversarial tone is quite striking when one compares this language to pre-2014 summits, which emphasized the cooperative nature of NATO–Russia relations. This shift is also obvious when one reads the 2010 Strategic Concept (adopted during the Lisbon Summit): "Notwithstanding differences on particular issues, we remain convinced that the security of NATO and Russia is intertwined and that a strong and constructive partnership based on mutual confidence, transparency and predictability can best serve our security."[7] Over the span of a decade, Russia has gone from partner to foe. The silver lining for the Baltic States is that NATO allies are now more aligned in their perception of threat on the eastern flank and have mustered the resources necessary to respond accordingly, following Russia's full-blown war in Ukraine.[8]

In this environment, many observers have asked if this is a return to the Cold War, back to a time where WPS norms did not even exist.[9] While the conventional nature of the response, with the deployment of battlegroups, is reminiscent of NATO troops that were (and some remained) permanently stationed in European countries, the threat is more hybrid in nature, with information operations and cyberattacks bolstering Russia's conventional and nuclear postures.[10] Prior to 2022, it was mostly below the threshold of war that NATO's WPS considerations were manifest; indeed, the gendered implications of conventional military conflict, like the mass mobilization of men in Ukraine or the gender composition of internally displaced people and refugees, were not fully appreciated until they became a reality. NATO has also steadily built up its infrastructure in the region, establishing divisional HQ as well as having American brigade combat teams on hand.[11] Military *mobility* and *readiness* are the two words constantly heard in expert discussions about NATO's ability to defend the Baltics, and those words now ring true across the eastern flank.[12] Since 2014, NATO has ramped up its readiness initiatives, reformed its command structure, and tabled new plans to enhance military mobility, even seeking greater cooperation with the European Union, since NATO would rely on European infrastructure to move troops eastward in case of direct conflict with Russia.[13] Moreover, since the Trump administration's open criticism of NATO, there are stronger doubts about American leadership within the alliance, which has pushed Europe further down the path of devising regional hedging strategies.[14] Biden's commitments to NATO offer only temporary reassurance.

Indeed, a key part of the mandate for enhanced forward presence, beyond deterrence, is to reassure allies in the region. When looking at indicators of operational effectiveness in the provision of NATO assurances, one must turn to the populations of the Baltic States and Poland, where sociodemographic, gender-disaggregated data can enhance security assessments. There are also more intuitive measures to determine the adequacy of assurance measures, for example, in the context of military-to-military interactions. At the time of my fieldwork, NATO forces were deepening their integration with their Baltic and Polish allies, and there was a sense that the longer the NATO forces were there, the more allies would be reassured. A physical presence demonstrates resolve, and resolve is a critical component of both deterrence and assurance. In this sense, every exercise, display, or demonstration of alliance solidarity counts. As far as deterrence goes, it is always a bit more challenging to measure; deterrence success is a non-event, precisely because nothing happens, while deterrence failures are much more obvious.[15]

According to NATO officials, the primary deterrence focus remains on increasing alliance capabilities, as well as the demonstration of those capabilities through forward presence and exercises. For the deterrence equation, having a growing alliance, with member states that are different in terms of size, political culture and geographic location, represents an important political constraint. This is perhaps most evident in NATO's communication efforts at the strategic level but also in theater, across the battlegroups.[16] Within NATO's Public Diplomacy Division (PDD) in Brussels, there is a relatively new task force that is responsible for deterrence messaging. PDD has tracked NATO's popularity in the past, for example, and is also tailoring some of its messaging at target audiences who display lower levels of awareness about NATO, including youth and women.

The challenge of the post-2014 environment is thus twofold for NATO: developing a new deterrence model and then pushing different directorates and divisions to adopt it.[17] Some of these approaches have been tested at the North Atlantic Council level, like running tabletop deterrence exercises in a hybrid environment to identify blind spots in decision-making.[18] These practical exercises are where WPS norms can work their way in and gain traction because special "injects" can be integrated into the scenarios. *Injects* are unexpected events that are introduced to make the exercise more unpredictable for participants and are tied to precise learning or training outcomes, with larger implications for shaping NATO's own interpretation of norms through practice. For instance, NATO's big annual war game, called CMX (which stands for Crisis Management Exercise), has introduced WPS injects like challenging participants to handle female refugees on the battlefield, which improves internal awareness about WPS norms across NATO's divisions.

More generally though, exercises like CMX, can be used as vehicles to test out deterrence approaches and to validate NATO's processes in a pre-crisis space, which is very much compatible with the deteriorating security environment that led to the creation of eFP. The multinational nature of deterrence activities, with multiple allies involved in eFP, can further contribute to assurance measures by sending a credible signal of NATO's commitment to countries on the eastern flank. In terms of capacity, more NATO countries contributing to eFP might not make Estonia more combat-effective, but the messaging aspect of having multiple allies on board might deliver both deterrence and assurance effects.[19] Put more bluntly, the military benefit of waving the Icelandic flag in Lithuania as part of eFP is nil, but the political benefit of demonstrating alliance unity is thought to be worth the trouble.[20] Understanding both the political and military dimensions of deterrence, therefore, is an important area of focus for NATO, even if the capability-based approach to deterrence remains dominant.[21] In terms of military capabilities, there is still a gap between Russia and NATO. Russia has a lagging economy but still mustered a military expenditure of $61.7 billion in 2020.[22] NATO's total military spending exceeds $1 trillion.[23] Russia's war in Ukraine has further demonstrated the limits of its military capabilities and overall operational effectiveness.

Finally, it is worth spotlighting the Baltic States' and Poland's contributions to collective defense more specifically, given their experience in hosting multinational battlegroups on their soil. These states made the 2% NATO defense spending guideline a priority, though, admittedly, this is much easier to achieve for countries with smaller gross domestic products compared to some of NATO's bigger economies. Politicians on the eastern flank understand that they cannot credibly call for NATO reinforcements if they are not seen as paying their fair share or improving their national forces.[24]

In sum, the Baltics and Poland have been strong supporters of eFP from the start, and their calls for a greater NATO presence on the eastern flank were finally taken seriously in 2014, after the annexation of Crimea. NATO solidarity and cohesion further solidified in 2022, prompting the deployment of more capabilities eastward. Although the initial four battlegroups could not have realistically halted or pushed back a massive Russian advance in the Baltics (the combined force level of eFP barely reached 5,000 troops), their very presence, along with the announced reinforcements, serve as a credible warning to Moscow that the alliance stands ready to defend the territories of its easternmost members. The next section delves deeper into eFP's original mandate and the key mission tasks carried out at the tactical level, demonstrating how the command structure, civil–military balance, and gender composition contribute to an uneven pattern of implementation when it comes to WPS norms.

Gender, Mission Tasks, and eFP's mandate

NATO spent the bulk of the post–Cold War period focused on security in the Balkans and then Afghanistan. The idea of shifting the alliance's focus

back to deterrence and to collective defense could not have been anticipated in the early 2000s as NATO–Russia relations were at their warmest and
President Vladimir Putin had kind words for NATO. In 2002, speaking about
the NATO–Russia Council during the Rome Summit, Putin even stated the
following:

> For Russia, with its geopolitical position, the enhancement of coopera-
> tion with NATO as equal partners is one of the real embodiments of the
> multiple approach, to which there is no alternative and which we intend to
> pursue resolutely. . . . Only by harmoniously combining our actions in all
> these areas will we open up wide-ranging possibilities for building a single
> security region—from Vancouver to Vladivostok.[25]

With NATO reprioritizing deterrence, its official posture has focused quite
narrowly on the appropriate mix of conventional and nuclear forces needed
to discourage Russia from performing another land grab, this time challenging NATO's resolve when it comes to invoking Article V. As such, there
is not much literature, nor is there a robust policy discussion, that examines
the intersection of deterrence and gender. In the context of this book, it is
worth asking whether this is because it is an underdeveloped field of study or
because there is no salient gender dimension to deterrence and collective defense. When we focus on NATO's ability to deter, which is rooted in credibly
communicating commitments to allies and demonstrating collective capabilities, we can assess if WPS norms are more important than traditionally
assumed.

To demonstrate the credibility of NATO's commitment in the Baltics,
the alliance initially set up an air policing mission, Standing NATO
Maritime Group 1 in the Baltic Sea, and then followed up with the four eFP
battlegroups, announced at the 2016 NATO Summit.[26] In 2022, capabilities
were further strengthened as war spread across Ukraine's territory. NATO's
real weakness, however, is not material. Even if regional experts preach that
more military capabilities are needed, such as the ability to deploy faster
reinforcements, bolstering air power, and acquiring more anti-tank weapons
and ammunition, alliance resolve is harder to demonstrate than capabilities
and is fundamentally political in nature. As a democratic alliance, NATO
relies on political unity among all of its member states in order to communicate its intentions. As Putin has well understood, undermining this unity
and further polarizing existing ideological cleavages is an effective strategy to

sow doubts about NATO's ability to deter its adversaries and defend its allies. Launching a full-scale military invasion in Ukraine appears as a strategic miscalculation in this respect, as allies tightened coordination and cooperation to rapidly improve their deterrence and defense capabilities.

When it comes to clearly signaling that NATO would be willing to fight Russia if provoked, can we really point to a cohesive alliance picture? Prior to 2022, what may have undermined cohesion is NATO's varying levels of public support across its member states, especially on defense spending and deploying troops on operations, with those levels of support varying across men, women, and youth.[27] Recognizing this, NATO both boosted public diplomacy efforts targeting women and raised the profile of WPS norms through its messaging. Additionally, and the 2022 invasion notwithstanding, allies have different perceptions of threat; and some NATO states, like Turkey and Hungary, have cultivated overtly friendly relations with Russia over the years. Other NATO states have been more subtle and, at times, covertly friendly toward Russia. For example, before the 2021 NATO Summit in Brussels, Germany at times appeared very muted in its criticism of Russia and resisted the view that it might constitute a threat to Europe or NATO.[28] Germany quickly revised its stance vis-à-vis Russia after the expansion of the war in Ukraine in 2022, almost immediately committing to meeting NATO's 2% pledge.

In 2022, the alliance found out just how far the Kremlin was willing to go to protect Russian influence in what it perceives to be its near abroad. While hindsight is 20/20, NATO could not predict or try to guess the Kremlin's calculations or next moves. As far as NATO's territorial integrity is concerned, it is just as easy to argue that the deployment of the battlegroups deters Russia than it is to argue that it has not changed anything. This ambiguity might be the exact security context that Russia is trying to shape and uphold, as reflected in its disinformation tactics, aimed to "deprive audiences of the ability to distinguish between truth and lie by creating as many competing narratives as possible in the global media space."[29] Moreover, Russia has also deployed a gender-based analysis in its propaganda efforts, through fake news and by targeting soldiers' mobile devices, especially in the Baltics. Young, male soldiers are the key demographic of these targeting efforts; the battlegroups' gender composition is almost exclusively male and, at least prior to 2022, there was a lot of downtime in the training areas, including free weekends. This has become so significant that "NATO officials now tell troops to treat their mobiles as potentially compromised." Estonia, Latvia, and Lithuania "have drafted strict rules on how mobiles can and cannot be used."[30] Hacking efforts range from modern-day honeypots—hackers posing as women to lure soldiers into online relationships—to "psyop" text messages that "falsely announce infidelity" or that aim to demoralize soldiers.[31]

While the Canadian and German commanders I spoke to in Latvia and Lithuania downplayed the significance of this threat, these were early days for the mission. More recent reports in the news have since indicated the problem has gotten more significant, not less. American personnel deployed in the Baltics and Poland have also been targeted: "the rising popularity of the internet and mobile apps for dating among younger Americans has given new life to one of the Soviet Union's trademark espionage collection techniques . . . in which intelligence operatives lure victims into illicit sexual encounters, which can be exploited for blackmail."[32] These types of threats are being studied by NATO's Centre of Excellence on Cyber Defence in Estonia, and cyber and information domain threats are increasingly being built into NATO exercises to improve preparedness and resilience; but NATO's reach within the eFP context was limited at first because of the prevailing command structure.[33]

While there is an overarching NATO mandate for eFP, SHAPE initially did not own the operational planning and force generation processes, giving the framework nations broad latitude in terms of how the battlegroups are structured.[34] Logistically, the division of labor between NATO and the framework nations is not immediately obvious because there are three main chains of command: NATO, the host country, the framework nation. And then sending nations (troop-contributing countries) also have a national chain of command to honor. The way that the Canadian-led battlegroup interpreted the mandate and ramped up its activities was to focus on deterrence and, if necessary, defense against an aggressor, with a readiness level at about 80%.[35] This defense and deterrence posture through eFP's first phase was meant to prevent conflict, not to escalate the tense NATO–Russia situation. Framework nations have had to be conscious of this dynamic when planning for training and exercises, as well as when deploying their strategic communication efforts. From my fieldwork, I could see that the Battlegroup in Latvia conducted training activities regularly and focused on tactical interoperability with the other contributing nations and integration with the other battlegroups.[36] By contrast, the German-led battlegroup in Lithuania was more focused on training activities, and it was not at the same readiness level when it comes to developing a combat-ready battalion.[37]

While eFP's mandate is rooted in NATO's principle of collective defense, it is also important to mention that, from an allied perspective, the relationship between framework nations and the host country is pivotal as it contributes to the assurance function that eFP battlegroups also serve. The lines of effort listed in the operational orders and concept of operations (CONOPS) capture these multiple dimensions: situational awareness, interoperability, readiness, strategic communications, presence, responsiveness, integration, force protection. Ultimately, if deterrence were to fail and Russia were to invade or impose a fait accompli through a land grab in the Baltics, then eFP forces would have to hold tight for reinforcements from the Very High Readiness Joint Task Force (which at the time involved 5,000 NATO troops that could deploy in a seventy-two-hour time frame) and the NATO Response Force (20,000 NATO troops that could deploy in a five- to thirty-day time frame).[38]

SHAPE and Other Chains of Command

As alluded to above, as eFP took shape, NATO did not count the battlegroups as part of its operations; rather, eFP was considered to be part of the alliance's portfolio of activities. Prior to the 2022 war, operational planning was coordinated between the framework (or lead) nations of eFP and the sending nations (or troop-contributing countries), rather than SHAPE. Four member states volunteered to act as framework nations for the four multinational battlegroups, and then, the host nations integrated these NATO contingents into their national force structures. All eFP forces worked and trained together under a common NATO flag, but in practice, the details were arranged via bilateral agreements between host states and contributing allies, in coordination with the framework nations.[39]

From 2016 to 2022 then, the NATO role is more circumscribed, when compared to KFOR or NMI. NATO's operational-level HQ for eFP, JFC-Brunssum, would keep the supreme Allied commander in Europe informed on the battlegroups, providing "joint operational guidance to the battlegroups, ensuring that all other elements of the chain of command remain informed and share responsibility for the task. In addition to that, JFC-Brunssum now has a clear role in assessing the capabilities of eFP battlegroups, and to ensure that they are able to fulfill their mission."[40] Using insights from the principal–agent framework outlined at the beginning of the book, I argue that this kind of command structure allows for greater discretion on the part of the original framework nations (Germany, the United Kingdom, Canada, and the United States) and their individual commanders, with less NATO oversight and control over how the mandate is implemented on the ground. When interviewing SHAPE officials, it was stressed that "NATO really is not in the loop" when it comes to "capabilities eFP framework nations are bringing to the table."[41] I was told that, even if there were no NATO requirement for certain capabilities, they would be deployed based on the framework nation's discretion and not generated through NATO's Combined Joint Statement of Requirements. While this does not necessarily affect the deterrence equation, it does undermine co-ordination efforts on the NATO side; and therefore, it results in different approaches to WPS as well.

At the time of my visit, what NATO provided to eFP was fairly min-imal. There were joint enablers, like the air policing assets and strategic communications, alongside some level of coordination capacity and lo-gistics channeled through the NATO Force Integration Units (NFIUs).[42] However, strategic communications are central to mission success, and the fact that NATO has developed an overarching strategic communica-tions framework provides some coherence to efforts across battlegroups.[43] This guidance document, which makes no reference to the gender per-spective or the broader WPS agenda, explains the nature of the threat to be countered and the key communication objectives related to deter-rence: demonstrating cohesion, preventing miscalculations, and coun-tering disinformation.[44] This is in tension with the WPS action plan, which specifies that "gender perspectives are included in strategic com-munications," as one of the stated outputs.[45] The strategic communications strategy notes that "Russia already conducts a significant Information Operations/disinformation campaign directed at NATO for both Russian domestic and international audiences, with particular aggressive efforts in the Baltic States" and it "will exploit any real, perceived or fabricated differences among Allies."[46] This kind of strategic-level guidance, coor-dination, and synchronization is supporting StratCom efforts but not the core of eFP's work that is focused on battlegroup training and exercises. Ironically, NATO mentions its adversaries' (though this seems primarily aimed at Russia) use of a gender perspective in its hybrid warfare activi-ties, claiming that "there is evidence showing how states are targeting spe-cific groups of a society, in many cases men, to steer riots and mistrust against the national authorities to gain support, or in other cases enter another country and retrieve land."[47]

In sum, while the eFP framework nation model provided speed and flexibility initially, it strayed from developing replicable procedure, predictable planning cycles, and systematic data collection, what SHAPE essentially lives by.[48] This trade-off between expediency and the quality of coordination impacted many aspects of the operation, including when WPS was taken into account and how.

Entry Points for Gender Considerations

The discussion thus far has focused on the political and strategic levels of analysis. Turning to the battlegroups and how they work now brings us to the operational and tactical levels, with more mission-specific entry points for gender-based considerations. Through their concepts of operations, operational orders, mission orders, and standard operating procedures, battlegroup commanders can reference NATO's WPS norms and directives. This might include the collection of sex-disaggregated data for NATO forces as well as sex-disaggregated data for local communities, especially when it comes to their level of support for eFP. Commanders might mandate gender awareness training designed by NATO, from the framework nations' own training repository, or both, as well as appoint or work with GENADs and gender focal points (GFPs; gender training requirements, if there are any, are specified in the force generation orders). The most ambitious plan for implementing WPS norms came from the Canadian-led battlegroup. The commander's intent was communicated as follows:

> I intend to integrate gender perspectives into Analysis Planning, Execution and Evaluation in order to maximize the effectiveness of the eFP activities by understanding and using all relevant data with regards to the different segments of the population and the impact our activities have on them. This will maximize the effectiveness of the BG [battlegroup] and will minimize detrimental effects stemming from our operations. I see this as a joint initiative amongst all sending nations. As a result, this will lead to the collection of lessons learned and the sharing of information amongst our allies. Overall, this will help perpetuate gender mainstreaming within NATO and its partner nations.[49]

Consistent with the argument developed in the first half of the book, WPS norms and NATO guidance are primarily about mainstreaming gender considerations into military planning and activities rather than improving the gender balance of the force. They are about NATO's own operational effectiveness, though preventing unintended consequences can serve both the alliance and local communities. This is explicitly reported in battlegroup standard operating procedures, where the stated aim is "to ensure compliance with all NATO direction on the consideration and incorporation of gender perspectives into BG planning and activities" to "reduce the risk of unintended consequences and increase our effectiveness."[50] This is achieved through a 1:75 ratio of GFPs to battlegroup personnel (at all levels and across ranks) to facilitate and monitor gender mainstreaming tasks, in line with the commander's intent.[51] In the GFP Mission Order, further instructions are provided with regard to training requirements. In the case of Latvia, the commanding officer mandated that all eFP members complete the CAF's Gender-Based Analysis Plus training, in addition to three different course packages available through NATO's learning platforms. The overall intent and plans are tied to NATO policies and directives but also to national-level documents, at the discretion of the battlegroup HQ.

Battlegroup Tasks

At the tactical level, there are both kinetic and non-kinetic tasks that are meant to deliver effects that support the broader strategic goals of deterrence and assurance. As this section will show, the gender dimension is embedded into operational plans and assessments but may not be carried out consistently at the tactical level. Additionally, it is worth noting that if women's representation is already skewed at the strategic level, it admittedly gets more pronounced as we get closer to the tactical level. The eFP battlegroups have the worst gender balance statistics of all NATO deployments. While Bi-Strategic Command Directive 040-001 on WPS leaves decisions on force composition to individual allies, there are many signposts encouraging countries to deploy more women in NATO operations. Female representation is also tracked and monitored through annual reports compiled by the International Military Staff's Office of the Gender Advisor.

The baseline assumption driving NATO's initial posture and activities on the eastern flank was that Russia was unlikely to launch a ground invasion but would instead pursue actions to undermine and destabilize NATO governments.[52] As such, deterrence in the Baltics must continue to evolve, considering both the hybrid threat environment and changes to regional security dynamics. While the four original NATO battlegroups trained to defend, which is also necessary for a credible deterrence posture, they also focused on non-kinetic tasks. As one of the battlegroup commanders put it, "it's building cohesion, one parade at a time."[53] In today's deterrence blueprint, this too can have a strategic effect. It means ensuring integration within the host brigades (each battlegroup is part of a national brigade within the host country) but also smooth multinational coordination within the battlegroup's HQ as every country is there representing its national interests and coordinating its own assets in support of training and exercises.[54]

Training and Exercises

In terms of kinetic tasks, there are many military exercises planned and executed during each rotation. For training activities, the main lines of effort are readiness, interoperability, strategic communications, and force protection. In a nutshell, they promote interoperability and cohesion internally while demonstrating the battlegroup's capabilities externally.[55] On the strategic communications side of things, the goal at the battlegroup level is to design deliberate messaging and social media engagement to broadcast training for both assurance and deterrence purposes.[56] During my visit, I noticed that the extent to which the battlegroups were going outside the training areas varied, perhaps most starkly when comparing the German-led battlegroup, which mostly stayed in its training area in Rukla, with the Canadian-led one, which carried out dispersed training outside its training area as well as more community engagement activities.[57]

When it comes to NATO's gender perspective, it is the last execution item of the operational orders, with a one-liner that states, "consideration of gender perspectives is an integral part of all NATO planning, including eFP."[58] In the tactical orders for battlegroup activities, there can be some specific instructions for the GENAD. In the case of Latvia, the tactical orders for exercise Tomahawk Smash (where the objective is stated as destroying the enemy to delay its advance long enough to "set conditions for NATO offensive action"), the GENAD directives specify that "same sex searches will be conducted when handling detainees, civilians or PWs [prisoners of war].

All reporting is to use sex disaggregated data when possible."[59] The exercises are meant to introduce a broad range of training, including anti-armor training, conducting coastal and littoral training, amphibious training, dismounted patrolling, training aviation resupply, executing joint training with local forces, and operational reconnaissance. These same exercises are often repeated from one rotation to the next and the battlegroup orders and CONOPS detail their execution.

Ultimately, these exercises (about fourteen key exercises over a nine-month period) support training to enable battlegroups to conduct full-spectrum operations across the host country and to demonstrate interoperability and deterrence within the Baltic region. Each rotation builds up their ability to project combat power with each exercise they run, while demonstrating cohesion and presence in their respective joint operation area and region. One of the rotation orders, for example, emphasizes the importance of demonstrating "how we fight within the environment" and how "readiness will be verified and enhanced through a progressive set of exercises both internal and external to the BG."[60]

Does the battlegroup's gender composition matter in this context then? The eFP battlegroup in Latvia, for example, was 97% male during the time of my visit (954 male personnel, 29 female personnel, 0 non-binary).[61] Essentially, save for some civil–military cooperation (CIMIC) and public affairs activities discussed further below, there is no evidence to suggest that the lack of women in the battlegroup impairs the execution of discrete mission tasks, though it undoubtedly has an impact on the battlegroup's internal dynamics. For good measure, I asked the GENAD to reflect on NATO's narrative regarding women and operational effectiveness. She nodded knowingly and said, "What I have noticed, as soon as you start including more women in the military process, it changes the tone and why things are done. I think it's a good thing. When we tend to have more females, it tends to become more inclusive. I understand the logic but it depends on what you are doing. If bullets are flying, I don't think it makes a difference. The big difference is with the civilian population."[62] When asking similar questions in Lithuania at the Rukla training area, soldiers expressed no issue with gender integration but talked about the divisions that exist in professional experience, between those with deployment experience in Afghanistan and those with no operational experience.[63]

To summarize, the original mission template for eFP activities at the battlegroup level was relatively straightforward: training and exercises contributing to deterrence through demonstrations of alliance solidarity, interoperability, and capability, while furthering assurance measures for members of the host nation's armed forces. To reassure local populations and counter Russian disinformation, strategic communications and CIMIC activities are discussed in greater detail below.

Strategic Communications, Public Affairs, and CIMIC

When trying to grasp the broader operational picture for eFP, interviews with the NFIU stationed in Vilnius, Lithuania, were informative as they further clarified the division of labor that was established between NATO and the individual battlegroups. The NFIU works with the host nation's armed forces to help prepare them in case of an invasion, which entails developing a national support plan, logistics, and transportation for all NATO troops. Its tasks also include strategic communications, and here there has been a big emphasis on schools, to disseminate information about, and acceptance of, the NATO troop presence. In terms of applying a gender perspective, I was told that there was some attempt to identify local women's organizations, especially in the business sector.[64] At the time of my visit, only five of the forty NATO officials at the NFIU were women, which meant they were asked more often to participate in public engagement, on average, as NATO officials were mindful of representation in engagement activities and through social media posts. Indeed, having at least one woman in uniform was identified as a good practice. Again, this is a capability that is leveraged when available; it is not specifically identified as part of the force generation criteria.

NATO's key strategic communications themes and messages are threefold.[65] The first theme deals with readiness and is primarily concerned with sharing information about the host country so that it is accessible across NATO divisions and HQ but also includes communication about the NFIU's role in "supporting forces and exercises in the region."[66] The second theme is about capability and adaptation as NATO is standing ready to scale up its commitment and presence in the region if the security environment changes which indeed it did fairly rapidly in 2022. In addition to supporting the movement of forces in the region based on a regular calendar of activities, NATO can, on a moment's notice, "facilitate the rapid deployment of the [Very High Readiness Joint Task Force]."[67] Finally, NATO's core role with regard to deterrence and defense is represented in its messaging, emphasizing the alliance's core collective defense purpose. The combination of eFP and the NFIUs ensures a continued presence in the Baltics. These messages are, of course, part of public affairs efforts through traditional and social media but also include key leader engagements; community outreach activities and public engagements; social responsibility projects, such as youth projects and working with charity organizations; and finally, briefing and liaising with defense stakeholders within each eFP country. These lines of effort support all overarching goals and reinforce strategic communication efforts. While WPS norms are not influencing the design of these three key messages, the gender perspective is considered in terms of how these messages are disseminated via engagement activities.

Countering fake news and Russian tactics in the information domain is another key area of focus, and these efforts target troll factories, outlets like Sputnik and Russia Today, as well as independent news channels in Russian. NATO has acknowledged this threat, emphasizing that "Russia's disinformation is aimed at forcing Western states to concentrate on mitigating the effects of the political damage done by Russian disinformation efforts, as well as reinforcing popular anti-Western discourses inside Russia."[68] To counter such tactics, NATO and eFP countries can increase awareness and knowledge about the alliance and its role in the Baltics, closely monitor traditional and social media, and work with civil society actors to improve independent fact-checking.

In Rukla, where the German-led eFP battlegroup is stationed, there is some community outreach as well. This ranges from lending the military band for local events to opening up the barracks for visits and equipment displays to "chopping wood for old ladies."[69] The key messages that are reinforced through these engagement opportunities are about having a diversity of countries present for the defense of Lithuania.[70] While Russian propaganda has ebbed and flowed, it is tracked closely by the battlegroup and has provoked certain policy changes. For example, the German-led battlegroup has a zero-alcohol policy because in Russia Today or Sputnik, adversaries would report that soldiers were picking fights with locals, and these incidents were exploited for propaganda purposes.[71]

In both Latvia and Lithuania, there are frequent parades in the capitals, with military vehicle displays. This happens in the capitals by design, even if that is not where the battlegroups are located, to boost the visibility of these outreach efforts. Soldiers are also provided with media training to respond to confrontational questions from Russian media outlets. There are certain differences in terms of how individual NATO countries will choose their messaging. While the Dutch soldiers emphasize deterrence against Russia specifically, Germany, by contrast, initially refrained from singling out Russia. But overall, the displays and responses to challenges are quite similar and coordinated across sending nations.

One of the examples of how gender was incorporated into day-to-day activities was with community outreach in rural areas, where the presence of NATO troops in certain regions did not seem to be well understood or accepted. At first, the Canadian battlegroup started to do outreach in schools by hosting hockey games with former National Hockey League players from Latvia, but the outcome was that only men were involved. The GENAD proposed and was successful in bringing the Canadian women's national team to balance things out. Another example was about the walking out policy, which refers to when (and how) the troops are allowed to leave the base for a few days. At first, CAF members were mandated to stay in groups of four, which meant that women who left usually ended up being with three guys who typically just wanted to go to bars. The GENAD revamped the personnel support programs to organize day trips over the weekend at the spa. In the end, a lot of men signed up for this activity as well.

A third example relates to medics because the GENAD identified that the only person who was authorized to do exams for sexual assault was a man. This was also changed so that there would be one male and one female on site who is trained for sexual assault response. To be clear, this is intended for the personnel on base; but if the situation were to change from deterrence to open conflict, NATO forces might also be providing medical care to civilians. A fourth example relates to threat assessment and intelligence. This came up with information operations early on in the mission, whereby the Russians played on the traditional values of the population in the area. They would attempt to undermine NATO credibility by referring to a disgraced Canadian Air Force colonel, Russell Williams (he was convicted of murder and sexual assault in 2010). The Russians thus exploit social norms to undermine the NATO presence, and the battlegroup then responds with strategic communication efforts that play up both national and NATO narratives.[72] The GENAD can step in to assist, along with the PAO, providing advice when there is an opportunity to do so.

One of the challenges with the non-kinetic tasks is deploying effective strategic communications in an environment where people are receiving primarily Russian news in Russian-speaking areas (the main target of strategic communications efforts).[73] While building trust with different segments of society is important, engaging Russian-speaking communities has proved more challenging given that NATO was not on TV, where most people tend to get their news and information in the Baltics. Understanding these patterns of life led to an adjustment. The battlegroups engaged in a range of CIMIC activities to raise awareness of eFP's presence in the Baltic region, from organizing hockey games to helping schools and orphanages or building playgrounds. Community outreach events are then publicized on NATO platforms and benefit from applying a gender-based analysis, although the extent to which that happens varies from activity to activity, based on the details included in the CONOPS. Ultimately, these outreach activities not only help to demonstrate NATO's presence and commitment but facilitate the forging of partnerships in the host country, improve situational awareness through interactions with the local population, and help in identifying the needs or concerns of relevant stakeholders across the Baltic region.

GENAD Roles and Constraints

The primary mechanism through which the gender perspective is incorporated within eFP are add-ons to operational orders that relate to overarching WPS policies and guidelines. Networks of GENADs and GFPs, when they exist, represent the means by which these efforts are kept on track. At the time of my visit, the Canadian-led battlegroup was unique in having a GENAD in the country, along with an active network of GFPs, despite this being a NATO requirement (Bi-Strategic Command Directive 040-001). The CAF GENAD is not at the battlegroup level but, rather, in the capital, within Task Force Latvia, while the GFPs are integrated into the battlegroup within the training area. This can create a bit of a disconnect as the GENAD is not as plugged into the day-to-day training and exercise activities and has fewer face-to-face interactions with the battlegroup commander.

Another important challenge, within eFP but also other theaters, relates to GENAD vacancies that take several months to fill. When I was conducting interviews for the book, I was able to speak to the outgoing GENAD virtually, but there was no one in the post when I visited the Canadian-led battlegroup in person.[74] In Lithuania, there was no GENAD at all, looking at both the German-led battlegroup and NFIU Lithuania. The closest GENAD in the command structure, therefore, was a GENAD in the Bundeswehr Joint Forces

Operations Command in Potsdam. Instead, while visiting Rukla, I was introduced to a junior enlisted Bundeswehr soldier, who was tasked with being the employment equity representative. The officer who volunteered to translate summarized her role as follows: "She is responsible for the 'gender' aspect, conflicts within BG, men's inappropriate behavior but for Germany only."[75] Then, a member from the mechanized infantry platoon was introduced to me as a "deputy spokesperson" to assist in disciplinary matters. I was told mechanically that there were no incidents because "there are few women and the soldiers are very disciplined."[76]

NATO regulations require GENADs and GFPs on operations, but, once again, since eFP was not technically a NATO operation, the alliance did not exercise this kind of oversight, though the command structure has evolved since then. As a NATO activity, it would then be up to the framework nation to follow through (or not) on requiring and deploying a GENAD. In other words, even if GENADs are a NATO requirement, it is the individual countries that have to provide this capability; and if the framework nation does not look after this requirement, NATO will not intervene given eFP's unique command structure. NATO countries also vary in their ability to force-generate GENADs. Certain countries have had GENADs for a long time, while others have started to train and deploy them more recently. Canada, for example, only issued its GENAD directive in 2016, so it is still fairly new, compared to Australia and Sweden, which deployed GENADs sooner.

Considering that the Canadians had a GENAD and GFPs, while the Germans did not, the discussion here will primarily focus on the battlegroup in Latvia. Because there are similar tasks across all battlegroups in the Baltics and Poland, it is reasonable to expect that the best practices from the GENAD deployed to Latvia could easily apply to the other battlegroups. But, first, a caveat is in order. Not every GENAD that takes up the position has prior knowledge or expertise on gender, and this indeed varied widely in terms of the GENADs I interviewed.

The GENAD of Task Force Latvia, for instance, was handpicked by her boss because she had gone through staff college prior to her deployment and written a research paper on gender integration in the forces.[77] In addition to this academic work, she was sent (like most GENADs) to the two-week gender awareness course in Sweden offered by the Nordic Centre for Gender in Military Operations, about a week after arriving in Latvia. An important piece of feedback offered by the GENAD was that, though the course in Sweden was professionally delivered, most of the examples and training material were better suited for work in the Middle East and Africa. There was a strong emphasis on cultural differences and how these impact gender assessments. Relating this back to eFP proved challenging because there is no active conflict in the Baltics and because both the sending nations and host countries share a lot of cultural similarities, so few examples from the course were seen to be applicable.

The challenge was replicated once in theater as the GENAD was left to her own devices in terms of developing her workplan. One of the key stumbling blocks was grappling with the question of how to translate high-level WPS norms to a setting where "female–male dynamics are very similar to back home in Canada and where culturally, there is no stark sex segregation, as might be the case in Afghanistan or Iraq."[78] Moreover, the fact that Latvia is not a conflict setting and that women participate wholly in the local economy makes it harder to really draw out the gendered implications for the force, she said. In her view, one thing that stood out is that the rate of domestic abuse is among the highest in the European Union, but this does not really have any implications for the application of the eFP mandate. She added that the first few weeks on the job, therefore, represented a big learning curve.

One already has to work hard as a GENAD to communicate to others what the position entails and then to get buy-in and support from peers and superiors so that everyone complies with gender directives. It makes sense then that when the entry points for gender considerations are harder to figure out, the job is harder. To seek help, the GENAD reached out to CAF colleagues from the training area, starting with the senior GFPs, who in turn can reach out to the sixteen GFPs across all subunits and nationalities represented in the multinational battlegroup. These GFPs come from different occupations and have different ranks, but they are all ultimately meant to assist the commander and GENAD in incorporating a gender perspective across military tasks. In the end, the main focus of the GENADs' and GFPs' efforts revolved around training. Gender considerations were integrated into the military exercise that focused on CIMIC. Through the prism of this exercise, the gender dimension was highlighted in the planning tasks for displaced persons so that the implications for both men and women, as well as children, were made clear, especially regarding the provision of medical assistance and the appropriateness of the installations. These materials were drawn from experiences that the CAF had encountered domestically while providing disaster assistance after major floods in Québec. The disaster assistance literature also corroborates the fact that in disaster situations women are more affected and suffer higher casualty rates.[79] As this exercise included both the Latvian armed forces and the American military, it was interesting to note that, while these concepts were familiar to the Americans, they were entirely new for the Latvians. The Latvians came on board in what might be a good example of cultivating deeper interoperability, creating greater familiarity with gender guidelines in operational planning and military activities.[80]

While it is commonly assumed that GENADs and GFPs are women, the majority of GFPs in Latvia were men because the battlegroup was overwhelmingly male. The Canadians accepted volunteers from other countries as well for GFP positions, and the training was conducted in Riga. There was some appeal to doing this off-base. First, it may have removed some of the stigma of being branded as a GFP (this varies from country to country), and soldiers generally view off-base opportunities as a desirable escape from their day-to-day tasks in the isolated training area. Since the training (provided by the Canadians) was held every six to eight weeks in Riga, the GFP role had its perks, which, of course, included eating non-military-issued food and spending time in Latvia's beautiful capital. Of course, intellectual curiosity may have played into the growing list of eager participants, but one can speculate that not as many people would have signed up if the training had been conducted in a tent in the middle of a field in the Adazi camp.

This is not to suggest that there is broad-based acceptance of the WPS training materials that were presented to soldiers. The GENAD relayed a few stories from her training encounters with battlegroup soldiers. When asking soldiers about the role of GENADs, many answered that "this position was not needed because men and women are treated the same but when the external dimension is brought in, like how it might be relevant to carry out the mission, it seems a bit more intuitive to people, especially those with prior operational experience."[81] Another common reaction, but from the Canadian soldiers specifically, was that these initiatives were seen as coming from the Liberal government even though the concept of GENAD and all of the aforementioned NATO guidelines predate Trudeau's 2015 arrival in office. What the GENAD emphasized in the training then is that WPS norms are "not bra-burning feminism" but, rather, represent an analysis of human and social factors on operations, emphasizing that "the name is unfortunate and the education piece is still missing."[82]

After conducting this interview, I could not help but think that, with such a strong majority of men in the battlegroup, finding the right angle or right examples to get buy-in as a female GENAD was probably challenging. The common misconception is that anything related to the WPS agenda and gender refers to women's place in the military, and sometimes this is perceived as a zero-sum game, namely that by placing this much attention on women, men are at a professional disadvantage, a theme that came up in different interviews with battlegroup personnel. Accordingly, the female GENADs I spoke with thought that when the GENAD is male he is able to command more time and that he gets more initial attention—the same barriers do not automatically go up as they do with his female counterparts.[83] Female GENADs, from high-level HQ, routinely told me that they had about thirty seconds to win or lose their audience, so pitch exercises were increasingly being built into GENAD trainings.

An additional challenge with the role of the GENAD on operations is cultural, meaning that there are major differences in terms of professional military education and training across sending nations. For example, within the CAF, LGBTQ2+ service members have been integrated; but with international audiences, this is not necessarily the case, and GENADs pick their battles, tailoring some materials to the audience in order "not to come off as preachy."[84] For the Baltic States, for instance, the GENAD's assessment was that the mentality is closer to what it was in Canada in the 1980s, which means that some material that is intended for a Canadian audience might shock or offend soldiers coming from other NATO countries, which could cause some friction within the battlegroup.

In sum, the bulk of the GENAD's work within eFP is focused on developing training packages and tailoring the materials to different groups within the mission setting. Additionally, the advisory function means providing a gender perspective for policies, plans, and meetings, as needed. This can be done with the battlegroup commander or other entry points within the national chain of command.

Conclusion

Once again, eFP from 2016 to 2022 stands apart as a case study given its unique command structure. Since eFP was initially designed as a NATO activity and not a SHAPE-directed operation, NATO guidelines applied (like Bi-Strategic Command Directive 040-001) but were not necessarily implemented systematically by the original four framework nations. This command structure, different from the cases of KFOR and NMI, helps explain some of the variation we can observe when it comes to the implementation of WPS norms across missions but also across the eFP battlegroups. Ultimately, the regular NATO command and reporting structure foster greater harmonization of reporting and activities, with broader implications for how the mandate is interpreted and then carried out from the strategic down to the tactical level.

What is common to all cases, however, is the extent to which COVID-19 impacted military activities, especially over the course of 2020 and 2021. With the pandemic, there was a spike in Russian disinformation activities around COVID-19. There is also an acknowledgment that it has become increasingly difficult to get reliable and accurate data on local attitudes toward the mission, given that CIMIC activities were curtailed because of public health measures. There have also been moments of heightened anxiety around Russian military exercises. This was the case with ZAPAD, an exercise conducted in Belorussia, but also in 2021–2022, with the Russian military buildup right on Ukraine's border, the precursor to a devastating war. The nightmare scenario of a Russian land grab and incursion into NATO territory remains relevant for eFP, but the parameters of what is considered to be a likely threat shifted dramatically on February 24, 2022.[85]

NATO and individual battlegroups have continued to counter Russian propaganda through their strategic communication efforts. Even the visibility of soldiers matters, and everyone from the battlegroups is told to wear their uniform when walking around so as to demonstrate the visibility of NATO's commitment and presence. For all public-facing engagement activities, there have been attempts to include women in the group of uniformed personnel interacting with the Latvian population or in the visual content that is posted on social media. A more tangible security outcome from eFP that should be mentioned here is the improvements to the national armed forces across the Baltic region, which continue to benefit from the training activities with the framework and sending nations. Armed forces in the Baltics have been in a rebuilding phase since their accession to NATO and still have some Soviet-era equipment. Interacting with other NATO forces on a daily basis, therefore, reinforces training and contributes to the harmonization of NATO practices. This could include developing greater familiarity with WPS norms and guidelines, but again, there is no consistent picture on this front, when comparing the four battlegroups.

When it comes to the practical applications of the gender perspective, there is evidence that, at the very least, commanders track sex-disaggregated data about their forces and about the joint operations area. This eFP case study stands apart also because NATO has not given precise guidelines on how WPS norms can be actualized to fulfill its collective defense pillar. This remains an ongoing challenge for NATO, as revealed by the analysis of key documents and interviews conducted in the NATO HQ, SHAPE, and JFC-Brunssum and with eFP military personnel. Since 2014, NATO has had to re-emphasize its traditional purpose of collective defense but has not fully fleshed out how gender matters in this context. The 2022 invasion of Ukraine will accelerate strategic thinking on this front. To be sure, the alliance has also not figured out a comprehensive assessment process for deterrence in a hybrid context either; uncertainty is not unique to WPS. Updating the alliance's approach to deterrence is an ongoing task, and incorporating a gender perspective will proceed unevenly until there is more solid strategic-level political–military guidance. For now, commanders and GENADs can learn from previous rotations in promoting awareness through gender training, the appointment of GFPs, and the collection of sex-disaggregated data for the battlegroup's own gender composition and for social assessments of the joint operation area. These activities continue to be framed and justified as supporting operational effectiveness, in a way that is rather disconnected from WPS norms about advancing gender equality. Gender considerations have superficially been integrated into strategic communications, CIMIC, and community engagement but remain out of reach for NATO's core focus on collective defense, deterrence, and assurance.

6

Advising and Assisting in Iraq

Joining a growing list of countries, from Australia to Afghanistan, Iraq is one of NATO's newest "partners across the globe," formalizing its ties to the alliance since 2011. As the country focuses on stabilization and on rebuilding the territories once controlled by the Islamic State, NATO allies are encouraging the greater participation of women in security forces and including *a gender perspective* into the curriculum of Iraqi military academies through the NATO Mission in Iraq (NMI). Because this is a relatively new mission, Women, Peace and Security (WPS) norms were embedded from the start within NMI's operational design, with a dedicated line of effort for integrating gender perspectives. Even with WPS as one of the stated priorities, NMI still suffers from a familiar credibility gap: it is failing to deploy a critical mass of women, both civilian and military, to role-model the importance of the agenda when interacting with Iraqi stakeholders. NATO's primary interlocutor in Iraq is the Ministry of Defense (MOD), an organization that is dominated by the military and predominantly male. Perhaps unsurprisingly, this audience is not always receptive to what the NMI gender advisor (GENAD) has to offer, and the opportunities to interact with Iraqis remain limited. This much is recognized at Joint Forces Command (JFC) Naples: "when engaging with countries from the Middle East or North Africa, we have to temper our approach, we use interest-based arguments [for WPS]."[1] As a military advisor to the commander, what the GENAD can do is to continue to raise the topic so that it is perceived as relevant across the mission's core tasks. In practice, this means increasing women's participation and visibility as part of NATO's training and capacity-building efforts, socializing gender-related concepts through these training and education efforts, as well as contributing to advisory tasks geared toward the Iraqi government and armed forces.

This chapter provides an overview of the mission and shows how WPS norms have been included since NMI's inception. With strong representation from the Canadian Armed Forces (CAF) in the first rotations, this meant heightened awareness of WPS; but there are still many obstacles in translating this NATO line of effort into clear tactical action. Internally, the

Deploying Feminism. Stéfanie von Hlatky, Oxford University Press. © Oxford University Press 2023.
DOI: 10.1093/oso/9780197653524.003.0006

importance of gender considerations and the role of the GENAD are not always well understood. The GENAD I met in Iraq recognized the importance of this internal dimension as it increases the buy-in and participation of other members of the contingent to embed WPS norms across advising and capacity-building tasks. In many ways, NMI has the best conditions to minimize norm distortion: a better civil–military balance than the Kosovo Force (KFOR) and enhanced forward presence (eFP), some women in key roles, as well as a NATO-led command structure providing guidance on a manageable set of military tasks. Compared to the case of eFP in the Baltics and Poland, discussed in the previous chapter, there is a clearer accountability structure within NMI, where there are established NATO reporting lines that flow up to other GENADs at the operational (JFC-Naples) and strategic (Supreme Headquarters [HQ] Allied Powers Europe [SHAPE]) levels. Failing to account for progress on NATO's WPS policy or its corresponding Bi-Strategic Command Directive can reflect poorly on the commander, who is accountable to higher-level HQ on all lines of effort. Yet a major obstacle relates to the challenge of introducing NATO-branded WPS norms to a security culture where women are largely absent. Nevertheless, when the mission's military tasks are broken down, one can see the entry points where NATO's gender perspective can take hold.

This chapter first provides an overview of the mission and historical context, the second section describes the integration of WPS norms as part of NMI's civilian and military tasks, and the third section introduces how the GENAD and those in other key positions interpret and implement gender policies and guidelines.

Mission Background and Historical Context

There are over three decades of Western intervention in Iraq. It started with Iraq's invasion of Kuwait in 1990, then the American invasion of Iraq in 2003, and finally, the creation of a global coalition to beat the Islamic State after it seized territory across the country and declared a new caliphate in 2014. NATO has had intermittent involvement, primarily in the area of training and capacity-building, starting with a small training mission in 2004, the NATO Training Mission in Iraq, which wrapped up in 2011.[2] The mission was focused on activities like "rebuilding the different levels of officer education," advising on developing education programs, and establishing a non-commissioned officer (NCO) corps and was less controversial than US-led military efforts.[3] Then, things picked up again more recently, when NATO joined the US-led Coalition to Defeat ISIS in 2017.[4] Unlike in 2003, the United States could count on more partners to intervene in Iraq this time around. Moreover, the legal basis for such an intervention was clearer, given the explicit request of the Iraqi prime minister at the time, Haider Al-Abadi. His successors also opened the door to a greater NATO role of assisting with training and capacity-building. The creation of NMI was announced in July of 2018 during the NATO Summit in Brussels. The key features of this mission are that it is a non-combat, training, and capacity-building effort and that it operates alongside Combined Joint Task Force–Operation Inherent Resolve (CJTF-OIR).[5]

In Iraq, NATO has to make the case for why its mission matters as there are many international actors competing for the Iraqi government's attention.[6] Consultation between international actors, from the United States, the United Nations (UN), the European Union, NATO, and others, appears to be an endless task, made all the more cumbersome by different rotational timetables.[7] Coordination efforts are time-consuming for commanders, but really, they weigh on every working relationship that exists between these organizations, including the GENAD, who routinely coordinates, or at least deconflicts, with counterparts from CJTF-OIR and the UN.[8] Working with international organizations is explicitly mentioned in the action plan for the implementation of NATO's WPS policy and identified as one of the mechanisms by which NATO can "advance gender equality, integrate gender perspectives and foster the principles of the WPS agenda."[9] NATO and EU activities in Iraq are the most closely aligned as they are both geared toward improving "Iraqi national security structures."[10] The engagement opportunities are, of course, much broader than seeking out counterparts because, in the words of the NMI commander, "you have to understand what everyone is doing, even the Russians who are here teaching soviet style vehicle maintenance."[11]

While NATO's training and advising mandate is rather narrow, the mission's performance indicators are not as precise as one might think. The mission does not have a set number of individuals to train, and the advising portfolio remains, by definition, hard to quantify or measure. For security sector reform (SSR) projects, progress is measured through milestones based on the completion of specific projects, but timelines for building longer-term training capability and reforming MOD processes are loosely defined and harder to capture in NATO reporting. The NATO mission can act as a gateway for a more stable partnership with Iraq, and, as the commander highlighted, "the training is a way to get them there."[12]

NMI builds on a relationship established between NATO and Iraq shortly after the US-led Coalition to Defeat ISIS was created. NATO presented a defense capability package for the Iraqi MOD in 2015 to facilitate the implementation of training and capacity-building efforts, primarily through the deployment of mobile training teams and financial commitments.[13] Under NMI, NATO trainers have continued to work with Iraqi trainers but have now established a permanent local presence on a US base. More concretely, areas of focus for technical training include countering improvised explosive devices, civil–military planning, armored vehicle maintenance, and military medicine. Then, there are broader training efforts like contributing to curriculum development in military academies.

The first commander of NMI, a two-star general from the CAF, had a critical number of Canadian officers and troops (250 CAF personnel out of a total of 580) as part of the NATO contingent. Canadian troops were already in theater as part of Operation Impact, which made the task of taking over this command logistically easier than it would have been for other countries that may have wanted the command role. The attribution of these leadership roles is typically (though not always) based on which country is offering the biggest contribution. Canada, in this case, had a good reputation in Iraq and could credibly act as an honest broker, in addition to already having assets in theater.[14] But of course, and in true NATO fashion, multiple allies have been contributing troops and assets since the mission's onset, from the Czech Republic to Turkey.

Looking at the force composition of the mission, one thing that is immediately clear is the high number of senior officers. In other words, there are many, many colonels and three generals. This rather top-heavy structure, however, was seen as necessary, given the advising function that NATO has with the Iraqi MOD. Because the Iraqi bureaucracy is itself top-heavy, with a higher-than-typical concentration of generals within the defense ministry, rank on the NATO side does matter to guarantee the right access. The mission is also structured along the J functions in the military, and the GENAD is meant to work with gender focal points (GFPs) from across these functions, although this was not yet the case at the time of my visit.

For the NMI commander, a novel feature of leading this mission was working so closely with a GENAD as part of his command team. He recalled his experience in Afghanistan where there was no GENAD, but this function was subsumed under the civil–military cooperation or intelligence capability. During our conversation, the commander readily admitted that there is not always a clear understanding of the advantages that a GENAD can bring to a mission: "It is not just about treating people more equitably, it is very practical. In Afghanistan, we needed to talk to the women and had varying levels of success doing so. In Iraq, this has to be understood within the team: everyone who talks to Iraqis should focus on our messages of rule of law, code of conduct, building integrity, gender perspectives, and inclusive security."[15] The commander also noted the importance of applying a gender analysis to threat environment assessments: "we hope to coach them [Iraqis] on how to deal with the weaponization of women, as women play an increasing role in the insurgency. We are going from brides of ISIS to mothers of the caliphate."[16] In the commander's own assessment of how NATO guidelines should be applied in a NATO context, there exists a balance between what the mission requires and how gender considerations can improve operational effectiveness but also the need to tap into the society's needs and getting a variety of viewpoints. With the inclusion of WPS as a main line of effort, there is an opportunity to broaden gender considerations beyond the requirements of operational effectiveness. This is a start; but while this is identified as a priority, there are important constraints for implementing this vision on the ground.

Gender, Mission Tasks, and NMI's Mandate

With NMI, even though you have one country in command (at first Canada, then Denmark), it does not put its imprint on the design of the mission to the same extent as a framework nation can in the context of eFP. However, the commander was influential in bringing other positions that he deemed necessary but that were not included in the initial crisis establishment.[17] In those cases, this represents an additional cost that Canada must agree to take on, alongside the contribution it offered to meet the NATO request as part of the force generation process.

In terms of operational design, there are several lines of operation. Each category is tied to a desired end state, and then tasks and milestones are reverse-engineered from this desired end state. The operational design is refined in consultation with the Iraqis, to better understand and integrate their needs; but NMI personnel and staff also conduct an independent assessment to identify potential problems or gaps. Ultimately, the ministries determine the priorities, but NMI provides a menu of options from which they can choose; and that is how a dynamic of mutual influence is maintained. Some organizations internal to the MOD are more receptive than others, which translates into programs being designed and delivered at different speeds.[18]

The focus areas of NMI are governance, policy, and strategy; legal (so that armed forces operate in a way that is consistent with the constitution); crisis management (e.g., what can be done with Mosul now that ISIS no longer controls territory in Iraq); integrity (corruption); operational law (international humanitarian law); gender/WPS; planning; and training. When we consider this mission design, what stands out, especially in comparison with the other cases, is that gender/WPS has its own line of effort, which leads to a number of clearly defined outcomes:

- Achieving a framework for gender mainstreaming within the MOD
- Integrating gender perspectives into the curriculum of training schools and education institutions
- Supportive effective implementation by the MOD of the Iraqi National Action Plan on UN Security Council Resolution (UNSCR) 1325
- Integrating a gender perspective into the MOD to increase awareness of WPS guidelines and how these apply in defense
- Gender mainstreaming into training schools and educational institutions and within Iraqi processes, policies, and documentation
- Providing a sustainable structure for "gender in operations" as part of existing processes

While many of these outcomes are long-term goals, it is important to note that there are some aspects of Iraqi governance that are just not in place, whether they relate to gender or not.[19] In sum, the visibility of WPS as a line of effort makes it more central to mission planning, execution, and assessment; but the performance metrics as outlined here remain vague because the overall performance metrics of the mission as a whole are vague. Over time, one might observe change through capacity-building efforts; but in the short term, progress is harder to capture. For example, when NMI proposes changes to the curriculum of military academies or offers new courses, there are no immediate tangible effects.

Nevertheless, the chief of planning, commenting on the gender line of operation, pointed out that gender is not an afterthought; it is integrated in all aspects of planning.[20] The commander supported it, and then the Spanish chief of staff mandated it. All NMI staff have at least taken the two NATO gender courses, so there is some baseline awareness. In addition to the leadership sending a strong signal, gender and integrity are in the operational order. NATO HQ and SHAPE also send down requests about gender, placing additional pressure on the command team not to ignore it.

Entry Points for Gender Considerations

An important feature of this mission is the extent to which it is integrated, in terms of civilian and military personnel. This integrated civilian and military structure was deemed important because of the nature of the mission's advisory function, which necessitates civilian engagement. Moreover, civilians "add continuity and greater expertise."[21] Although more balanced in terms of its civil–military composition than KFOR and eFP, the military is squarely in the lead: there were ten civilian positions within NMI, only a handful of which were filled at the time of my visit.[22] The mission is also different from the Resolute Support Mission in Afghanistan, in that there is no special representative who reports to the International Staff at the NATO HQ. The difference stems from NMI being presented as an apolitical mission, and because of this, there is no political advisor either (although in practice there is a staff person who fills that role). NATO's senior civilian representative for the mission reports to the commanding two-star general. In the remainder of this section, I assess how military and civilian personnel perform their tasks with gender and WPS principles in mind, focusing on advising and training tasks but also more generic military tasks and positions.

NATO's Advisory Function

Providing advice in the NMI context involves two main components: at a lower level, it involves improving Iraqi training schools for the military, and at a higher level, it involves talking to MOD directors to promote institutional change.[23] What is obvious from the interviews I conducted is that the civilian leadership and the chief of defense have a hard time collaborating within the MOD. Civil–military cooperation is challenging under the best of circumstances, but this situation has been made worse by decades of operations, meaning that the integrity of the system overall has suffered. One solution would be to advise the MOD as civil–military teams, but NMI does not do that systematically. For one, there are not enough civilian advisors within NMI, and moreover, the civilian advisors work out of the British Embassy, which means they are physically disconnected from the military core of the NATO mission.

I asked the military officer in charge of advising if he worked with the GENAD, and he admitted that it did not happen frequently. He offered, displaying a noticeable grin, that when you have a job (i.e., GENAD) that not everyone is fond of, it is good to have social skills.[24] Operationally speaking, he said that he was exposed to the complexity of gender issues in Afghanistan, but also in various command roles, observing how gender dynamics play out within teams. With NMI, he said that gender considerations came up in something as benign as translating a document: "For our out-of-country courses, the Iraqi brigadier asked if both men and women could attend. I replied that all courses are open for men and women at NATO . . . the brigadier then pointed out that if you translate this into Arabic, it implies that it is for men only, since gender neutral translates into male. As a result, we had to make it really explicit, writing that all courses are open to male and female. . . . But in the end, I'm not sure if there are many Iraqi women soldiers."[25]

For the Spanish military officer, a legal advisor (LEGAD) at the colonel rank, who advised the Iraqis on planning, the importance of relationships was really brought home; but this is an area where deployed women could potentially face challenges.[26] Even at the highest levels, this seemed to be an issue. When NMI welcomed a woman as commander, the "Iraqi chief of defense [was] open to her, but the minister of defense, not so much."[27] The Spanish advisor offered that women may face a disadvantage because building relationships while advising counterparts happens "man to man," adding the following:[28]

> When you engage with your counterpart, the more feelings you have in your relationship, the better you can develop your work, it is based on these personal feelings. This is the base for this kind of work, advising at the strategic level. Advising at the tactical level is different, it is different, because I do what I usually do like fight or deploy a battalion to

provide security. This is what I did when I was advising the Afghan battalion in Afghanistan. This work is easier because it is just you and your counterpart.[29]

Another potential connection to be made in this context, as was the case for KFOR, is cross-cultural: "they [the Iraqis] are quite interested in knowing the organization of other ministries of defense. Our Croatian colonel briefed his Iraqi counterpart on his ministry of defense. Croatia had to reorganize after the war. It is a good example from his point of view."[30] In addition to the relationships that are built, the cultural diversity of NATO becomes an asset that is sometimes not much talked about. Not only did it appear to be relevant in all three cases but it was leveraged when convenient, even if not explicitly articulated in NATO directives. It seems to have occurred organically, based on personal connections and happenstance.

Not everything that NATO proposes works out however, and there are obstacles that come with attempting to reform the military and the MOD's practices. The Spanish military advisor noted that, "The staff officers are supposed to help the commander in making decisions based on the options they provide. When they are playing a role in the MOD at the strategic level, because of their mentality, they don't play this staff officer role. According to their mentality, they say I cannot tell my commander what he has to decide. You don't have to decide what to decide but you have to give him options. That is your job!"[31] With power struggles and a top-heavy military bureaucracy in Iraq, NATO can be a good conduit for more open discussions across a range of topics, including gender.

The colonel ended our conversation by sharing that he had completed his gender training, both in Spain and via NATO, noting that this has been a big change in the last decade or so. While he experienced working with GENADs in Afghanistan and Kosovo, this contrasts to most NMI staff officers I interviewed, who were working with a GENAD for the first time in a mission context. Nevertheless, he did not identify a role for gender issues in fulfilling *his* planning functions, which demonstrates a misreading of the existing guidance that WPS be considered across the board. Finally, the officer conceded that bringing in female officers would be important for the demonstration effect when dealing with Iraqis.[32] This is important, but ultimately, having more women deployed as part of NMI to conduct targeted engagement is not part of NATO's lines of effort, even if complementary, nor is it a formal part of the force generation process.

NATO's Training and Education Function

The training and education component of NMI can be considered the "front-line" of the mission. "The mission of NMI is training the trainer to build the Iraqi military," as summarized by one of the US Army trainers for NATO.[33] Though the core of the mission resides in Baghdad, given the importance of its advisory component, training and education activities were also taking place in Taji and Besmaya at the time of my visit. In each of those locations, you had embedded training and advisory teams (ETATs) to provide training advice or deliver courses with a force protection team in tow. The English colonel in charge of overseeing the ETATs summed it up this way: "ETAT is three people, allocated to a school, from a single nation."[34] This means different contributing states have different training emphases. For example, the Polish teams might be responsible for the school of mechanical and electrical engineering, while the NCO school might be run by a different NATO state.

The training institutions can be focused on tactical training, like tank maintenance or bomb disposal, but can also be focused on professional military education, through military academies. Tactical helicopter detachments also ensure mobility between Baghdad, Taji, and Besmaya because there are force protection concerns: "you couldn't go from Baghdad to Taji by road as casualties would be unpalatable."[35] When more in-depth work is needed, NATO can also deploy a mobile training team (MTT) to assist the Iraqis for a determined period of time. For MTTs, states have to pony up even more troops in an environment where the core of the mission is still under its crisis establishment, meaning many positions are unfilled. During my fieldwork, for example, there were 430 people out of the required 585.[36]

Setting up training means, once again, building relationships with Iraqi partners. The first step consists in identifying existing training schools and institutions, as was done, for example, with a computer school. The NATO team would set up a meeting with the commanding officer and instructors, analyze the curriculum, and provide preliminary advice on how to improve it. One could call this a preliminary needs assessment. The Iraqi partners may be more or less open to change but I was told that, most of the time, they appear receptive if it comes from NATO (as opposed to the United States). NMI can then offer to supplement the curriculum by introducing new courses and training the trainers modules so that the on-site Iraqi instructors can then take over course delivery. In the example of the computer school, the NMI instructor was able to teach a group of fifteen for a three and a half-week period. There are some security considerations when it comes to the provision of this kind of training. Students had to be screened, which led to one student being excused. The other security provision dealt with transporting the training team from Union III, where the NMI HQ is located, to the training site. Every morning, there were three vehicles to do the trip, with six or more guardian angels, the name that was commonly used to refer to the force protection teams. The instructors themselves would be armed; they would remove the gear and their M4 but would still have their M9 pistol on their person in the classroom.

There were some challenges encountered when working with military academies, like getting course materials or equipment that the school was lacking, which NATO would not fund. Another limitation was the language barrier. It was decided that the slides would not be translated (there were 1,500 total), given that translators and interpreters were always in short supply for NMI. Instead, an interpreter was dispatched alongside the instructor to support course delivery. The interpreter happened to have a computer degree and was able to help out, although it was exhausting work. She also happened to be a woman; "but no one disrespected her," I was told, which signaled to me that disrespectful behavior toward women may have happened in other similar contexts.[37] There were also women guardian angels, and some students were surprised to see women in uniform wielding guns and standing by in front of the classroom. Overall, students in these Iraqi military academies were accepting of the NATO presence: "Students were so kind, they brought us lots of food. Everyone eating from the same bowl. The students were more than grateful. They were taking selfies and bringing presents."[38]

Obviously, these kinds of favorable reviews are welcome from a NATO perspective; but the main objective when it comes to training and education is to influence the curriculum, and NATO wants gender to be part of that curriculum. Like most people I talked to at Union III, the ETAT head had never been in an operation with a GENAD: "What I can help with is in the training course we do, we'll have content that will support these ideas. . . . It can be quite subliminal: like showing the picture of a woman [in uniform] teaching on a slide. I would like to have women in my team. I don't have any in the ETATs, that's something that maybe should be positively addressed."[39] Here, too, officers in the NMI HQ directly point out the discrepancy between the objectives underlying NATO's gender guidelines and the fact that the NATO presence lacks women to fulfill certain objectives.

However, the concept of "inclusive security" is put forward to integrate gender perspectives as part of briefings to ETATs and MTTs, who then go on to work directly with Iraqis in terms of designing and delivering curriculum. Inclusive security, even if the term also does not seem to be well understood, "may not be as shocking to the Iraqis" as explicitly referring to women or gender, the GENAD offered.[40]

The training branch does not operate in isolation, and trainers coordinate with advisors who work with the Iraqi MOD to identify and highlight these training and curriculum gaps with their ministerial contacts. Beyond gender, interoperability is another value the mission is trying to embed into its training and advisory activities. And so, NMI is encouraging exchanges of personnel across different functions and occupations to promote mutual understanding and awareness of different competencies. The bigger role, from an advisory perspective, is to introduce some kind of career management system so that the military can be managed more professionally and reliably.

As illustrated with the training example and the lack of course materials and equipment, NATO only has a little bit of money to incentivize change. Leverage, however, can be found in the fact that Iraq wants to remain a NATO partner; and modernizing its armed forces is a direct benefit from this relationship, or at least this is how the lead advisor put it: "Iraq has to understand we are offering intellect, not F16s."[41] The out-of-country courses offered by NATO's centres of excellence represent another incentive: they are a welcome escape from day-to-day military routines and tasks. These courses are sought after, and they can be very relevant for Iraqi training priorities, like those offered at the Slovak Centre for Excellence on bomb disposal. Iraq, in other words, could aspire to be like Jordan, which has developed a privileged relationship with NATO, in addition to cultivating close bilateral ties with many NATO allies. Part of being on the road to a deeper partnership with the alliance is also socializing Iraqi partners in terms of NATO values, which means emphasizing certain themes like international humanitarian law and WPS norms, often just referred to as "gender issues" by participants during the interviews. These themes are present and embedded across the training, education, and advising packages of NMI. There is recognition that the material must be adapted, however. NATO personnel will take the standardized course package, for example, the basic instruction techniques course, "throw ideas into it and then make it acceptable to the Iraqis."[42] I am told that NATO personnel and staff pay attention to certain "cultural sensitivities" when it comes to WPS material, avoiding the word "gender" when possible. Ultimately, some compromise exists between what would be considered NATO standard and what is palatable to Iraqi stakeholders in this context. Thinking back on the mechanism of norm distortion, I am reminded of something a GENAD said about NMI in our interview: "you don't follow the regulation to the letter, you make it your own so that it works."[43]

Even though the mission is still in its early days, the senior military personnel I talked to expressed optimism: "there will be a tipping point where it all falls into place," and this applies across lines of effort.[44] For example, the training acquired at bomb disposal school can make a real difference as defusing ordnance will be a major part of normalization since ISIS left behind tons of mines and improvised explosive devices. The Iraqis are moving toward a UN standard training course and are substantially investing in building this capability within their own security forces, and awareness is gently being raised about WPS.

Force Protection

Other than the GENAD, the other women in uniform I encountered on the base were all with the force protection unit (FPU), the unit tasked with protecting NATO military personnel and staff who are on the move in armored convoys (including me, throughout my fieldwork). I met with three members of the FPU on the rooftop of the NMI building at Union III so that they could have a smoke while we discussed their day-to-day tasks. Their battle rhythm was very similar from one day to the next. They would get up, eat, and then prepare the vehicles that might be going out for the day, in response to orders about the various convoy missions. In general, the FPU routine is predictable: they escort; remain on standby for the duration of the engagement, whether it is a meeting or course delivery; and then get back to camp. One of the female infantry officers said that when she is the one driving, the checkpoint clearance is a lot quicker. The three soldiers all recognized that the most important gender aspect at play in this mission is the demonstration effect of having women in military roles within Iraqi society, where such things are rare. In a separate conversation about force protection, the J3 (who manages operations on the joint staff) concurred, acknowledging that having women as part of the FPU or the helicopter detachment did demonstrate to Iraqis that women could perform those roles: "they are visible and that can make an impact."[45]

This demonstration effect can also play out internally within the mission as the Turks expressed surprise at the number of women infantry soldiers doing force protection. It might also impact workplace dynamics: having mixed teams leads to different types of interactions than homogenous teams. For example, the (self-declared) oldest woman of the group confided that the men like to share stories with her: "they call me mom, jokingly."[46] The medic within the FPU also noted the importance of having a choice for the provision of care: to have a man or a woman depending on the circumstances. But all three FPU soldiers stressed that the younger generation does not care so much: "so long as you pass the tests, it's ok," and a mixed force is increasingly seen as normal.[47] The conversation also veered toward the state of military installations on base, with mixed tents or sleeping quarters; and they all indicated that their preference is always to stay with their platoon: "If you are separated, then you're out of the loop. You want to be part of the team," one of the female soldiers from the FPU said.[48] Over time, then, the separate sleeping quarters for men and women have been adapted from the old ways of doing things. This seems to vary from mission to mission though, and different contributing countries might have different policies when it comes to sleeping quarters.

Civilian Staff

Unlike the two other missions, the civilian staff at NMI is more visible and active, in addition to being more favorably embedded into the command structure of the mission, which provides some mechanism for civilian oversight at the tactical level. This is partly due to the advisory mandate of NMI, which I was repeatedly told is not political but still has an important policy component. Nonetheless, it is a small team. In a NATO security and defense sector reform environment, civilian tasks are focused on defense capacity, building integrity, and gender. There are two branches of operations: training and advisory. The training component is dominated by the military (the aforementioned MTTs and ETATs), and on the advisory side of NMI, the civilian leadership exercises a prominent role; but all decisions still must go through the commander, who has the final say. Within the civilian component of the mission, there are two divisions. One is the ministerial advisory and liaison branch, led by a Dutch ambassador, and the other is the specialized program office, led by a senior civilian from Turkey. Together, the branches total ten people (two of whom were women when I visited), so it is quite a small footprint within NATO's total crisis establishment of over five hundred personnel and staff.

However, the civilian women, especially the senior civilian representative, hold a highly visible role within NMI. This is recognized by the Turkish lead of special programs: "When the Iraqis see an ambassador like her, very experienced and able to do her work very well, they are really influenced by the knowledge, the experience. This makes a difference. It's a new model."[49] And that's just it, a senior civilian representative, with the title of ambassador, *is* uniquely positioned to get things done; but I wondered whether being a woman also influenced those dynamics. In her previous role, she was posted to Iraq, so she already had extensive contacts and a solid understanding of national and regional politics, which no doubt contributed to the influential role she played. Though formally subordinate to the NMI commander, she seemed to have found a military leader eager to give the perception of a balanced civil–military leadership team.[50] This role involves meeting with civilian representatives of the MOD, attending national security council meetings, accompanying the commander to other meetings, interacting with civil society, etc. The senior civilian representative is also perhaps best placed to be the conduit between civil society, the MOD, and other NMI representatives; reaching out to women's groups and assessing their unique security needs fulfills one of the broader mission goals related to gender, which is consistent with how WPS norms are meant to operate. However, since the mission is rather Baghdad-focused, with few civil society interlocutors in Taji and Besmaya, she said her work was impaired by limited mobility and reach within the country, a constraint that was also identified by the GENAD. If NMI representatives want to go to places like Ramadi, Babylon, or Basra, then they would have to hitch a ride from other organizations (read armored convoys or helicopters if the location is more remote). Many people I spoke to expressed frustration at not being able to move around and to more directly engage with Iraqi stakeholders. Even for the trainers, force protection concerns increasingly limited their freedom of movement over the course of the mission, due to a worsening security climate and, later, because of the COVID-19 pandemic.[51]

Overall, it is the advisory work that is really at the heart of the civil–military component of the mission. On the training side, there is still an advisory function, but mobile teams or embedded teams of military advisors work with military training and education institutions. The senior civilian representative's official title is SSR coordinator, unlike how the role was de-fined in Afghanistan. Indeed, the role is meant to be more technical than political, and that distinction is reflected in the title. The SSR coordinator confided that as the lone woman and often the lone civilian in meetings, she stands out yet profits immensely from having the title of ambassador (the senior civilian position does not come with the title; she came to the role with it) and from having previously worked in Iraq.

Another undeniable advantage she identified, pre-empting my question, is her access to women: "I have better access to women. That is a fact in this country."[52] Even if she's fourth in the pecking order of the mission, she has established a visible presence by the commander's side. Other senior officers I talked to within the mission routinely referred to the ambassador and the commander as a team. The ambassador noted that she created a position spe-cifically for WPS, which had a hard time getting filled. That person would eventually be able to look at the Iraqi WPS National Action Plan, talk to women's groups, and build relationships with civil society and other inter-national organizations; and, in turn, that work would translate into a better understanding of the environment. So here, too, the view is that there should be more women and perhaps more civilians, given that advice is a core part of the mission. On the military side, the only women I encountered were the GENAD, female soldiers with the FPU, and the commander's assistant: I am repeatedly told that NATO should be doing better, given that NMI is encour-aging the Iraqis to have more women in their security apparatus.

GENAD Roles and Constraints

The first thing I found striking about the NMI gender structure is that there was a GENAD but no GFPs. While this may have changed in subsequent rotations, the decision not to have GFPs was a conscious and deliberate one by the GENAD. Her rationale for essentially flying solo was quite straight-forward and disheartening. She said that there was already some resistance to her presence and that, this early in the mission's existence, she wanted to establish a solid basis for her work before recruiting GFPs who would es-sentially be dual-hatted.[53] This is significant because she was doing her work without respecting the NATO gender structure, while also not benefiting from extra staff time to fulfill her goals as GENAD. She received questions about this decision by higher-level HQ, including SHAPE, but managed to delay setting up the GFP structure. The plan, for the next rotation, would be to have one GFP per location (Baghdad, Taji, Bismayah) supporting the ETATs, which would be different from the NATO model that has GFPs in each branch. It appears that the GENAD at the tactical level can exercise some discretion in terms of implementing NATO's gender guidelines more narrowly than intended, but that at least in this case, oversight was exercised by higher-level HQ to see why GFPs were not in place, as per NATO's specified gender structure. The GENAD also mentioned that with her position, supported by GFPs, there might be a sense from the rest of the staff that "gender" is all taken care of, that it is not everyone's responsibility.

The paper trail for how GENADs conduct their day-to-day tasks is well codified given NATO's reporting requirements, detailed in its *Gender Functional Planning Guide*. More generally, an action plan guides the gender dimension of the mission, which details the lines of effort and tasks, and identifies the enablers versus disablers. The NMI GENAD's activities, therefore, are articulated around three objectives. The first objective consists of working internally to establish and socialize a code of conduct within the mission and to provide internal training on NATO's gender policies and guidelines, which are primarily focused on understanding the different impacts the mission might have on women and men within the host country. Here, the primary challenge is finding ways to integrate Iraqi women into NATO programming, given that there are none present in the MOD or military training and education institutions where NATO delivers the bulk of its work. There is also a gender annex (Annex RR) within the operations plan to guide this work, but the instructions are fairly generic; for example, there is mention of including gender perspectives in training activities, without specifying how this might be done. The GENAD has to adapt these guidelines to the mission's day-to-day activities, which is harder to achieve when delivering training on, say, vehicle maintenance as opposed to planning key leader engagement with MOD stakeholders. The commander of NMI offered public support for the GENAD's work at the outset, saying "I chose her because she can move things forward. I support her 100%."[54] Before that happened, there was little interest internally and even overt resistance on behalf of certain fellow NATO officers, providing some confirming evidence for feminist claims about how military culture clashes with WPS prescriptions. This further contributes to a narrow reading of how WPS norms get translated on the ground. GENADs do their work on the basis of what they think their peers will accept.

The second objective of the GENAD's activities consists of working directly with the Iraqis, providing materials to promote greater gender awareness in Arabic that would be well suited for the core stakeholders within the ministries and throughout the training and education institutions with which NATO engages. Going a step further, NATO would see it to be within its mandate to support Iraq's own National Action Plan on WPS; but realistically, NATO is hampered by a narrow mandate, limited mobility, few material resources, including money, as well as a lack of civilian and military women deployed as part of NMI who could support these types of engagement opportunities (with mostly female Iraqi stakeholders). Compared to the UN, the European Union, embassies, or international non-governmental organizations, NATO is ill equipped and badly located to undertake more direct community-based interactions with Iraqi civil society and women's groups.

The third objective serves to ensure a coordination function within the mission. Much like the case of KFOR, this entails making sure that NMI is plugged into the international networks in Iraq and with the other main partners, namely the US-led coalition, the European Union, the UN, the embassies, and US agencies, such as USAID. Being aware of what other organizations do is necessary to avoid duplication, but there are also opportunities to collaborate at times, through workshops or conferences. If there is progress in advancing Iraq's National Action Plan on WPS, NATO's just not part of it—it barely stays in the loop. What is being achieved can be credited to NATO's political guidance embedding WPS as part of NMI's lines of efforts, more civil–military integration in NMI's leadership, and having few but well-placed women to raise WPS norms (in addition to the commander) and to serve as role models when interacting with Iraqi stakeholders.

More than that though, NATO's pitch on WPS is tailor-made for a military audience; it is a selection of arguments and data points designed to pre-empt resistance. Every GENAD I talked to highlighted this persistent problem: appealing to audiences who already have a negative predisposition toward the topic of gender. For some, the solution lies in making it personal, like talking about their family and non-traditional gender roles. As an example to share with her Iraqi audience, the NMI GENAD talked about her military work–life balance, mentioning that her husband is the primary caregiver in their family. "They were surprised," she admitted; and that opened the door to them wanting to know more about her story, which created an opportunity to talk about WPS norms or, rather, inclusive security.[55] She adds that "once that door is open, you can introduce more formal instruction on gender, but that first pitch is key."[56] It seems to be a similar dynamic with NATO personnel and staff from the mission, namely that the GENAD has one chance to present the right arguments to justify being there. Those arguments invariably focus on operational effectiveness. Case in point: the pamphlet developed by the GENAD for NMI is titled *Gender as a Force Multiplier*. Some GENADs have even avoided mentioning their titles, not wanting to elicit negative responses or resistance from uttering the word "gender"; they simply say that they are advisors to the commander instead.

This was a new challenge for the NMI GENAD, who never anticipated being tapped on the shoulder to fulfill this role, although she enthusiastically accepted the post for the opportunity to deploy abroad.[57] A logistics officer in the Canadian Army for thirty years, she was with the Allied Rapid Reaction Corps when she was offered this GENAD opportunity. Shortly after her appointment as NMI GENAD, she took the GENAD course in Sweden before deploying to Iraq. She had also previously been a harassment advisor, a useful prior assignment for developing the code of conduct within the mission, a task that has fallen to the GENAD. I would call this "learning on the job," and it is fairly typical of the other GENAD trajectories I have encountered. The training and credentials required for GENADs are much lighter than they are for other advisors, for instance, a LEGAD.

As far as the training goes, there is a consensus among the GENADs I interviewed, including the NMI GENAD, that it was not well suited for what they faced in theater. She noted that the course she took to be certified was focused on peer-against-peer operations, which are far removed from scenarios that could resemble her day-to-day in Iraq.[58] In terms of training, the GENAD referred to the Gender Training of the Trainers Course, Gender-Based Analysis Plus (GBA+; a Canadian online training package that the CAF members have been required to take), as well as the online courses offered by NATO's Allied Command Transformation. The challenge then was to standardize the knowledge within the NATO contingent, and the GENAD was supported by the chief of staff in mandating that everyone take the pre-deployed course on gender.[59] The GENAD also provided additional training on-site, based on the perceived demand and needs. Here, too, the GENAD's role is as much about internal training—meaning delivering training on gender to other members of the contingent—rather than implementing the gender directives themselves, as spelled out in NATO documents. Yet GENADs find it hard to do the latter when there is no baseline awareness on why gender matters for the mission and why GENADs are advising the commander, so they design and conduct training to generate more awareness and acceptance.

On paper, the activities that the GENAD carries out in theater should flow from directives, operational orders, and standard operating procedures.[60] Then there is monthly reporting to higher-level HQ, to record how implementation is progressing. The core focus is to integrate "a gender advisory capability into Iraq military institutions and PME [professional military education]."[61] In practice though, the GENAD's tasks involve supporting the NMI commander and staff, overlooking the integration of a gender perspective across HQ functions, conducting key leader engagement, carrying out activities with local government or security institutions, as well as cooperating with international organizations or civil society. At the beginning of the mission, the GENAD was not necessarily active across the board, but from month to month, the reports demonstrate clear progression, with more engagement with key leaders and local institutions over time. There are also international engagement opportunities, even for the tactical-level GENADs, meaning engagement at SHAPE and NATO HQ, speaking about the GENAD's function in Iraq to other NATO stakeholders or representatives from the international community who are eager to hear about experiences from the field.

The key to any GENAD's success, I am told, is to be proactive in finding opportunities to show that gender is relevant across functions and military tasks. The planning meetings remain one of the main conduits for influence. For instance, the coordination and synchronization meetings about training are paramount because this is when the contents of the courses are determined. The GENAD will also inform the development of key NMI documents, like an operational risk document or standard operating procedure reviews. The other important meeting for the GENAD is the commander's update brief. In terms of tools, the NMI GENAD was developing a gender soldier card and wanted to develop a gender media card with talking points and an easy pitch to remember for NATO personnel.[62] Nagging is another strategy GENADs typically admit to using, though in moderation. The NMI GENAD mentioned that when the training teams come back from the field, she will ask them if they raised gender. "Sometimes it's yes, sometimes it is no"; but she keeps asking, and the teams know they will get the question each time. She is insistent, but does not want to rush things.[63] "Trainers who don't want to talk about gender but feel forced to will do a bad job," she says, "and this can be more damaging."[64] Sometimes she is invited by the schools too, in which case she can build relationships, start asking questions about curriculum, and look at the installations to see if they might be appropriate to welcome women. Toward the end of our conversation, she said more women within the mission are needed for key leader engagement. It ends up being mostly her, but sending women on key leader engagements, with male officers, really seems to make an impression. Having women role models appears to be a simple and evocative way to make the WPS norms come to life.

Outside NMI, I had a chance to speak to the two CJTF-OIR GENADs, who echoed a lot of the concerns I had previously heard about the ways in which WPS norms are perceived in military operations and the role of GENADs more specifically: "The perception we are fighting is that of a pink chair: that's what non-ops positions are called. It's assumed that you don't have an impact. We are making inroads as 'special staff.' You have to do some key leader engagement internally and find the champions. You have to show that it is a force multiplier from the J1 to J9."[65] They have examples on hand, highlighting the operational benefits of women's roles when it comes to checkpoint searches: "ISIS knows the coalition has fewer women to do searches, so they use women to carry stuff."[66] From those conversations, I also took away that diversity is more important for some mission tasks than others; but overall, it is still very much perceived through the prism of operational effectiveness.

The Australian GENAD echoed the words of her Canadian colleague: "You have two minutes to sell it, and they do teach you that strategy in GENAD courses."[67] Much like with the NMI GENAD, the words used to describe the WPS portfolio are carefully chosen. The language around operational effectiveness is adopted so as not to solicit unnecessary resistance internally, which is typical when talking about WPS or UNSCR 1325.[68] The Canadian GENAD from CJTF-OIR perhaps summed it best: "It's the hardest job I've ever had. This job is harder because you need to be an influencer everywhere, but no one reports to you. They don't have to listen."[69]

Other Key Advisors

Although the work of the GENAD is obviously central to integrating NATO's policies and directives on WPS, other special advisors contribute too. The

LEGAD, for instance, must also highlight women's rights and the gender considerations that are inherent to the application of international humanitarian law. The LEGAD's primary mandate is to provide legal advice to the commander. These considerations are related to protecting vulnerable populations, such as women and children in internally displaced people camps. This is how you highlight women's rights and principles of gender equality: "you use homeopathic doses," as one of the LEGADs put it.[70] These notions are also inculcated to the training teams, who then go off to deliver the training in Baghdad, Taji, or Besmaya. Women's rights get covered in discussions about human rights.

The LEGAD may also introduce specific projects such as the institution of a code of conduct within the Iraqi MOD. The LEGAD developed ten simple rules, with a manual that explains to the trainers and advisors the historical, legal, ethical, and moral foundations of the rules in the code of conduct. Other items on the LEGAD's docket include clarifying the rules of engagement, training Iraqi LEGADs (there are very few of them), and reforming their military justice system. But all of this work is very slow, given the cultural and language barriers. The work cannot be done without interpreters, but NATO personnel can get information through other means, such as their conversations with other international organizations and non-governmental organizations: "we are in the dark, walking slowly, we have a very incomplete picture and then, we refine our message as we go."[71] This is understood at the operational level too: "for NMI, the challenge is the political complexity and maintaining the consent of the Iraqi government for each aspect of the mission."[72] Added to this are lots of administrative tasks, like drafting memoranda of understanding with partners and coordinating or clarifying certain things with allies or the coalition.

Interestingly, the LEGAD is French and has never worked with a GENAD in theater before because he says there are no GENADs in France (I chose not to contradict him, but I know I have interviewed French GENADs at Allied Command Transformation before). He emphasized the role of GFPs only but with the caveat that "France does not pay as much attention to gender as NATO does."[73] Clearly, for this French LEGAD, working under the NATO umbrella was an adaptation of sorts, a redefinition of his role that implies coordination with the GENAD: "I've performed GENAD tasks in the past without knowing it, through work dealing with sexual violence, or targeting for civil–military cooperation. Now that I know what a GENAD does, I certainly see the value."[74]

At the NMI HQ, I also had the opportunity to interview members of the Commander's Initiative Group (CIG), handpicked military personnel who directly support the commander. This is a core group of trusted (all-male) staff on whom the commander relies for advice, to get urgent things done or when more focused attention on a problem is needed. The loyalty is to the commander primarily before the mission: "We are the three musketeers. We protect the king."[75] In terms of gender, members of the CIG were all Canadian, so they had done the mandatory GBA+ training and had been exposed to the GFP within their division back home. The problem with GENADs is that they often get forgotten: "if gender gets left behind in reports or if the GENAD has not been consulted, then the CIG can catch it and correct course."[76] The dynamics within the CIG are perhaps most closely related to executive-level or board interactions, where diversity has been shown to improve decision-making.[77] It is also where, provided that the commander has set the right climate, critical thinking can take place, which can be difficult within the rigid hierarchy of the military. The CIG might therefore greatly benefit from having diversity built into its DNA. There is no multinational diversity either as the CIG is composed primarily of staff drawn from the commander's inner circle.

Another area where the gender dimension is prominent within NMI is in terms of its public diplomacy. If this holds up at the tactical level, then we should see the public affairs officer (PAO) featuring some key messages on women's participation or, at the very least, integrating a gender-based analysis as part of the communications strategy. The PAOs I interviewed began by outlining their priority audiences: starting with audiences in NATO countries, then Iraqi populations, and finally, a more personal audience of deployed service members' families.[78] Those are the people who tend to be attentive to NATO's messaging efforts at the tactical level. On Facebook, the posts are in both Arabic and English, and a number of consistent messages are articulated: that NMI is a non-combat mission, that Iraqi sovereignty is being respected since the government invited NATO into the country, and finally, that NMI's mandate is counterterrorism through capacity-building.[79]

Although the gender breakdown was not monitored by the PAOs, they estimated that the audience on Facebook is 75% male and 25% female. Perhaps surprisingly, the Facebook post which focused on gender played really well and became one of the top posts—it was about one of the engagements that the GENAD did.[80] One of the explicit ways that the gender dimension is infused through content is by featuring photos of both men and women. There is much diversity, for example, in the team of Iraqi interpreters. However, some of them are reluctant to have their pictures posted on Facebook because of the perceived security risk.

Because the lack of women was repeatedly brought up during interviews, I sought out the J1 (military personnel) to ask questions about the force generation process and what mechanisms would need to be in place to increase the representation of women in the mission, based on requests coming from the commander. One identified limitation of the force generation process is that it is militarily driven, even though it is a joint civilian and military mission: indeed, it was obvious that NMI had staffing challenges on the civilian side and no efficient way to quickly fill vacant civilian positions.[81] The force generation process goes through the senior military representatives at SHAPE, but there is no mechanism to ask Global Affairs Canada, the US State Department, or the UK's Foreign and Commonwealth Office for civil servants to fill those posts. A few were subcontracted as a result, but a number of positions were left unfilled. Moreover, force generation would be the mechanism to get more women on the military side, but this is not activated. The J1 officer also pointed out the hypocrisy of calling on Iraqis to increase women's participation when there are fewer than 5% on NMI (counting both civilian and military personnel).[82] Indeed, in the very first NMI monthly report submitted by the GENAD to higher-level HQ (dated January 2019), there is a note on the underrepresentation of women. With fourteen women out of 375 within NMI, representation sat below 4% for women (2.4% in the military). In the report, the GENAD included a rationale for why there should be more women deployed as part of NMI: it is directly tied to the ability of NATO to implement UNSCR 1325 and the extent to which men "revert to the traditional view."[83]

When one looks at where the women are within NMI, the picture is even more interesting. The ETATs, seen as the frontline of the mission, are all-male teams, which is described as suboptimal; part of NMI's mandate is to promote greater gender equality, so this was raised as a potential obstacle and a credibility gap by several of the military personnel and civilian staff interviewed. Because ETATs work directly with and within Iraqi institutions, there are barriers tied to infrastructure (no bathrooms for women) and/or social issues, whereby women are treated differently in a variety of local contexts (flirtatious behavior was explicitly mentioned here). During my visit, I was told that there were discussions about finding ways to include women as part of the team. However, the argument about having more women in theater is primarily demonstrative, as proven above, as it shows to the Iraqis the value of having women in the military and helps raise specific concerns related to gender, such as the suitability of military installations or codes of conduct. Overall, the takeaway is that it is hard to promote a WPS agenda, a commitment that has been taken up by NATO, the UN, and the Iraqi government, with no or few women present.

Within the tactical aviation detachment and the FPU, there were women (in combat arms and medical trades). But this is not by design as the deployment of women to the mission was left up to the state, not stipulated in SHAPE's Combined Joint Statement of Requirements, which is NATO's wish list for its missions. In practice, to increase the participation of women, there needs to be an effort at all levels, from the feedback issued at the tactical level to the operational level (JFC-Naples) and to the strategic level (SHAPE). By activating the command structure in this way, pressure could be applied and even formalized through the force generation process, the process by which SHAPE solicits contributions from NATO member states, from one rotation to the next. While the process itself seems pretty clear, my conversations at all levels really showed that there is a general lack of will to build this as a bona fide military requirement that would be part of the force generation process. I would go as far as to say it is a sensitive topic based on how people reacted to my questions about it, which ranged from shifty body language to a hurried "no, this will never happen," based on who I talked to. This resistance is interesting given the fact that it is not unprecedented.[84] For example, the UN mandates that troop-contributing countries count 15% of women as part of their contingent. When I raised the UN example though, the NATO officials and commanders I interviewed did not see this as a positive thing because they view targets as controversial, with the potential to lead to backlash and resentment.[85]

Conclusion

The NMI commander stood apart in his approach to the GENAD, when compared to the other cases, because he explicitly and publicly insisted she come to all planning meetings. He also told his staff to listen and pay attention, understanding how the GENAD's position can be perceived by some: "what she says goes or NATO risks facing a credibility gap."[86] The commander is not alone in thinking this; many people I interviewed felt uncomfortable with the fact that NATO is telling the Iraqi government to make room for more women when NMI often shows up with all-male teams to meetings. Some solutions to the credibility gap are quite straightforward: get more women in theater for that demonstration or role-modeling effect. This has been the case for the UN, so why could NATO not achieve the same result? Across all missions I visited, the percentage of women in uniform was quite low, hovering around 5% or slightly higher if the civilian staff were counted. Moreover, you cannot just deploy women and assume there will be tangible benefits; they have to be of the right occupation and rank for the jobs they are asked to take on in theater. By going through NATO's force generation process, you could achieve this. Right now, women are thrown into certain roles because NATO needs female representation for certain tasks, meaning those women are diverted away from their current job (often health, logistics, or administrative roles). Such a solution would require rethinking NATO's force generation process so that a specified number of women are deployed as part of every rotation, based on a specific operational rationale.

The Iraq case also demonstrates the importance of GENAD networks in theater. There were two GENADs with Operation Iraqi Freedom, and the European Union and the UN also had their own GENADs. This can significantly boost the visibility of the position and help with institutional memory so that important information is retained from one rotation to the next. With multiple GENADs in the Baghdad area, there are always other GENADs around who can show the newcomer the ropes. The other source of institutional knowledge is through the NATO chain of command, with GENADs situated within JFC-Naples at SHAPE and at the NATO HQ. The GENAD at JFC-Naples is the primary point of contact for the tactical-level GENAD and provides all of the information and guidance about the position.

Within NMI, people's opinion and understanding of what the GENAD does varied greatly. This was apparent during my fieldwork since, for most of the people I interviewed, it was their first time working with a GENAD. It is admittedly personality-driven too, to some extent. What seemed to have worked particularly well at NMI is the collaboration that emerged between the GENAD and the LEGAD, who can address both the Law of Armed Conflict and gender perspectives within the same briefing to Iraqi stakeholders. It is also quite apparent that the Iraqis have an appetite to talk about gender perspectives within a post-conflict context but are less willing to engage when it comes to promoting women's participation in their security forces.

The challenge ahead for Iraq is quite daunting. It entails reforming the security sector and the force structure to have a defensive posture, now that ISIS has been conventionally defeated. It also means staying alert for a potential low-lying insurgency. Within the ministries, restoring a balance within civil–military relations is another priority task, as is building integrity (read fighting corruption) across all public institutions and organizations. Building integrity and WPS are two cross-cutting themes that surface in almost everything that is being done through SSR efforts, but it remains unclear how any of this is really moving the gender equality needle.

In support of stabilization, participation from a broad range of societal actors, including women's groups and civil society, will be necessary to properly identify priorities and needs, making sure that men and women have equal voice and access in the decisions made. This is a core operating principle for NATO and should be monitored as funds are disbursed and training is delivered.[87] However, when WPS norms were discussed during my interviews, two things stood out: first, how engaging with women can translate into a better reading of the security environment for NATO and, second, how having more women on the mission would be desirable because of the role-model effect and/or because NATO "talks the talk, but does not walk the walk" (in terms of women's representation). These types of arguments, deployed to actualize NATO's gender policies and directives, perpetuate a narrow and militarized interpretation of WPS norms, consistent with the logic of norm distortion. And to be fair, while the idea of better identifying the needs of local women is expressed, this is almost exclusively raised by the civilian staff and is clearly aspirational, given that limited mobility impairs any regular community-based engagement with Iraqi women (which only got worse after the assassination of Soleimani and with COVID-19, of course).

Since this is a relatively young NATO mission, one would expect it to have the gender perspective better integrated into the plans and procedures of the operation. This stands in contrast to older operations, like KFOR, which was launched in 1999, when guidance and many of the directives were not in place and when the position of GENAD had not yet been invented. Yes, for NMI, WPS principles are built into the curriculum for the military, and, yes, female staff and personnel can be paraded around; but the implementation of WPS norms should be more directly tied to gender equality goals that benefit women and Iraqi society as a whole. One such consideration, for example, is that war has transformed women's roles in society, with certain groups, like the Yazidi women who were subjected to sexual slavery by ISIS, being disproportionately affected.[88] As Angeline Lewis notes, organizations like NATO should refrain from "assuming a universality of priorities, concerns and interests among women of different backgrounds, merely as a result of their gender."[89] But, more generally, decades of war have severely limited women's access to employment, confining their role to the home. The defeat of ISIS represents a turning point in rebuilding political institutions and making sure women have the same or better access to education and employment than they did under Saddam Hussein's regime. It is important to take into account that resentment has built over the years as conditions for women have not necessarily improved under foreign occupation. This is especially true for the many war widows who have to run the household with little support and have uneven access to services when it comes to water, sanitation, and electricity.

While civil society and international organizations have been pushing for change, they have had little traction when it comes to introducing new legislation. Measures encouraging women's political participation or the use of quotas "have ensured that women are represented in the Iraqi parliament, but the mere presence of women has not necessarily resulted in the inclusion or championing of women's issues in the overall political agenda."[90] Evidently, there are barriers to women's participation in Iraq that are not present in Kosovo or in the Baltics, which sets NMI apart in many ways and specifically limits the possibility of direct engagement with women. Male attitudes and, in some cases, male consent are barriers when introducing measures to increase women's participation in the labor force or in politics more specifically. As for the impact of conflict, the situation in Iraq again stands in contrast to those of Kosovo and the Baltics and might be more comparable to that of Afghanistan. It is reported that 14,000 women have suffered violent deaths since 2003, with an additional 5,000–10,000 being abducted or trafficked.[91] Sexual violence was particularly acute during conflict, with abhorrent accounts of systematic rape that happened in ISIS-controlled areas.[92] There is an obvious need for more personnel and staff, especially women staff, to support survivors, while making services accessible considering the barriers that deep social stigma imposes. While these considerations should emerge from the application of WPS norms across its activities in Iraq, NMI is more narrowly focused on raising awareness through training and advisory tasks. The GENAD insisted that this is a necessary first step and that things should improve over time.

7

Conclusion

Is NATO a Feminist Alliance?

Emerging from the human security focus of the 1990s, the United Nations (UN) introduced more gender-responsive global norms with the adoption of UN Security Council Resolution (UNSCR) 1325. Women's groups and feminist scholars participated in the advocacy efforts that contributed to the inauguration of the Women, Peace and Security (WPS) agenda, which to date includes UNSCR 1325 as well as nine follow-on resolutions. These norms have been adopted by states and international organizations alike, to make the link between gender equality and conflict more explicit, encourage women's greater participation in conflict resolution and peacebuilding processes, address sexual and gender-based violence, and include gender analysis in international programs and missions. While feminist ideas inspired the emergence of these norms on gender and conflict, military organizations have been on the frontlines of translating these norms into practice. The result is that these WPS norms are interpreted through the prism of a military culture that values one thing above all else: operational effectiveness. This book tells the story of how the military has been delegated authority to advance gender equality as part of its activities, proposing a mechanism to explain why the military interpretation of WPS norms often leads to norm distortion. Indeed, armed forces are trained to stay focused on mission objectives and to lay out military tasks and lines of effort, making the implementation of WPS norms almost a given but not necessarily as intended.

Based on fieldwork and interviews in NATO headquarters (HQ), Iraq, Kosovo, and the Baltics, this book details the process by which WPS norms are militarized and put at the service of operational effectiveness. The pursuit of operational effectiveness is at the heart of military culture, and it is at the heart of NATO's organizational culture as well, given the political–military nature of its activities.

Deploying Feminism. Stéfanie von Hlatky, Oxford University Press. © Oxford University Press 2023.
DOI: 10.1093/oso/9780197653524.003.0007

The Limits of Operational Effectiveness

Deploying Feminism recounts NATO's journey as it adopted and integrated new norms of military cooperation into the day-to-day business of running the world's largest military alliance. At the end of the Cold War, these norms were moving away from deterrence and collective defense, instead embracing the concept of cooperative security and a more global approach to international cooperation than had been pursued since its inception in 1949. Several of the NATO civilian staff or military personnel I met during the course of this project thought that, with the adoption of a WPS agenda, NATO had gone too far. Why should a military alliance be tasked with promoting gender equality? Why should the military be involved? Ironically, these types of objections can also be heard at the opposite end of the spectrum, from feminist activists, since gender equality is seen as an antithetical pursuit to NATO's hardwired military preoccupations. But what if feminist principles could make NATO better? After all, NATO's post–Cold War forays into being more than an alliance by pursuing out-of-area operations have largely been a failure, with Afghanistan and Libya being the most obvious examples. Even in the Balkans, more than twenty years after NATO's decisive action put an end to ethnic cleansing, a continued NATO presence remains necessary. Is this what success looks like?

An alternative picture could emerge if military organizations thought of operational planning in broader terms, beyond a strict reading of military capabilities and personnel, along with the bullets and beans that keep the machine running. Indeed, a core lesson learned from the failure of the 1990s and early 2000s interventions has been that a better understanding of the operating environment is necessary for success and that this should include cultural norms and patterns of life, considerations that are fully consistent with WPS norms. Yes, this makes the business of operational planning much messier because it opens the door to time-consuming and intellectually demanding gender, social, and cultural analyses. Further, this requires change and adaptation on behalf of the civilian and military institutions that support the alliance's operations and activities.

On the one hand, the military can be well suited for change as military leaders are told what to do by civilian decision makers and then have a clear chain of command to get the job done. But what happens when the proposed change is seemingly at odds with the prevailing military culture? The military is touted as one of the most (if not the most) patriarchal institutions within society; can it really transform its practices to be in sync with WPS norms? By introducing the concept of norm distortion, I argued that the feminist principles that led to the adoption of the WPS agenda can get lost in translation when these norms are filtered through the prism of military culture, which dictates a focus on operational effectiveness. This distortion is why NATO's implementation of WPS norms has not furthered gender equality goals to the same extent that it has instrumentalized local engagement with women to benefit military tasks. The broader theoretical argument is that the meaning of WPS norms, adopted by international security organizations, changes in the process of implementation by military actors. This mechanism becomes visible when we examine how international security organizations like NATO carry out their day-to-day activities, from their HQ to their theaters of operation.

How NATO Works

When compared with other international organizations that deploy troops on missions, NATO stands out in one key respect: it develops its own doctrine and has an integrated military command structure. While there are always at least two chains of command at play, the NATO chain of command and the national chain of command, having common doctrine leads to a degree of harmonization across allied contributors. Ultimately, this makes a significant difference when it comes to implementing WPS norms through policies and directives. This tight control over NATO standards, ensured through common training and clear reporting lines, makes tracking and measuring change over time possible.

By contrast, there are areas where NATO has less control in the pursuit of WPS objectives, like in the realm of force generation, especially when compared to other organizations like the UN. NATO is not requiring that allies deploy more women as part of its operations; it is merely suggesting it. Although NATO collectively identifies the capabilities needed for missions through its Combined Joint Statement of Requirements, the provision of those capabilities is a national responsibility. Individual allies and partners must pony up the resources to support NATO's missions, but NATO has not been explicit in setting targets for women's representation within deployed forces, even when there is a clear operational requirement to do so. Pressure might be exercised on states to do more, either bilaterally or with mild public shaming; but capitals send what they send, and NATO has little to no control on that front. NATO can really only move the needle internally, when it oversees the hiring process for certain positions within its own organizational structure, supported by the diversity and inclusion officers of NATO's International Staff.

This leads to one of the most glaring findings from the book: that NATO is limited in its ability to fulfill WPS norms in operational theaters because it has so few women representing the mission. There is an obvious credibility gap when NATO shows up with an all-male team to advocate for women's participation in the security forces of host countries. Moreover, certain military tasks, like interacting with women's groups and stakeholders in Iraq and Afghanistan, require the presence of uniformed women, who are in too short supply to meet those demands. NATO could reform its force generation process to remove systemic barriers for the deployment of women and change its approach to force generation so that women's representation is considered an operational requirement. As things stand, NATO has not done enough to increase women's representation across its military operations and activities, even if it has at times appointed women in key command roles. Where NATO has done better is in adopting formal policies and directives inspired by WPS norms.

Indeed, this book makes clear that there has been a significant institutionalization of new procedures for building more gender analysis into operational planning, facilitated through a gender structure composed of gender advisors (GENADs) and gender focal points, as well as its training tools. This is important because regardless of whether a commander is sympathetic or not to the idea of considering gender as a planning factor, they must now comply with the requirement and report on it. The commander may even get briefing requests from higher-level HQ on this specific topic. That commander might come from a country where this is not done or required through the national chain of command, but within a NATO operation, the alliance's common doctrine and reporting overseen at Supreme HQ Allied Powers Europe (SHAPE) will prevail; there is at least minimal oversight. How gender mainstreaming is performed, however, varies from mission to mission and within each mission, as clearly laid out in the three previous chapters. Ultimately, the operational context will influence execution because the range of military tasks is different in each setting. Military plans, as designed at the strategic level, can be quite general; and somewhere between the operational and tactical levels, more precise lines of effort take shape.

This process of interpretation, from planning to execution, from the strategic level to the tactical level, influences every military task. But it is also important to account for variations across or within cases that is not due to the operational context itself as these will always be somewhat unique. My findings show that what best accounts for the variation in norm distortion are the command structure and the mission's staffing composition, in terms of its civil–military balance and gender balance. Whether or not NATO is leading command arrangements and operational planning matters because the alliance has an integrated command structure to oversee the consistent application of a "NATO standard" across its operations. Moreover, greater diversity within the mission's composition, which can be understood as professional (civilian or military) or personal (gender), generates more capacity to implement WPS norms. This diversity helps prevent a narrow interpretation of the norms that is strictly seen through the prism of operational effectiveness.

Gender Mainstreaming

When comparing the cases of the Kosovo Force (KFOR), enhanced forward presence (eFP), and the NATO Mission in Iraq (NMI), the variation in how WPS norms are implemented on the ground fully comes to light. For eFP, WPS implementation could be qualified as the bare minimum or entirely absent depending on the battlegroup because, prior to 2022, NATO had less control over how battlegroup activities were designed and carried out. There was little civilian oversight and low diversity in terms of women's representation. Within KFOR, gender considerations were more consistently mainstreamed through operational planning but limited to the execution of discrete military tasks, like engaging with the local population. The case study also revealed that the absence of civilians and women undermined the pursuit of certain key objectives: when a unit did not have any women, it was curtailed in its ability to engage with local women; when there are no civilians, deference to military actors is greater and the dynamics of oversight, looser. NMI, for its part, presents the most ambitious model as gender considerations are a distinct line of effort for the mission. Despite the practical constraints identified in the case study, like mobility across Iraqi territory, or the overall lack of women within NMI's contingent, having WPS-informed mission tasks and metrics creates a tighter accountability mechanism across the strategic, operational, and tactical levels. Moreover, even if the average representation of women remains low, they have secured key positions within the leadership structure, like the role of the security sector reform coordinator and the second commander of NMI, who was a woman general. Civil–military integration at this level, along with the presence of women in key posts, elevated WPS norms as a key consideration for the mission, even if the narrative on operational effectiveness was still dominant.[1]

While identifying and explaining these differences are important from both a scholarly and a practical standpoint, there were also some interesting similarities across cases that are worth highlighting. The most obvious similarity is the extent to which GENADs struggle when it comes to generating awareness about their role, as well as about NATO's broader WPS policies and directives.[2] Because that is the case, the GENAD invests a lot of time in developing training intended for an internal audience, that is, the personnel from NATO allies and partners. The challenges faced by GENADs, whether they are staff officers in higher-level HQ or deployed on operations, have been well documented and are further corroborated in this book. They include deficiencies in resources and training but also resistant attitudes from colleagues both up and down the chain of command.[3]

One improvement that was made by NATO in this respect is to have commanders include GENADs as part of their command teams. But *the way* in which this advice is framed is first and foremost as a matter of operational effectiveness. WPS norms, at their core, focus on women's participation and differentiated needs in volatile environments, with the overarching goal of promoting greater gender equality. This is a different focus compared to instrumentalizing gender analysis for tactical gain, but these lines are blurred across NATO's missions. The claim on the militarization of WPS norms is unambiguously confirmed across mission settings. The fact that sex-disaggregated data is being collected is a positive development, however. For example, the KFOR GENAD emphasized that his reporting requirements to higher-level HQ, Joint Forces Command-Naples and SHAPE, were focused on analyzing different segments of the population, as well as their unique needs or vulnerabilities. The next step will be for GENADs to offer advice on what can be done with this information to further gender equality and human rights in the country, which ultimately contribute to greater security and stability. By the same token, security measures should include how different groups within the population perceive and experience security improvements (or not). This is admittedly a broader measurement task than simply accounting for operational effectiveness, understood as the successful completion of predefined military tasks. However, it is a more sustainable and accurate reading of how NATO is doing in a particular operational setting.

Another point of commonality across missions is the extent to which gender is considered as part of public affairs, strategic communications, and outreach activities. At the strategic level, it is obvious that WPS is leveraged for public diplomacy purposes. At the tactical level, there is baseline awareness when it comes to recognizing the importance of representing men, women, and children in NATO's communication efforts. Whether that is done through social media posts or community-level engagement, more balanced representation of stakeholders was often raised by both civilian and military interlocutors without prompting. Nevertheless, given the low representation of women in deployed forces, NATO is often constrained in its ability to follow through with sending mixed teams for in-person engagement opportunities. The same women end up being tapped on the shoulder for every outreach opportunity in order to avoid all-male engagement teams. Even if this constraint was raised often during my fieldwork, there was also a recognition that NATO would not go the UN route in mandating specific targets for the deployment of women. NATO's experience with WPS norms in military operations, therefore, is primarily through the integration of a gender perspective in its activities, rather than through a concerted effort to increase women's representation and participation.

Women's Representation

Consistent with NATO's interpretation of WPS norms as improving operational effectiveness, let us consider how the representation and participation of women affect the equation. At the UN and NATO, deploying women soldiers on operations is seen as desirable because they are role models for local women and girls. Another perceived benefit is that, because women are often viewed as less threatening, they can lower tensions through dialogue. As shown in Chapters 4–6, there are specific conditions under which women do have a comparative advantage on operations. While the deployment of women can be seen as an operational requirement for certain tasks, it depends on the context. As an example, we can point to missions that rely on human intelligence, which includes both intelligence gathering and information operations. For human intelligence, the absence of women actually impedes mission success. While this might be more obvious in certain cultural settings, especially in societies where gender roles are more traditional, this applies more generally, given that women are an important segment of the population and bring a distinct security perspective within their communities. As for deployed personnel, because women are generally seen as more approachable, even when wearing body armor, they will have an easier time talking to female contacts and, as NATO's experiences in Afghanistan have shown, even male contacts. While this benefits the mission, better intelligence does not necessarily translate into military actions that are informed by gender equality concerns. Narrowing that gap could be an area of improvement for NATO.

While the literature emphasizes the unique contributions made by women or all-female units in the context of counterinsurgency operations and other population-centric operations (e.g., disaster assistance missions or peace support operations), the findings presented in this book demonstrate that this is true across the operational spectrum, from deterrence-type missions to peacekeeping missions. One must be careful not to overemphasize this point, however, as this comparative advantage is only for the performance of certain tasks. Whether we look at the patrolling of main roads in conflict zones or random checks in airports all over the world, women searching women has become a dominant practice. There is thus a clear requirement for female personnel or staff for those tasks. By contrast, when soldiers execute infantry and armored maneuvers across the Baltics, there is no clear operational rationale for imposing a specific gender composition requirement. In other words, whether a woman or a man performs those tasks should not make a difference, operationally speaking. In Latvia, for example, NATO infantry units are training together to improve interoperability and to conduct military exercises to deter Russia. Those infantry units are 98% male and would work no differently in terms of executing their military tasks if they had gender parity. When soldiers are fully kitted out and running tank maneuvers, you simply cannot tell the difference. The lack of women in this context makes clear that military organizations have failed to recruit and retain female personnel in combat trades, but it ultimately would not impair the execution of these discrete mission tasks on the ground.

For tasks where the gender composition of deployed personnel matters, it should be flagged as an operational requirement and taken into account during the force generation process. For staff positions in NATO HQs, the push toward greater diversity should continue, perhaps more ambitiously than has been the case thus far. Looking at the UN might be instructive here. As the UN was celebrating the fifteenth anniversary of its landmark resolution, it also had to come to grips with just how little progress had been made. At all levels of UN activity, the participation of women remained low; and this was particularly apparent in peace operations, where on average 4%–5% of the military personnel deployed were women. The UN then set out to codify specific targets for women's representation, calling on the secretary-general to steer efforts in order to double the number of women in peace operations within a five-year timeline. Secretary-General Guterres took a further step in stating that he would work toward achieving gender parity at the UN. The UN Strategy on Gender Parity was implemented with tangible results in terms of increasing the UN's diversity, both for HQ positions and in the field, with additional financial incentives provided by the Elsie Initiative, a trust fund that was set up to assist troop-contributing countries in their efforts to deploy more women in peace operations.[4]

For any initiative which aims to increase the representation of women in military operations, unintended consequences need to be carefully considered and mitigated. While deploying more women will probably continue to be pitched according to the logic of gender and operational effectiveness, because it seems to work in securing buy-in from predominately male organizations, it risks placing unfair scrutiny on the few women who are deployed on operations. Commanders therefore have an important responsibility to set the right climate for fair gender integration and swiftly intervene if there is any backlash or incidents unduly targeting women. It is unfair, ultimately, that the performance of men is not scrutinized to the same extent or, worse, that "the participation of men in operations is not made contingent upon some evidence-based claims about their effectiveness."[5]

From Feminist Theory to Policy Innovation

In the introductory chapter, I emphasized that, to put it bluntly, there is no consensus on whether WPS is a positive development in international politics or the co-optation of feminist ideas by patriarchal military organizations.[6] Some scholars take a pragmatic view and reject the idea that pursuing military effectiveness through WPS is necessarily co-optation, arguing that pushing gender equality for its own sake will just not gain any traction with the military.[7] Institutionalization of the WPS agenda, however imperfect, represents steady progress.[8] Kronsell also provides a fairly optimistic view but on different grounds, offering that "the attention paid to gender issues is an indication of a sea change, particularly when these concerns come into the organization's operational level and into daily practices, because it means that a discussion is raised and people are forced to reflect on gender issues."[9] In Afghanistan and in other NATO operational settings, women did become more visible, but this is a minimal first step; this is a much narrower WPS focus than what was intended. WPS norms, as originally intended, should push us to rethink security beyond traditional military metrics, by putting gender equality at the center of the security equation. As Enloe reminds us, "security does not have to be militarized," which entails thinking about metrics that matter for the most vulnerable people in conflict settings and understanding that these vulnerabilities will differ across social demographics. She suggests that "this alternative interpretation of 'security' would accord less authority to military experts and more authority to local women's groups whose activists have been collecting information about women's daily lives and devising ways to prevent rape and domestic violence."[10] This represents a significant broadening of the norm system embodied by militarism.[11]

WPS norms propose a reconciliation of two goals that have often been pitched as competing goals: on the one hand, creating military organizations that can effectively respond to strategic challenges and, on the other, making sure these military organizations are compatible with the values and principles espoused by the UN.[12] In national contexts too, the tension between the pursuit of military effectiveness and respect of societal values has been highlighted in the literature on civil–military relations, and it is at play here.[13] Staying true to WPS norms while securing organizational buy-in is a delicate balance to strike, as acknowledged by a former GENAD from NATO's Allied Command Operations:

> On the one hand, the change process must be continuously and firmly grounded within the transformative WPS mandate: the demand of primarily preventing conflict and ensuring women's participation together with the objective of achieving gender equality. On the other hand, for this change process to be successful and effective, it must also be on the organization's own terms.[14]

Some reject outright that the two can be reconciled, especially when it comes to reconciling gender equality with military effectiveness.[15] This objection was already highlighted on feminist grounds, but military organizations also have cause to push back as they "may not see gender equality as part of what they are responsible for."[16]

NATO's proposal is that the two can be mutually reinforcing; that to stay effective, the alliance must adopt WPS norms. Indeed, because WPS norms have been diffused across international institutions and their member states, it is not surprising that different interpretations and priorities tied to the agenda have emerged.[17] Organizations with strong military cultures, like NATO, can make gender equality a true planning priority by broadening their metrics of operational effectiveness to include more long-term indicators of security to assess operational success. Implementation will be enhanced by increasing deployment opportunities to both civilian and military women, through reforms of force and staff generation processes. NATO and its member states should also continue to enhance the professional incentives staff and personnel face when it comes to demonstrating competent performance on WPS. While NATO has done this for all of its HQs, standards at the national level for individual allies vary widely and are beyond the scope of what NATO controls.[18] NATO can, however, push for change with partners and individual allies that are champions of WPS, using diplomacy to share best practices and knowledge with allies that are either recalcitrant or falling behind.

Beyond the strict NATO context, states that have adopted feminist foreign policies could also be doing more. Canada, Sweden, France, Spain, Mexico, and Luxembourg have all endorsed feminist principles as part of their international policy statements, though some have been more vocal than others in doing so. While working through organizations like NATO and the UN can achieve concrete results, like policies and directives, countries with feminist foreign policies could build a unique partnership, which reflects their commitment to gender equality.[19] In the wake of COVID-19, it is easy to understand how starting with gender equality as a lens through which global challenges should be assessed makes sense, given the uneven impact the pandemic has had on different segments of society. Indeed, women and racialized people have been affected in unique ways. In a NATO context, allies who claim to pursue a feminist foreign policy could help further refine principles of intervention by taking sexual and gender-based violence as a key indicator of threat perception and an important consideration when deciding on NATO's military involvement.[20] Yes, women are disproportionately targeted when it comes to sexual and gender-based violence, but men and boys, as well as members of the LGBTQ community, also suffer from these types of atrocities.[21] Drawing from an intersectional lens supports a more thorough understanding of these insecurities, which is an other area that is ripe for improvement in the NATO context. Ultimately, it is just not possible to build sustainable security outcomes by leaving so many people out of the equation. Conveying, as *The Economist* did after the collapse of Afghanistan, that "nations that fail women fail," should be at the heart of the narrative that states and international organizations employ.[22]

Conclusion

When NATO set out to increase the representation of women within its structures and introduced a gender perspective into operational planning and missions, it was not an intuitive journey for a military alliance forged during the Cold War. But NATO has nonetheless championed the WPS agenda, even if it has adapted these norms to suit its own purposes. These WPS norms—and the more precise objectives that they morph into—are often subject to interpretation and take on new meanings in the practice of day-to-day civilian and military activities. It is unlikely that NATO and feminist objectives will ever be completely aligned.[23] From an international relations perspective, the interesting question is why NATO's journey has taken this particular turn and how these new norms are shaping patterns of military cooperation.

This book shows that WPS norms, as well as their corresponding policies and directives, have been institutionalized in significant ways. First, NATO's common doctrine has facilitated implementation because policies adopted by the alliance have been integrated into its planning documents and embedded within a gender structure (a network of GENADs and focal points). Second, NATO has deployed training to ensure that there is a baseline understanding of WPS principles and how they apply in operational contexts. Third, personnel and funding have been dedicated to support NATO's WPS agenda, which results in material incentives for further institutionalization. However, while this is tangible evidence of change, it would be a stretch to suggest that there is broad acceptance of these WPS norms within the alliance. Instead, what I have observed is awareness across the organization that these norms exist but strong inconsistencies in how these norms are understood and acted on.

The path of least resistance has been to push the operational effectiveness rationale, a rationale that has been tepidly endorsed by the military. Considering the evidence presented in this book, arguing that WPS norms and gender considerations translate into operational benefits is the primary way to get traction, even if this obscures these norms' true purpose: advancing gender equality through NATO's programming and actions. Everyone I talked to seemed to buy into the proposition that more comprehensive social analysis, which necessarily includes a reading on how both women and men experience conflict, can improve NATO's understanding of its operating environment. Civilian and military personnel with prior field experience or deployments in NATO or UN missions are quick to point to the benefits of understanding local communities as one of the most important variables of mission success. Whether or not these local actors then benefit from NATO's better situational awareness is unclear, but that could change.

I am often asked if there is even a realistic alternative to the argument on operational effectiveness. It is tempting to bypass the question by answering that this is NATO policy, period; policies need to be implemented and orders, carried out; or that buy-in will come with time and the detractors will eventually fall in line. But the bigger question of identifying what is needed to successfully implement the WPS agenda is a complex one. NATO, much like the UN and EU, decided to endorse the WPS agenda and then proceeded to underscore the importance of gender analysis as part of its policies and operational planning methodologies. This is easier said than done as gender analysis is a time consuming exercise, which necessitates prior knowledge and training. On the gender representation front, NATO only has control over its own appointments, so it is constrained in the extent to which it can boost female representation across its missions. What NATO member states choose to do, whether they prioritize women's increased representation or not, is their business. NATO policies, thus, can only lead so far.

Another set of incentives for implementation, then, involves national priorities. NATO member states have adopted national action plans on WPS, which would give them a mandate to implement this at home but also through organizations to which they belong, like NATO. The problem here is that national action plans grow and shrink in importance depending on the government of the day. Canada will obviously push for action on WPS norms if it is pursuing a feminist foreign policy, just as Sweden might.[24] So depending on which government is vocal on WPS norms, there will be clusters of enthusiastic countries when it comes to promoting women's representation or "the gender perspective." Capitalizing on this political momentum is another avenue for change.

Then, the argument that has the least traction in military circles, perhaps ironically, is the argument which forms the core of the WPS agenda; it is a moral, rights-based argument in support of gender equality.[25] Even if common values are enshrined within NATO's foundational treaty, WPS norms clash with certain states' political culture. While they might refrain from opposing WPS norms publicly, those states (Turkey, Hungary, Poland, to name a few) will not go out of their way to champion the vision of NATO as a feminist alliance.[26]

This leaves us with the question of what a truly transformative WPS agenda, rooted in feminist principles, would look like. To some, it entails "high quality gender mainstreaming processes and concrete improvements in gender equality worldwide."[27] To others, it entails a more radical project of dismantling security and military organizations as "problematic institutions."[28] Regardless of which vision prevails, the WPS agenda has left its imprint on the norms of military intervention in a noticeable way, from the highest-level HQ to command teams at the tactical level. Moving forward, the most important priority is the development of clearer guidance on how gender equality can be furthered by NATO's political and military objectives. That requires more decisive civilian leadership and active civil–military cooperation on WPS, with no exit strategy or end state in sight.

Notes

Chapter 1

1. Center for Army Lessons Learned, *Commander's Guide to Female Engagement Teams* (Fort Leavenworth, KS: Center for Army Lessons Learned, 2011), 60, https://call2. army.mil/toc.aspx?document=6818&filename=/docs/doc6818/11-38.pdf. Though I'm citing this guide as an example, the FET concept emerged earlier.
2. Center for Army Lessons Learned, *Commander's Guide*, 63.
3. This has contributed to framing issues of gender inclusivity in terms of military "capacity rather than rights," as argued by Ben Wadham et al., "'War-Fighting and Left-Wing Feminist Agendas': Gender and Change in the Australian Defence Force," *Critical Military Studies* 4, no. 3 (February 2016): 266.
4. Gender will mostly be discussed in binary terms, as analyzed through the prevalent narratives employed in NATO documents and interviews.
5. Katharine A. M. Wright, Matthew Hurley, and Jesus Ignacio Gil Ruiz, *NATO, Gender and the Military: Women Organizing from Within* (New York: Routledge, 2019); Megan Bastick and Claire Duncanson, "Agents of Change? Gender Advisors in NATO Militaries," *International Peacekeeping* 25, no. 4 (August 2018): 554–577.
6. Cynthia Enloe, *Maneuvers: The International Politics of Militarizing Women's Lives* (Los Angeles: University of California Press, 2000), 298.
7. Cynthia Cockburn, "Snagged on the Contradiction: NATO, UNSC 1325, and Feminist Responses" (paper presented at the annual meeting of No to War—No to NATO, Dublin, Ireland, April 2011, https://no-to-nato.net/wp-content/uploads/2013/03/NATO13251.pdf).
8. Claire Duncanson and Rachel Woodward, "Regendering the Military: Theorizing Women's Military Participation," *Security Dialogue* 47, no. 1 (December 2015): 3–21.
9. Wright, Hurley, and Ruiz, *NATO, Gender and the Military*, 61. It should be noted that in 2016 the Civil Society Advisory Group was created to promote deeper engagement with feminist activists and civil society organizations.
10. Laura J. Shepherd, "Making War Safe for Women? National Action Plans and the Militarisation of the Women, Peace and Security Agenda," *International Political Science Review* 37, no. 3 (March 2016): 324–335. See also Bastick and Duncanson, "Agents of Change?," and Stéfanie von Hlatky, "Building a Feminist Alliance," *Open Canada*, November 18, 2020, https://opencanada.org/building-a-feminist-alliance/.
11. Originally recounted in Christopher D. Kolenda, *The Counterinsurgency Challenge: A Parable of Leadership and Decision-Making in Modern Conflict* (Mechanicsburg, PA: Stackpole Books, 2012).

12. United Nations, Office of the Special Adviser on Gender Issues and Advancement of Women, "Landmark Resolution of Women, Peace and Security," http://www.un.org/womenwatch/osagi/wps/.

13. All available NAPs can be found at Women's International League for Peace & Freedom, "1325 National Action Plans (NAPs)," http://1325naps.peacewomen.org.

14. This link has been established in the academic literature. See, for example, Valerie M. Hudson et al., "The Heart of the Matter: The Security of Women and the Security of States," *International Security* 33, no. 3 (Winter 2008–2009): 7–45 and the WomanStats Project Database: https://www.womanstats.org.

15. The idea that the military is designed to "kill people and break things" is mentioned sporadically in public commentary and debates, for example, Thomas E. Ricks, "The Military's Purpose Isn't to Break Things and Kill People, but It Should Be," *Foreign Policy*, September 24, 2015, https://foreignpolicy.com/2015/09/24/the-militarys-purpose-isnt-to-break-things-and-kill-people-but-it-should-be/.

16. To illustrate, Anthony King says that women in the military are made to belong to one of three categories by their male peers: bitches (hetero and sexually unavailable), whores (prone to fraternization), and dikes (homosexual, sexually unavailable). See Anthony King, "The Female Combat Soldier," *European Journal of International Relations* 22, no. 1 (2016): 122–143. Laura Sjoberg's earlier work had also shown how women are categorized by their male counterparts in a finite number of essentializing categories, such as "mothers, monsters, whores." See Laura Sjoberg and Caron E. Gentry, *Mothers, Monsters, Whores: Women's Violence in Global Politics* (London and New York: Zed Books, 2007). Similarly, Melissa S. Herbert examines how the military marginalizes women in all settings, degrading femininity in how they socialize soldiers, in *Camouflage Isn't Only for Combat: Gender, Sexuality, and Women in the Military* (New York and London: New York University Press, 1998).

17. NATO, *NATO Bi-Strategic Command Directive 040-001, Integrating UNSCR 1325 and Gender Perspectives* (Mons, Belgium: SHAPE, 2017), 5, https://www.act.nato.int/images/stories/structure/genderadvisor/nu0761.pdf.

18. NATO, *NATO Bi-Strategic Command Directive 040-001*, 7.

19. Jennifer F. Klot, "UN Security Council Resolution 1325: A Feminist Transformative Agenda," in *The Oxford Handbook of Transnational Feminist Movements*, ed. Rawwida Baksh and Wendy Harcourt (New York: Oxford University Press, 2015), 4, 10.

20. Torunn L. Tryggestad, "Trick or Treat? The UN and Implementation of Security Council Resolution 1325 on Women, Peace, and Security," *Global Governance* 15, no. 4 (2009): 544–548; Felicity Hill, Mikele Aboitiz, and Sara Poehlman-Duombouya, "Nongovernmental Organizations' Role in the Buildup and Implementation of Security Council 1325," *Signs: Journal of Women in Culture and Society* 28, no. 4 (2003): 1256–1259.

21. UN Women, "HeForShe," accessed January 23, 2016, http://www.heforshe.org/en/our-mission (webpage discontinued).

22. Jens Stoltenberg and Angelina Jolie, "Why NATO Must Defend Women's Rights," *The Guardian*, December 10, 2017, https://www.theguardian.com/commentisfree/2017/dec/10/why-nato-must-defend-womens-rights.

23. Karin Aggestam, Annika Bergman Rosamond, and Annika Kronsell, "Theorising Feminist Foreign Policy," *International Relations* 33 (2018): 23–39.

24. Government Offices of Sweden, "Feminist Foreign Policy," accessed January 23, 2016, http://www.government.se/government-policy/feminist-foreign-policy/. For a feminist analysis of Sweden's feminist foreign policy, see Karin Aggestam and Annika Bergman-Rosamond, "Swedish Feminist Foreign Policy in the Making: Ethics, Politics, and Gender," *Ethics & International Affairs* 30, no. 3 (2016): 323.

25. United Nations, Office of the Special Adviser on Gender Issues and Advancement of Women, "Landmark Resolution of Women, Peace and Security," http://www.un.org/womenwatch/osagi/wps/.

26. Etienne Wenger, *Communities of Practice: Learning, Meaning, and Identity* (Cambridge: Cambridge University Press, 1998); Emmanuel Adler, "The Spread of Security Communities: Communities of Practice, Self-Restraint, and NATO's Post-Cold War Transformation," *European Journal of International Relations* 14, no. 2 (2008): 195–230.

27. Cynthia Enloe, *Globalization and Militarization: Feminists Make the Link* (London: Rowman & Littlefield, 2016); on feminist international relations, see, for example, Enloe, Cockburn, Cohn, Kronsell, Duncanson, Basham, Millar, Henry, Belkin.

28. Bastian Giegerich and Stéfanie von Hlatky, "Experiences May Vary: NATO and Cultural Interoperability in Afghanistan," *Armed Forces & Society* 46, no. 3 (2019): 495–516.

29. Matthew Hurley, "The 'Genderman': (Re)Negotiating Militarized Masculinities when 'Doing Gender' at NATO," *Critical Military Studies* 4, no. 1 (January 2018a): 85.

30. Some parts of this section are drawn from Stéfanie von Hlatky, "The Gender Turn in Canadian Military Interventions," in *Canada among Nations*, ed. Fen Osler Hampson and Stephen M. Saideman (Waterloo: Centre for International Governance Innovation, 2015), 161–176.

31. Paul Kirby and Laura J. Shepherd, "The Futures Past of the Women, Peace and Security Agenda," *International Affairs* 92, no. 2 (March 2016b): 373–392; Paul Kirby and Laura J. Shepherd, "Reintroducing Women, Peace and Security," *International Affairs* 92, no. 2 (March 2016a): 249–254.

32. Carol Cohn, Helen Kinsella, and Sheri Gibbings, "Women, Peace and Security Resolution 1325," *International Feminist Journal of Politics* 6, no. 1 (January 2004): 130–140; Nicola Pratt and Sophie Richter-Devroe, "Critically Examining UNSCR 1325 on Women, Peace and Security," *International Feminist Journal of Politics* 13, no. 4 (December 2011): 489–503.

33. Laura J. Shepherd and Jacqui True, "The Women, Peace and Security Agenda and Australian Leadership in the World: From Rhetoric to Commitment," *Australian Journal of International Affairs* 68, no. 3 (May 2014): 257–284; Rebecca Tiessen, "Gender Essentialism in Canadian Foreign Aid Commitments to Women, Peace, and Security," *International Journal* 70, no. 1 (March 2015): 84–100, https://doi.org/10.1177/0020702014564799.

34. Laura J. Shepherd, "WPS and Adopted Security Council Resolutions," in *The Oxford Handbook of Women, Peace, and Security*, ed. Sara E. Davies and Jacqui True (New York: Oxford University Press, 2019), 98–109; Soumita Basu, "Gender as National Interest at the UN Security Council," *International Affairs* 92, no. 2 (March 2016): 255–273; see also Sahla Aroussi, "Women, Peace, and Security and the DRC: Time to Rethink Wartime Sexual Violence as Gender-Based Violence," *Politics & Gender* 13, no. 3 (September 2017): 488–515.

35. Aiko Holvikivi and Audrey Reeves, "Women, Peace and Security after Europe's 'Refugee Crisis,'" *European Journal of International Security* 5, no. 2 (June 2020): 135–154, https://doi.org/10.1017/eis.2020.1; Sawi Parshar, "The WPS Agenda: A Postcolonial Critique," in *The Oxford Handbook of Women, Peace, and Security*, ed. Sara E. Davies and Jacqui True (Oxford University Press, 2019), 829–839.

36. Shepherd, "Making War Safe for Women?"

37. Tiessen, "Gender Essentialism."

38. Matthew Hurley, "Watermelons and Weddings: Making Women, Peace and Security 'Relevant' at NATO through (Re)Telling Stories of Success," *Global Society* 32, no. 4 (October 2018b): 440.

39. On tensions between the different variants of feminism, see David Duriesmith and Sara Meger, "Returning to the Root: Radical Feminist Thought and Feminist Theories of International Relations," *Review of International Studies* 46 (2020): 357.

40. Brooke A. Ackerly, Maria Stern, and Jacqui True, "Feminist Methodologies for International Relations," in *Feminist Methodologies for International Relations*, ed. Brooke A. Ackerly, Maria Stern, and Jacqui True (New York: Cambridge University Press, 2006), https://ebookcentral-proquest-com.proxy.queensu.ca/lib/queen-ebo oks/reader.action?docID=268249&ppg=33.

41. Annica Kronsell, "Gendered Practices in Institutions of Hegemonic Masculinity," *International Feminist Journal of Politics* 7, no. 2 (June 2005): 288; Naidu, Maheshvari, "Wrestling with Standpoint Theory . . . Some Thoughts on Standpoint and African Feminism," *Agenda* 83 (2010): 25.

42. Abigail Brooks, "Feminist Standpoint Epistemology," in *Feminist Research Practice*, ed. Sharlene Hesse Biber and Patricia Lena Leavy (Thousand Oaks; London; New Deli: Sage Publications, 2007), 54–55, https://us.sagepub.com/sites/default/files/ upm-binaries/12936_Chapter3.pdf; on standpoint feminism and intersectionality, see Agnes Liljegren, "A Double Occupation: The Struggle within the Struggle" (bachelor's thesis, Lund University, 2020), 8, http://lup.lub.lu.se/luur/downl oad?func=downloadFile&recordOId=9033851&fileOId=9036737.

43. Connie Brownson, "The Battle for Equivalency: Female US Marines Discuss Sexuality, Physical Fitness, and Military Leadership," *Armed Forces & Society* 40, no. 4 (2014): 765–788.

44. Orna Sasson-Levy, Yagil Levy, and Edna Lomsky-Feder, "Women Breaking the Silence: Military Service, Gender, and Antiwar Protest," *Gender & Society* 25, no. 6 (2011): 740–763; Rose Weitz, "Vulnerable Warriors: Military Women, Military Culture, and Fear of Rape," *Gender Issues* 32, no. 1 (2015): 164–183, https://doi.org/ 10.1007/s12147-015-9137-2.

45. Joshua S. Goldstein, Jon C. Pevehouse, and Sandra Whitworth, *International Relations*, 2nd ed. (Toronto: Pearson/Longman, 2008); Robert O. Keohane, "International Relations Theory: Contributions of a Feminist Standpoint," *Millennium* 18, no. 2 (June 1989): 245–253.

46. Regina F. Titunik, "The Myth of the Macho Military," *Polity* 40, no. 2 (April 2008): 137–163.

47. Jens Stoltenberg, "Digital Dialogue about the Future of Women, Peace and Security at NATO" (NATO Zoom webinar, October 15, 2020, https://www.youtube.com/watch?v=3HuHZQBCmM8).

48. Heidi Hudson, "Gender and the Globalization of Violence: The Treacherous Terrain of Privatised Peacekeeping," *Agenda: Empowering Women for Gender Equity* 59, 1 (2004): 42–55; Johanna Valenius, "A Few Kind Women: Gender Essentialism and Nordic Peacekeeping Operations," *International Peacekeeping* 14 (2007): 515; Vanessa F. Newby and Clotile Sebag, "Gender Sidestreaming? Analysing Gender Mainstreaming in National Militaries and International Peacekeeping," *European Journal of International Security* 6 (2021): 160.

49. United Nations Peacekeeping, "Women in Peacekeeping," United Nations Department of Peacekeeping, accessed October 10, 2019, https://peacekeeping.un.org/en/women-peacekeeping.

50. Claire Duncanson, "Forces for Good? Narratives of Military Masculinity in Peacekeeping Operations," *International Feminist Journal of Politics* 11, no. 1 (March 2009): 63–75; Claire Duncanson, *Forces for Good? Military Masculinities and Peacebuilding in Afghanistan and Iraq* (New York: Palgrave Macmillan, 2013).

51. Paul Higate and Marsha Henry, "Engendering (In)Security in Peace Support Operations," *Security Dialogue* 35, no. 4 (December 2004): 493; see also Henri Myrttinen, Lana Khattab, and Jana Naujoks, "Re-thinking Hegemonic Masculinities in Conflict-Affected Contexts," *Critical Military Studies* 3, no. 2 (May 2017): 103–119, https://doi.org/10.1080/23337486.2016.1262658.

52. Sandra Whitworth, *Men, Militarism, and UN Peacekeeping* (Boulder, CO, and London: Lynne Rienner Publishers, 2004), 16.

53. Claire Duncanson, "Beyond Liberal vs Liberating: Women's Economic Empowerment in the United Nation' Women, Peace and Security Agenda," *International Feminist Journal of Politics* 21, no. 1 (2019): 113–114.

54. Laura Sjoberg, "Feminist Security and Security Studies" in *The Oxford Handbook of International Security*, ed. Alexandra Gheciu and William C. Wohlforth (New York: Oxford University Press, 2018), 45–60, 47.

55. Claire Duncanson, "Beyond Liberal vs Liberating: Women's Economic Empowerment in the United Nations' Women, Peace and Security Agenda," *International Feminist Journal of Politics* 21, no. 1 (2018): 111–130, 114.

56. K. Kopsa, "Gendering Crisis Management: Examining the Role of Gender in the Report of the Parliamentary Committee on Crisis Management" (Bachelor's thesis, Malmö University, 2021).

57. Kopsa, "Gendering Crisis Management"; see also Helena Carreiras, *Gender and the Military: Women in the Armed Forces of Western Democracies* (London and New York: Routledge, 2006), 88.

58. Caroline Kennedy-Pipe, "Liberal Feminists, Militaries and War," in *The Palgrave International Handbook of Gender and the Military*, ed. Rachel Woodward and Claire Duncanson (London: Palgrave Macmillan, 2017), 23–37, 34.

59. Not all self-identified "critical feminist" accounts, however, take an anti-military view. For instance, Wright, Hurley, and Ruiz, in their book *NATO, Gender and the Military*, identify their approach as critical feminist security studies yet put military women's activism at the core of their inquiry. See also Duncanson and Woodward, "Regendering the Military."

60. Maya Eichler, "Militarized Masculinities in International Relations," *Brown Journal of World Affairs* 21, no. 1 (Fall/Winter 2014): 81–93.

61. Carreiras, *Gender and the Military*, 204.

62. Claire Duncanson, *Gender and Peacebuilding* (Cambridge: Polity, 2016); Megan MacKenzie and Nicole Wegner, eds., *Feminist Solutions for Ending War* (London: Pluto Press, 2021).

63. Laura J. Shepherd, "Sex, Security, and Superhero(in)es: From 1325 to 1820 and Beyond," *International Feminist Journal of Politics* 13, no. 4 (December 2011): 504–521; Audrey Reeves, "Feminist Knowledge and Emerging Governmentality in UN Peacekeeping: Patterns of Cooptation and Empowerment," *International Feminist Journal of Politics* 14, no. 3 (2012): 348–369, https://doi.org/10.1080/14616 742.2012.659853; Laura Sjoberg, *Gender, War & Conflict* (Cambridge: Polity, 2014).

64. Cohn, Kinsella, and Gibbings, "Women, Peace and Security Resolution 1325"; Isabelle Côté and Limingcui Emma Huang, "Where Are the Daughters? Examining the Effects of Gendered Migration on the Dynamics of 'Sons of the Soil' Conflict," *Studies in Conflict & Terrorism* 43, no. 10 (2018): 837–853; Laura Sjoberg and Caron E. Gentry, "Reduced to Bad Sex: Narratives of Violent Women from the Bible to the War on Terror," *International Relations* 22, no. 1 (2008): 5–23.

65. Pratt and Richter-Devroe, "Critically Examining"; Maria Martin de Almagro, "Producing Participants: Gender, Race, Class, and Women, Peace and Security," *Global Society* 32, no. 4 (October 2018): 395–414; Chantel de Jonge Oudraat, "The WPS Agenda and Strategy for the Twenty-First Century," in *The Oxford Handbook of Women, Peace, and Security*, ed. Sara E. Davies and Jacqui True (Oxford University Press, 2019), 840–849; Katharine A. M. Wright, "NATO's Adoption of UNSCR 1325 on Women, Peace and Security: Making the Agenda a Reality," *International Political Science Review* 37, no. 3 (2016): 350–361; Nicola Pratt, "Reconceptualizing Gender, Reinscribing Racial–Sexual Boundaries in International Security: The Case of UN Security Council Resolution 1325 on 'Women, Peace and Security,'" *International Studies Quarterly* 57, no. 4 (December 2013): 772–783.

66. Martin de Almagro, "Producing Participants."

67. Natalie Hudson, "The Challenges of Monitoring and Analyzing WPS for Scholars," in *The Oxford Handbook of Women, Peace, and Security*, ed. Sara E. Davies and Jacqui True (Oxford: Oxford University Press, 2019), 850–862.

68. Deborah D. Avant, *Political Institutions and Military Change: Lessons from Peripheral Wars* (Ithaca, NY: Cornell University Press, 1994); Peter Feaver, *Armed Servants* (Cambridge, MA: Harvard University Press 2003); Peter Feaver, "The Civil–Military Problematique: Huntington, Janowitz, and the Question of Civilian Control," *Armed Forces & Society* 32, no. 2 (January 1996): 149–178; Eric Rittinger, "Arming the Other: American Small Wars, Local Proxies, and the Social Construction of the Principal–Agent Problem," *International Studies Quarterly* 61, no. 2 (June 2017): 396–409; Sean Gailmard, "Accountability and Principal–Agent Theory," in *The Oxford Handbook of Public Accountability*, ed. Mark Bovens, Robert E. Goodin, and Thomas Schillemans (Oxford University Press, 2014), 90–105.

69. Gailmard, "Accountability and Principal–Agent Theory," 90–105.

70. David P. Auerswald and Stephen M. Saideman, *NATO in Afghanistan: Fighting Together, Fighting Alone* (Princeton, NJ: Princeton University Press, 2014).

71. Giegerich and von Hlatky, "Experiences May Vary."

72. Duncanson, *Gender and Peacebuilding*, 33; Kwadwo Appiagyi-Atua, "United Nations Security Council 1325 on Women, Peace, and Security—Is It Binding?" *The Human Rights Brief* 18, no. 3 (2011): 2–6; See also Jody M. Prescott, "NATO Gender Mainstreaming and the Feminist Critique of the Law of Armed Conflict," Georgetown Journal of Gender and the Law 14 (2013a): 85–127. https://heinonline.org/HOL/Page?handle=hein.journals/grggenl14&div=6&g_sent=1&casa_token=eRQLM EkmOC0AAAAA:qmMnvnFh02XxzW7UdIQ2KJY_LYnhiNG1jXI-rGNNbza1___ IFQLyQlLosRqKYLkr7TVuZp_kr-mU&collection=journals.

73. Martha Finnemore and Kathryn Sikkink, "International Norm Dynamics and Political Change," *International Organization* 52, no. 4 (1998): 887–917. Kreft applies this model to the application of 1325 in a UN context. See Anne-Kathrin Kreft, "The Gender Mainstreaming Gap: Security Council Resolution 1325 and UN Peacekeeping Mandates," *International Peacekeeping* 24 (2017): 132, https://www.tandfonline.com/doi/pdf/10.1080/13533312.2016.1195267?needAccess=true.

74. Amitav Acharya, "How Ideas Spread: Whose Norms Matter? Norm Localization and Institutional Change in Asian Regionalism," *International Organization* 58, no. 2 (April 2004): 244.

75. Jeffrey T. Checkel, "International Institutions and Socialization in Europe: Introduction and Framework," *International Organization* 59, no. 4 (October 2005): 813.

76. Norm contestation could refer to the localization of transnational gender mainstreaming norms. See Lara Klossek and Elisabeth Johansson-Nogués, "The Female 'Boot on the Ground': Indian Ambivalence over Gender Mainstreaming in UN Peacekeeping Operations," *International Peacekeeping* 4 (2021): 542, https://www.tandfonline.com/doi/pdf/10.1080/13533312.2021.1880899?needAccess=true.

77. Antje Wiener talks about cultural validation as one of three processes by which the meaning of norms is established, see *The Invisible Constitution of Politics: Contested Norms and International Encounters* (Cambridge: Cambridge University Press, 2008), 1–253.

78. Thomas Risse, "International Norms and Domestic Change: Arguing and Communicative Behavior in the Human Rights Area," *Politics & Society* 27, no. 4 (December 1999): 529–559.

79. Heidi Hardt and Stéfanie von Hlatky, "NATO's About Face: Adaptation to Gender Mainstreaming in an Alliance Setting," *Journal of Global and Security Studies* 5, no. 1 (2020): 136–159.

80. Hardt and von Hlatky, "NATO's About Face." From this same project, we published our NATO Gender Guidelines Dataset (available at https://dataverse.harvard.edu/ dataset.xhtml?persistentId=doi:10.7910/DVN/VUHDGW) and the Gender Training Course Package (with Darleen Young, Sara Greco, and Charlotte Duval-Lantoine; available at https://www.queensu.ca/cidp/research/gender-awareness-applications-nato-community).

81. Ernest B. Haas, *When Knowledge Is Power: Three Models of Change in International Organizations* (Berkeley: University of California Press, 1990); Frank Dobbins, Beth Simmons, and Geoffrey Garrett, "The Global Diffusion of Public Policies: Social Construction, Coercion, Competition, or Learning?" *Annual Review of Sociology* 33, no. 1 (2007): 449–472; Jacob Levy, "Learning and Foreign Policy: Sweeping a Conceptual Minefield," *International Organization* 48, no. 2 (Spring 1994): 279–312; Finnemore and Sikkink, "International Norm Dynamics"; Thomas Risse, Stephen C. Ropp, and Kathryn Sikkink, *The Power of Human Rights: International Norms and Domestic Change* (Cambridge: Cambridge University Press, 1999).

82. Laura Sjoberg, *Gender and International Security: Feminist Perspectives* (New York: Routledge, 2010); J. Ann Tickner, *A Feminist Voyage through International Relations* (New York: Oxford University Press, 2014).

83. John Baylis, James J. Wirtz, and Colin S. Gray, *Strategy in the Contemporary World: An Introduction* (Oxford: Oxford University Press, 2016).

84. For an example of how this kind of analysis is performed in the EU context, see Nadine Ansorg and Toni Haastrup, "Gender and the EU's Support for Security Sector Reform in Fragile Contexts," *Journal of Common Market Studies* 56 (2018): 1127.

85. Roberta Guerrina and Katherine A. M. Wright, "Gendering Normative Power Europe: Lessons of the Women, Peace and Security Agenda," *International Affairs* 92, no. 2 (March 2016): 293–312.

86. NATO also conducts maritime operations and does so primarily in the Mediterranean Sea. Operation Sea Guardian is engaged in surveillance and is ready to engage in interdiction operations linked to counterterrorism and protection of the maritime environment. There are also a number of support operations which NATO provides to the African Union, by lending its assets to ongoing operations in Africa and to the Baltics, through an air policing mission. Since the Baltic States do not have their own air force, NATO assets patrol the skies against Russian incursions. Key arguments about applying WPS norms in an operational setting mention few Navy- or Air Force–specific applications, so maritime domain and aerial missions are not included in the study.

87. It bears reminding that NATO countries had failed to secure a UN resolution to authorize the strikes.

88. NATO, "Mission," JFC Naples, accessed September 4, 2018, https://jfcnaples.nato.int/kfor/about-us/welcome-to-kfor/mission.

89. Christian Leuprecht, Joel Sokolsky, and Jayson Derow, *On the Baltic Watch: The Past, Present and Future of Canada's Commitment to NATO's Enhanced Forward Presence in Latvia* (Ottawa: Macdonald-Laurier Institute, 2018), 1–36, https://macdonaldlaurier.ca/files/pdf/20180327_MLI_LATVIA_WebF.pdf.

90. NATO, "NATO's Enhanced Forward Presence," March 2021d, https://www.nato.int/nato_static_fl2014/assets/pdf/2021/3/pdf/2103-factsheet_efp_en.pdf.

91. NATO, *The Secretary General's Annual Report 2018* (Brussels: NATO, 2019), 59, https://www.nato.int/nato_static_fl2014/assets/pdf/pdf_publications/20190315_sgar2018-en.pdf.

92. Lee Ann Fujii, *Interviewing in Social Science Research: A Relational Approach* (New York: Routledge, 2018).

93. Fujii, *Interviewing in Social Science Research*, 4.

94. Fujii, *Interviewing in Social Science Research*, 8–9.

95. Many participants have authorized me to use their name; but for the sake of consistency and to protect the identity of those who preferred to remain anonymous, I refer to interview participants by their position and rank and I do not specify the date of the interview, though I have specified the year range here.

96. Shepherd, "Making War Safe for Women?"

97. Hardt and von Hlatky, "NATO's About Face," 136–159.

98. Gülay Calgar, "Gender Mainstreaming," *Politics & Gender* 9, no. 3 (September 2013): 336–344.

99. For example, Mila O'Sullivan, "'Being Strong Enough to Defend Yourself': Untangling the Women, Peace and Security Agenda amidst the Ukrainian Conflict," *International Feminist Journal of Politics* 21, no. 5 (October 2019): 746–767.

Chapter 2

1. Tryggestad, "Trick or Treat?"

2. Rosalind Boyd, ed., *The Search for Lasting Peace: Critical Perspectives on Gender-Responsive Human Security* (Burlington, VT: Ashgate, 2014), 3–12.

3. Hardt and von Hlatky, "NATO's About Face," 136–159.

4. Megan Bastick and Claire Duncanson, "Agents of Change? Gender Advisors in NATO Militaries," *International Peacekeeping* 25, no. 4 (August 2018): 554.

5. Enloe, *Maneuvers*, 291.

6. Mia Bloom, "Female Suicide Bombers: A Global Trend," *Daedalus* 136, no. 1 (Winter 2007): 94–102.

7. Nyssa Fullmer, Stephanie Lipson Mizrahi, and Elizabeth Tomsich, "The Lethality of Female Suicide Bombers," *Women and Criminal Justice* 29, nos. 4–5 (2019): 266–282.

8. NATO Committee on Gender Perspectives—Department Head for Gender in Military Operations and Allied Command Transformation, "Gender Perspective

in Military Operations: Strategic/Operational Level" (PowerPoint presentation, accessed September 26, 2019), slide 9.

9. Andrea N. Goldstein, "'Why Are You Trying to Destroy the Last Good Thing Men Have?' Understanding Resistance to Women in Combat Jobs," *International Feminist Journal of Politics* 20, no. 3 (July 2018): 385–404.

10. Ricks, "The Military's Purpose."

11. Carreiras, *Gender and the Military*, 73.

12. Annica Kronsell, *Gender, Sex, and the Postnational Defense: Militarism and Peacekeeping* (New York: Oxford University Press, 2012).

13. Maxwell J. Mehlman, "Captain America and Iron Man: Biological, Genetic and Psychological Enhancement and the Warrior Ethos," in *Routledge Handbook of Military Ethics*, ed. George Lucas (New York: Routledge, 2015), 406–420.

14. Megan MacKenzie, *Beyond the Band of Brothers: The US Military and the Myth That Women Can't Fight* (Cambridge: Cambridge University Press, 2015b).

15. Linda Bird Francke, *Ground Zero: The Gender Wars in the Military* (New York: Simon & Schuster, 1997), 23.

16. Christina S. Jarvis, *The Male Body at War: American Masculinity during World War II* (DeKalb: Northern Illinois University Press, 2004), 5.

17. Jarvis, *The Male Body at War*, 66.

18. Wright, Hurley, and Ruiz, *NATO, Gender and the Military*, 21.

19. Bernard Nalty, *Strength for the Fight: A History of Black Americans in the Military* (New York: Free Press, 1986), 133.

20. Jarvis, *The Male Body at War*, 146–148.

21. I should add that the reversal of policies is also possible, as illustrated with the transgender ban during the Trump administration, later overturned by President Biden.

22. Quoted in Jenny Newton, "The Long Road to Gender Integration in the Canadian Armed Forces," *SITREP* 67, no. 3 (May–June 2007): 3–7, .

23. Franke, *Ground Zero*, 36.

24. Alice H. Eagly and Linda L. Carli, *Through the Labyrinth: The Truth about How Women Become Leaders* (Boston: Harvard Business School Press, 2007), 2.

25. *Background Study Use of Women in the Military*, 2nd ed. (Office of the Assistant Secretary of Defense for Manpower, Reserve Affairs, and Logistics, 1978), quoted in Francke, *Ground Zero*, 5.

26. For a critique of this approach, see Bipasha Baruah, "Short-Sighted Commitments on Women in Peacekeeping," *Policy Options*, November 23, 2017, .

27. Judith A. Hall, "Women's and Men's Nonverbal Communication: Similarities, Differences, Stereotypes, and Origins," in *The SAGE Handbook of Nonverbal Communication*, ed. Valerie Manusov and Miles L. Patterson (Thousand Oaks, CA: Sage, 2006), 201–218; Marc A. Brackett et al., "Relating Emotional Abilities to Social Functioning: A Comparison of Self-Report and Performance Measures of Emotional Intelligence," *Journal of Personality and Social Psychology* 91, no. 4 (2006): 780–795.

28. Nick Perry, "Australian Troops Unlawfully Killed 39 Afghan Prisoners, Civilians: Report," *Global News*, November 18, 2020, ; Angus Watson, "Long a Source of

National Pride, the Moral Integrity of Australia's Military Is Now at Stake," CNN, November 20, 2020, .

29. Sandra Whitworth. "Militarized Masculinities and the Politics of Peacekeeping," in *Critical Security Studies and World Politics*, ed. Ken Booth (Boulder, CO: Lynne Rienner Publishers, 2005), 89–106. On how military masculinity is used in different contexts and exhibits fluidity, see Marsha Henry, "Problematizing Military Masculinity, Intersectionality and Male Vulnerability in Feminist Critical Military Studies," *Critical Military Studies* 3, no. 2 (2017): 182–199.

30. US Equal Opportunity Employment Commission, "Charges Alleging Sex-Based Harassment (Charges filed with EEOC) FY 2010—FY 2019," accessed September 26, 2019, .

31. Remus Ilies et al., "Reported Incidence Rates of Work-Related Sexual Harassment in the United States: Using Meta-analysis to Explain Reported Rate Disparities," table 2, *Personnel Psychology* 56, no. 3 (2003): 607–631.

32. Mindy E. Bergman et al., "The (Un)Reasonableness of Reporting: Antecedents and Consequences of Reporting Sexual Harassment," *Journal of Applied Psychology* 87, no. 2 (2002): 230–242; John B. Pryor, "The Psychosocial Impact of Sexual Harassment on Women in the U.S. Military," *Basic and Applied Psychology* 17, no. 4 (1995): 581–603.

33. For the Australian Defence Force (ADF), see *Pathway to Change*, a series of reviews undertaken by the Department of Defense to reform ADF culture: Australian Government, *Pathway to Change—Evolving Defence Culture* (Canberra: Department of Defence), accessed September 26, 2019, http://www.defence.gov.au/PathwayToChange/. For the Canadian Armed Forces, a similar process was initiated following the publication of a damning external review report called the Deschamps Report: Marie Deschamps, *External Review into Sexual Misconduct and Sexual Harassment in the Canadian Armed Forces* (Ottawa: External Review Authority, March 2015),. Another independent external comprehensive review led by former Supreme Court justice Louise Arbour was launched in 2021.

34. Sandy Welsh, "Gender and Sexual Harassment," *Annual Review of Sociology* 25 (1999): 169–190.

35. Olivera Simić, "Does the Presence of Women Really Matter? Towards Combating Male Sexual Violence in Peacekeeping Operations," *International Peacekeeping* 17, no. 2 (2010): 189.

36.

37. Sophia Jones, "The Dangers of Forcing Gender Equality in Afghanistan," *New York Times*, November 21, 2017, .

38. Special Inspector General for Afghanistan Reconstruction, *Quarterly Report to the United States Congress* (Arlington, VA: SIGAR, 2016), 9, .

39. Stéfanie von Hlatky, "Gender and Peacekeeping," *Policy Options*, November 8, 2017, .

40. PfPC SSRWG and EDWG, *Teaching Gender in the Military: A Handbook* (Geneva: DCAF and PfPC, 2016), .

41. Hardt and von Hlatky, "NATO's About Face," 136–159; see also Kirby and Shepherd, "The Futures Past."

42. Francke, *Ground Zero*, 74.

43. Francke, *Ground Zero*; MacKenzie, *Beyond the Band of Brothers.*
44. Lana Obradovic, *Gender Integration in NATO Military Forces: Cross-National Analysis* (London and New York: Routledge, 2014), 8.
45. These statistics are regularly updated on both organizations' websites.
46. Joshua Goldstein, *War and Gender: How Gender Shapes the War System and Vice Versa* (Cambridge: Cambridge University Press, 2001).
47. Laura Sjoberg, "Seeing Sex, Gender and Sexuality in International Security," *International Journal* 70, no. 3 (2015): 434–453; Sjoberg and Gentry, "Reduced to Bad Sex."
48. Robert Egnell, "Gender Perspectives and Military Effectiveness: Implementing UNSCR 1325 and the National Action Plan on Women Peace and Security," *Prism: A Journal of the Center for Complex Operations* 6, no. 1 (2016): 77.
49. Megan MacKenzie, "True Grit: The Myths and Realities of Women in Combat," *Foreign Affairs*, August 12, 2015a, https://www.foreignaffairs.com/articles/2015-08-12/true-grit.
50. Sabrina Karim and Kyle Beardsley, "Gender, Peace, and Security: Implementing UN Security Council Resolution 1325," in *A Systematic Understanding of Gender, Peace, and Security: Implementing UNSC 1325*, ed. Ismene Gizelis and Louise Olsson (London: Routledge, 2015), 62–95.
51. According to Belkin, military masculinity is "a set of beliefs, practices and attributes that can enable individuals—men and women—to claim authority on the basis of affirmative relationships with the military or with military ideas," in Aaron Belkin, *Bring Me Men: Military Masculinity and the Benign Façade of American Empire, 1898–2001* (New York: Columbia University Press, 2012), 3.
52. Aaron Belkin, "Combat Exclusion RIP. Will Patriarchy's Demise Follow," *Critical Studies on Security* 1, no. 2 (August 2013): 250.
53. Simić, "Does the Presence of Women Really Matter?"
54. A documentary was made of Lioness Teams in Iraq: Meg McLagan and Daria Sommers, dirs., *Lioness*, aired November 13, 2008, on PBS, .
55. Matt Pottinger, Hali Jilani, and Claire Russo, "Half Hearted: Trying to Win Afghanistan without Afghan Women," *Small Wars Journal*, February 18, 2010, .
56. Sippi Azarbaijani-Moghaddam, "Seeking Out Their Afghan Sisters: Female Engagements Teams in Afghanistan" (CMI Working Paper 1, Chr. Michelsen Institute, Bergen, Norway, March 2014, http://hdl.handle.net/11250/2474930).
57. Pottinger et al., "Half Hearted," 1–10.
58. Tyra A. Harding, "Women in Combat Roles: Case Study of Female Engagement Teams" (strategy research project, US Army War College, 2012), 14.
59. Janet R. Holliday, "Female Engagement Teams: The Need to Standardize Training and Employment," *Military Review* 92, no. 2 (2012), 94.
60. Harding, "Women in Combat Roles," 20.
61. Ida Irby, "'FET' to Fight: Female Engagement Team Makes History," US Army, April 18, 2013, accessed 18 September 2018, .
62. Irby, "'FET' to Fight."

63. Gayle Tzemach Lemmon, *Ashley's War: The Untold Story of a Team of Women Soldiers on the Special Ops Battlefield* (New York: Harper Collins, 2015).

64. MacKenzie, "True Grit."

65. Lemmon, *Ashley's War.*

66. Sahana Dharmapuri, "Just Add Women and Stir?" *Parameters* 41, no. 1 (Spring 2011): 61, .

67. Donna Bridges and Debbie Horsfall, "Increasing Operational Effectiveness in UN Peacekeeping: Toward a Gender-Balanced Force," *Armed Forces & Society* 36, no. 1 (2009): 120–130. This argument has been criticized since women in the military should not have the burden of civilizing their male peers, in addition to everything else that is expected of them. They should have the right to just do their jobs, in other words, rather than to police the behavior of other soldiers within their unit.

68. Wright mentions Sweden specifically, noting that 1325 has been used as a diplomatic tool, in "NATO'S Adoption of UNSCR 1325."

69. Jody Prescott, "NATO Gender Mainstreaming: A New Approach to War amongst the People?" *RUSI Journal* 158, no. 5 (2013b): 56–62.

70. Tarja Väyrynen, "Gender and UN Peace Operations: The Confines of Modernity," *International Peacekeeping* 11, no. 1 (2004): 125–142; Henry Carey, "'Women and Peace and Security': The Politics of Implementing Gender Sensitivity Norms in Peacekeeping," *International Peacekeeping* 8, no. 2 (2001): 49–68.

71. Diane Otto, "Power and Danger: Feminist Engagement with International Law through the UN Security Council," *Australian Feminist Law Journal* 32, no. 1 (June 2010): 97–121; Carol Cohn, "Mainstreaming Gender in UN Security Policy: A Path to Political Transformation?," in *Global Governance: Feminist Perspectives*, ed. Shirin M. Rai and Georgina Waylen (Basingstoke, UK: Palgrave Macmillan, 2008), 185–206.

72. Klot, "UN Security Council Resolution 1325," 6; Betty A. Reardon and Asha Hans, eds., *The Gender Imperative: Human Security vs. State Security* (London and New York: Routledge, 2010); Cynthia Cockburn, "Gender Relations as Causal in Militarization and War," *International Feminist Journal of Politics* 12, no. 2 (June 2010): 139–152.

73. For a review of WPS in NATO's Strategic Concept and Summit communiqués, see Morgan Fox, "How Will Women, Peace, and Security Fit into NATO's Next Strategic Concept?," *Contact Report*, August 13, 2021, .

74. Wright, Hurley, and Ruiz, *NATO, Gender and the Military*, 1.

75. Wright, Hurley, and Ruiz, *NATO, Gender and the Military*, 3.

76. Wight, Hurley, and Ruiz, 4, 34. For more on NATO as a teaching machine, see Cynthia Enloe, *Does Khaki Become You?* (London: Pluto, 1983); Wright, "NATO's Adoption of UNSCR 1325," 350–361.

Chapter 3

1. Military personnel on missions typically rotate in and out of missions every six to nine months, with some exceptions like command appointments.

2. NATO, *Diversity and Inclusion Annual Report 2019* (Brussels: NATO, 2019), https://www.nato.int/nato_static_fl2014/assets/pdf/2021/2/pdf/2019-annual-diversity_inclusion_report.pdf.

3. Interview with an official from the NATO International Staff, Operations Division (Skype). European Union, *Final Report on Gender Work inside EUFOR RD Congo* (Potsdam: EU Operation Headquarters, 2006); European Union, *Comprehensive Approach to the EU Implementation of the United Nations Security Council Resolutions 1325 and 1820 on Women, Peace and Security* (Brussels: Council of the European Union, 2008).

4. NATO, "North Atlantic Treaty: Washington D.C.—4 April 1949," last updated April 10, 2019b, https://www.nato.int/cps/en/natolive/official_texts_17120.htm.

5. National reports from 2008 to 2014 are available here: https://www.nato.int/cps/en/natohq/topics_132097.htm.

6. Interview with the JFC-Naples GENAD (Naples, Italy).

7. NATO, "Brussels Summit Declaration: Issued by the Heads of State and Government Participating in the Meeting of the North Atlantic Council in Brussels, 11–12 July 2018," last updated August 30, 2018a, https://www.nato.int/cps/en/natohq/official_texts_156624.htm.

8. NATO, "Brussels Summit Declaration."

9. Interview with a civilian official from national delegation staff (#1; Brussels, Belgium).

10. Interview with a civilian official from national delegation staff (#2; Brussels, Belgium).

11. Interview with military official from national delegation staff (#4; Brussels, Belgium).

12. While NATO as an organization can (and does) have internal diversity policies to increase the representation and advancement of women within the alliance and greater diversity overall, it does not dictate how countries should staff positions they have the responsibility of filling. In other words, it is only when NATO is doing the hiring that these policies apply. The same applies to operations: NATO does not have targets or quotas to improve the gender balance within the units that deploy on its operations, although individual countries might have their own targets, based on their own national policies. So while NATO tracks the number of women in the military, that is all that it does, tracking and sharing.

13. Interview with JFC-Naples GENAD (Naples, Italy).

14. For a comparative account of WPS, illustrating this variation, see Carreiras, *Gender and the Military*; Robert Egnell and Mayesha Alam, eds., *Women and Gender Perspectives in the Military* (Washington, DC: Georgetown University Press, 2019).

15. NATO, "The NATO Policy on Preventing and Responding to Sexual Exploitation and Abuse," last updated April 21, 2021a, https://www.nato.int/cps/en/natohq/official_texts_173038.htm. It is worth noting that there is an appendix, "Standards of Behaviour" in Annex RR, which reflects NATO's Policy on Preventing and Responding to Sexual Exploitation and Abuse. This guidance is for deployed NATO forces and meant to socialize a common standard of behavior across contributing countries, mostly through pre-deployment training.

16. NATO, "NATO Policy on Preventing and Responding to Conflict-Related Sexual Violence," last updated May 31, 2021b, https://www.nato.int/cps/en/natohq/official_texts_184570.htm.

17. NATO, *Action Plan for the Implementation of the NATO/EAPC Policy on Women, Peace and Security 2021–2025* (Brussels: NATO), last updated October 21, 2021c, https://www.nato.int/cps/en/natohq/official_texts_187485.htm.

18. In addition to the policy and action plan, as described above, there is an implementation plan, which specifies more precise indicators of performance for the purposes of NATO reporting and assessment. An external consultant was hired to design a monitoring and evaluation framework. The NATO secretary-general's special representative for WPS also took training on evaluation upon taking the position to improve implementation. The implementation plan is not releasable to the public, as confirmed by the Office for Human Security, headed by the SR for WPS (e-mail correspondence).

19. Swedish Armed Forces, *Course Catalogue,* 24. While the tasks are varied, their depiction in both official documents and the literature is fairly consistent. See Keirsten H. Kenney, "Gender Advisors in NATO: Should the U.S. Military Follow Suit?," *Military Law Review* 224 (2016): 1052–1072.

20. Bastick and Duncanson, "Agents of Change?," 559.

21. According to the NATO regulations, there is a network inside of the HQ made up of GFPs referred to as *GFP net*. It is composed of people from all branches and divisions of the HQ. They are dual-hatted positions, and individuals volunteer or are nominated for these posts. Some people view it as more work; others are genuinely committed to making sure gender guidelines are considered in their branch or division.

22. In these committees, the work is centered around building support toward concrete actions/decisions. In other words, all discussions are formal and on the record.

23. For more on the NCGP, see https://www.nato.int/cps/en/natohq/topics_101372.htm.

24. The SR for WPS chairs those meetings and generally provides an overview on how this portfolio is progressing, but some sessions can also include special briefings, lectures, or stocktaking. These meetings are informal and off the record, and they can help air out some issues that are too touchy to be raised in a formal committee setting.

25. Allied Command Operations, *Gender Functional Planning Guide* (Mons, Belgium: Allied Command Operations, 2015), 1–E–3, https://www.forsvarsmakten.se/siteassets/english/swedint/engelska/swedint/courses/genad/07-aco-gender-functional-planning-guide.pdf.

26. Allied Command Operations, *Gender Functional Planning Guide*, 1.

27. For a course description, see NATO School Oberammergau, "Improving Operational Effectiveness by Integrating Gender Perspective," Course Catalogue, accessed November 4, 2019, https://www.natoschool.nato.int/Academics/Resident-Courses/Course-Catalogue/Course-description?ID=187&TabId=155&ID=178&Legal-Notice&language=en-US.

28. Allied Command Operations, *Gender Functional Planning Guide*, 2.

29. Allied Command Operations, *Gender Functional Planning Guide*, 2.

30. Interview with JFC-Naples GENAD (Naples, Italy).

31. The main part of the OPLAN is the intent of the operation and guidance for execution and the OPLAN document has an annex on every conceivable topic, including gender. The OPLAN is the plan for the operation, while OPORDER is the execution

of the plan. OPLANs are sent from SHAPE to NATO headquarters in Brussels, nego-
tiated by national representatives and the military committee.

32. NATO, *Comprehensive Operational Planning Directive* (Mons, Belgium: Allied
Command Operations, 2013), 4–10, https://www.forsvarsmakten.se/siteassets/engl
ish/swedint/engelska/swedint/courses/nato-copc/07-ch-4-op-v2.0-04-oct-13.pdf.

33. This is the process on paper. In practice, however, the tactical level also further refines
plans as it is difficult, if not impossible, for the operational level to provide plans that
will be detailed enough for personnel in theater.

34. Interviews with J5 military staff from Allied Command Operations (Mons, Belgium).

35. In total, there are nine J functions or branches: personnel (J1), intelligence (J2), operations (J3), logistics (J4), plans (J5), signals (J6), military education and training (J7),
resource management (J8), and civil–military cooperation (J9).

36. For planning, the main reference is the COPD; and for assessments, the key document is NATO, *NATO Operations Assessment Handbook* (Brussels, NATO, 2015).
https://natolibguides.info/ld.php?content_id=30192868

37. The J2 branch conducts joint intelligence preparation of the environment assessments,
in coordination with all advisors. On the basis of theses assessments, as approved by
the commander, J5 integrates this assessment into how the plans are developed. See
Joint Intelligence, *Joint Publication 2-0* (Washington, DC: Joint Chiefs of Staff, 2013),
I-1-V-13, https://www.jcs.mil/Portals/36/Documents/Doctrine/pubs/jp2_0.pdf.

38. Thanks to Steve MacBeth (former Canadian Armed Forces visiting defense fellow at
the Queen's Centre for International and Defence Policy) for this insight.

39. NATO, *Comprehensive Operational Planning Directive*, A-2.

40. Charlotte Isaksson, "Integrating Gender Perspectives at NATO: Two Steps Forward,
One Step Back," in *Women and Gender Perspectives in the Military: An International
Comparison*, ed. Robert Egnell and Mayesha Alam (Washington, DC: Georgetown
University Press, 2019), 240.

41. This is the only part of NATO decision-making that is not by consensus since one
nation's defense capability package must be approved by the twenty-nine other
member states (as opposed to being a consensus decision at thirty).

42. For an overview of the process, see https://www.nato.int/cps/en/natohq/topics_50
316.htm.

43. NATO, *Comprehensive Operational Planning Directive*, A5.

44. In addition to general reporting, SHAPE commissions strategic assessments, which
function a little bit like a review or audit. They entail data collection and consultation
(with academics and subject matter experts) to deliver comprehensive assessments
which are complementary to (and supportive of) the periodic mission review process. These efforts are meant to support and help military lines of effort and can bring
in more raw data.

45. Stuart Skeates, "Command Group Corner," *Northern Star* (March 2019): 3.

46. Skeats, "Command Group Corner," 3. The JFCs act as out-of-theater operational
headquarters for military operations but also plan and support NATO's joint military
exercises like Trident Juncture (2018) and Trident Jupiter (2019), carried out by JFC-
Naples and JFC-Brunssum, respectively.

47. Lt. Col. Miguel Angel Martinez Avila, "NATO and Gender: What Does Gender Mean in the Operational Level," *Northern Star* (March 2019): 20.
48. Interview with GENAD at JFC-Brunssum (Brunssum, the Netherlands).
49. Interview with GENAD at JFC-Brunssum (Brunssum, the Netherlands).
50. Interview with GENAD at JFC-Brunssum (Brunssum, the Netherlands).
51. Interview with GENAD at JFC-Brunssum (Brunssum, the Netherlands).
52. This involves providing information or supporting J2, J5, the Joint Operations Planning Group, and the ACO GENAD, in addition to relevant civilian organizations.
53. Allied Command Operations, *Gender Functional Planning Guide*, 8-4.
54. Since my interviews were conducted at SHAPE, NATO introduced the *Gender-Inclusive Language Manual*, discouraging use of the term *manpower*, in favor of *workforce/staff/labor force*. Office of NATO Secretary General's Special Representative for Women, Peace and Security, *NATO Gender-Inclusive Language Manual* (Brussels: NATO, 2020).
55. This includes coordinating between the J3 (operations) staff, which executes the directives received by J5.
56. Allied Command Operations, *Gender Functional Planning Guide*, C-1.
57. Allied Command Operations, *Gender Functional Planning Guide*, C-1.
58. Interview with NATO Defense College commandant (Rome, Italy).
59. Interview with a military official (#1) at JFC-Naples (Naples, Italy).
60. Bastick and Duncanson, "Agents of Change?," 568.
61. Group interviews with the J5 (Plans) team at SHAPE (Mons, Belgium).
62. Helene Lackenbauer and Richard Langlais, eds., *Review of the Practical Implications of UNSCR 1325 for the Conduct of NATO-Led Operations and Missions* (Stockholm: Swedish Defence Research Agency, 2013), https://www.nato.int/nato_static_fl2014/assets/pdf/pdf_2013_10/20131021_131023-UNSCR1325-review-final.pdf.
63. Interview with GENAD at JFC-Brunssum (Brunssum, the Netherlands).

Chapter 4

1. This was the oft-used tagline and how most of my interviews began.
2. Group interview with civilian and military personnel from JFC-Naples (Naples, Italy).
3. Filip Ejdus and Marko Kovačević, "Penetration, Overlay, Governmentality: The Evolving Role of NATO in the Western Balkan Security Dynamics," *Journal of Intervention and Statebuilding* 13, no. 5 (October 2019): 570–571.
4. Ejdus and Kovačević, "Penetration, Overlay, Governmentality," 570–571.
5. Ian Traynor, "Fourteen Dead as Ethnic Violence Sweeps Kosovo," *The Guardian*, March 18, 2004, https://www.theguardian.com/world/2004/mar/18/balkans.
6. Patrick Kingsley and Kenneth P. Vogel, "Pushing for Serbia–Kosovo Peace Deal, U.S. Roils Allies," *New York Times*, June 20, 2020, https://www.nytimes.com/2020/06/20/world/europe/serbia-kosovo-peace-elections.html?auth=login-email&login=email.

7. Government of the Republic of Kosovo, *Draft Law on Kosovo Security Force* (Kosovo: Government of the Republic of Kosovo, 2018), 3–4, https://kryem inistri-ks.net/wp-content/uploads/2018/09/PROJEKTLIGJI-P%C3%8BR-FORC%C3%8BN-E-SIGURIS%C3%8B-S%C3%8B-KOSOV%C3%8BS1.pdf.

8. Group interview with civilian and military personnel from JFC-Naples (Naples, Italy).

9. Interview with KFOR PAO (Priština, Kosovo).

10. Kimberley Kruijver and Visar Xhambazi, *Kosovo's NATO Future: How to Square the Circle?* (The Hague: Clingendael [Netherlands Institute of International Relations]), 2020), 1–2, https://www.clingendael.org/sites/default/files/2020-12/Kosovos_NATO _future_Correct.pdf.

11. Group interview with civilian and military personnel from JFC-Naples (Naples, Italy).

12. Quoted in JFC-Naples, "KFOR Troops Showcase Support of Women, Peace and Security Initiatives," NATO, 2017, https://jfcnaples.nato.int/newsroom/news/2016/ kfor-troops-showcase-support-of-women--peace-and-security-initiatives.

13. NATO, "Views from the Field: Interview with Major-General Jennie Carignan, Commander NATO Mission Iraq, and Major-General Michele Risi, Commander NATO's Mission in Kosovo" in *The Women, Peace and Security Agenda Continues to Have the Power to Transform. We Must Persist in Our Determination to Create Lasting Change* (Brussels: NATO, 2020a), 13, https://www.nato.int/nato_static_fl2014/assets/ pdf/2020/11/pdf/2011-WPS-Newsletter-Autumn-ENGLISH.pdf.

14. This coordination happens between GENADs but more broadly between counterparts at different levels. For instance, the legal advisor (LEGAD) must link up with the other missions (and the UN Mission in Kosovo in particular) so that the mission stays within the UNSCR 1244 framework. On EU–KFOR coordination, see Nina Græger, "European Security as Practice: EU–NATO Communities of Practice in the Making," *European Security* 25, no. 4 (2016): 478.

15. NATO, "Resolution 1244 (1999): Adopted by the Security Council at its 4011th Meeting on 10 June 1999," Basic Documents, updated June 30, 1999, https://www. nato.int/kosovo/docu/u990610a.htm.

16. NATO, "Resolution 1244."

17. NATO, "NATO's Role in Kosovo," last updated November 16, 2020b, http://www. nato.int/cps/en/natolive/topics_48818.htm.

18. It should be noted here that, as a NATO partner (not an ally), Austrian personnel and staff, I was told, do not benefit from full access to information via NATO systems.

19. Interview with the KFOR commander (Priština, Kosovo).

20. Clive Baldwin, "Implementation through Cooperation? Human Rights Officers and the Military in Kosovo, 1999–2002," *International Peacekeeping* 13, no. 4 (2006): 492–493.

21. Malte Brosig, "The Interplay of International Institutions in Kosovo between Convergence, Confusing and Niche Capabilities," *European Security* 20, no. 2 (June 2011): 196.

22. Interview with the KFOR commander (Priština, Kosovo).

23. Interview with the commander of MNBG-West (Peć, Kosovo).
24. Interview with the commander of MNBG-West (Peć, Kosovo).
25. The field houses are for LMTs who work and live among the communities in their assigned municipality. The field office is a space that is known as a *KFOR office*, where members of the community can come and interact with military personnel.
26. Group interview with LMT (Peć, Kosovo).
27. The decision on what to provide is made at the joint regional detachment level. The LMT commander will submit the request and then may or may not get approval.
28. Group interview with LMT (Peć, Kosovo).
29. Group interview with LMT (Peć, Kosovo).
30. NATO, "Views from the Field," 13.
31. Li Hammar and Annika Berg, eds., *Whose Security? Practical Examples of Gender Perspectives in Military Operations* (Stockholm: Nordic Centre for Gender in Military Operations, Swedish Armed Forces, 2015), 35, https://www.forsvarsmakten.se/sit easset/english/swedint/engelska/swedint/nordic-centre-for-gender-in-military-ope rations/whose-security-2015-low-resolution.pdf.
32. Interview with the deputy commander of MNBG-West (Peć, Kosovo).
33. For more on KFOR and the monks, see Elina Penttinen, "Harmless Moments in Peace-Keeping: The Politics of Telling Stories That Do Not Fit into Critical Security Studies Narratives," *Critical Studies on Security* 5, no. 2 (May 2017): 131, 133–134.
34. Interview with Italian NCO (Dečani, Kosovo).
35. Interview with Italian NCO (Dečani, Kosovo).
36. Interview with the KFOR LEGAD (Priština, Kosovo). LEGADs are part of the Command Group, and the commander also works with the senior national representatives, who are responsible for all the national regulations, administration, and policies within their contingent. This level of coordination ensures that what is being done in a multinational environment is compatible.
37. Interview with the commander of the multinational specialized unit (MSU; Priština, Kosovo).
38. Interview with the commander of the MSU (Priština, Kosovo).
39. Interview with a Carabinieri officer of the MSU (Priština, Kosovo).
40. Interview with a Carabinieri officer of the MSU (Priština, Kosovo).
41. Interview with a Carabinieri officer of the MSU (Priština, Kosovo).
42. Swedish Armed Forces, *Whose Security? Practical Examples of Gender Perspectives in Military Operations* (Kungsängen, Sweden: Nordic Centre for Gender in Military Operations, 2015): 14–15.
43. Interview with the Carabinieri commander of the MSU (Priština, Kosovo).
44. Liora Sion, "Peacekeeping and the Gender Regime: Dutch Female Peacekeepers in Bosnia and Kosovo," *Journal of Contemporary Ethnography* 37, no. 5 (October 2008): 561–585; Valenius, "A Few Kind Women."
45. Interview with EOD officer with MNBG-East (Sojevë, Kosovo).
46. Interview with EOD officer with MNBG-East (Sojevë, Kosovo).
47. Interview with Radio K4 manager (Priština, Kosovo).
48. Interview with Radio K4 manager (Priština, Kosovo).

49. Interview with medical officer with MNBG-East (Sojevë, Kosovo).
50. There are lethal and non-lethal effects: artillery is lethal; info ops are non-lethal effects.
51. Interview with CIMIC officer at MNBG-East (Sojevë, Kosovo).
52. Interview with CIMIC officer at MNBG-East (Sojevë, Kosovo).
53. Interview with CIMIC officer at MNBG-East (Sojevë, Kosovo).
54. GENADs have also commented on the importance of women serving as role models in other operational contexts, such as Afghanistan. See Bastick and Duncanson, "Agents of Change?," 567.
55. Interview with two military members of the Effects Cell (Sojevë, Kosovo).
56. Interview with KFOR GENAD (Priština, Kosovo).
57. The battalion itself was also deployed to respond to violence in 2011. See John DeRosa, *Strategic Defense Review of the Republic of Kosovo* (Kosovo: GAP Institute, 2013), https://www.institutigap.org/documents/81456_SDR.pdf.
58. Interview with junior officer #1 from KTRBN (Novo Selo, Kosovo).
59. Interview with junior officer #2 (Novo Selo, Kosovo).
60. Interview with junior officer #1 (Novo Selo, Kosovo).
61. Nicole Farnsworth, ed., *1325 Facts & Fables* (Prishtina, Kosovo: The Kosova Women's Network, 2011), 37, https://womensnetwork.org/wp-content/uploads/2018/10/20130120165559661.pdf.
62. Interview with the KFOR commander (Priština, Kosovo).
63. Interview with KFOR GENAD (Priština, Kosovo).
64. Interview with KFOR GENAD (Priština, Kosovo).
65. Interview with KFOR GENAD (Priština, Kosovo).
66. Interview with KFOR GENAD (Priština, Kosovo).
67. Interview with the KFOR POLAD (Priština, Kosovo).
68. Interview with the KFOR POLAD (Priština, Kosovo).
69. Interview with the KFOR POLAD (Priština, Kosovo).
70. Interview with the KFOR POLAD (Priština, Kosovo).
71. Interview with the KFOR POLAD (Priština, Kosovo).
72. Interview with the KFOR POLAD (Priština, Kosovo).
73. Interview with a NATO official from the International Staff (Brussels, Belgium).
74. Interview with a NATO official from the International Staff (Brussels, Belgium).
75. Interview with the KFOR LEGAD (Priština, Kosovo).
76. Lackenbauer and Langlais, *Review of the Practical Implications*, 58–60.

Chapter 5

1. Office of NATO Secretary General's Special Representative for Women, Peace and Security, *NATO/EAPC Women, Peace and Security: Policy and Action Plan 2018* (Brussels: NATO, 2018), 1–28, https://www.nato.int/nato_static_fl2014/assets/pdf/pdf_2018_09/20180920_180920-WPS-Action-Plan-2018.pdf.

2. These two battlegroups were selected as the two main fieldwork sites for eFP as they were the most multinational of the four battlegroups, which allowed for more varied perspectives from NATO member states. I did include a trip to Estonia, to conduct background interviews for the chapter, even without a battlegroup-level visit.

3. NATO, *NATO's Eastern Flank: Stronger Defence and Deterrence* (Brussels: NATO, 2022b), https://www.nato.int/nato_static_fl2014/assets/pdf/2022/3/pdf/2203-map-det-def-east.pdf.

4. NATO, "Brussels Summit Declaration."

5. NATO, "Brussels Summit Communiqué: Issued by the Heads of State and Government Participating in the Meeting of the North Atlantic Council in Brussels 14 June 2021," last updated June 24, 2021, https://www.nato.int/cps/en/natohq/news_185000.htm.

6. NATO, "Madrid Summit Communiqué: Issued by the Heads of State and Governments Participating in the Meeting of the North Atlantic Council in Madrid 29 June 2022," 2022a, https://www.nato.int/cps/en/natohq/official_texts_196 951.htm.

7. NATO, *Strategic Concept for the Defence and Security of the Member of the North Atlantic Treaty Organization* (Brussels: NATO, 2010), https://www.nato.int/lisbon2 010/strategic-concept-2010-eng.pdf.

8. The increase in European defense spending in the recent past can certainly be credited to Russian actions, though of course the rise of Islamic State also emerged at that time and has certainly contributed to a higher operational tempo for the United States and its NATO allies.

9. Holly Williams, "From the Trenches of Russia's Undeclared War on Ukraine, a Warning for America about Putin's Intentions," CBS News, June 15,2021, https://www.cbsnews.com/news/biden-putin-meeting-russia-intentions-ukraine-war-zelenskyy-cbs/; Mackenzie Institute, "NATO and Russia: Towards a New Cold War," July 31, 2019, https://mackenzieinstitute.com/2019/07/nato-and-russia-towards-a-new-cold-war-3/.

10. Katrine Hauane, "Deterrence Strategy in a Hybrid Threat Landscape: An Analysis of NATO's Deterrence Strategy in Estonia, Latvia, and Lithuania Concerning Russian Hybrid Threats and the Concept of Cross-Domain Deterrence" (master's thesis, University of Oslo, 2020), 3, https://www.duo.uio.no/bitstream/handle/10852/80080/5/K--Hauane--STV4992.pdf.

11. Adam Koniuk, "How Could the Baltic States Better Cooperate to Improve Their Capabilities and Facilitate the Extended Deterrence?," *Security Forum* (2018): 43, https://wsb.edu.pl/files/pages/634/security_forum_02_20183.pdf.

12. Latvian Public Broadcasting, "Namejs 2018 Military Exercise Underway," August 20, 2018, https://eng.lsm.lv/article/society/defense/namejs-2018-military-exercise-underway.a289322/. This was also apparent in the deliverables from the Brussels Summit, with readiness initiatives such as the Four 30s. The Four 30s initiative promised 30 battalions, 30 combat ships, and 30 squadrons of aircraft in 30 days. While NATO already had the Very High Readiness Joint Task Force, which promises quick reinforcement, its readiness was still counted in weeks. The goal now is to narrow that

time frame, by improving the infrastructure needed across Europe to move troops to the east. Defense experts and officials in the region also want to see air defenses improved (beyond the current NATO Air Policing mission), to at least deny Russian access to Baltic air space, especially in the event of a conflict.

13. Philip Breedlove and Alexander Vershbow, *Permanent Deterrence: Enhancements to US Military Presence in North Central Europe* (Washington, DC: Atlantic Council, 2018), 3, https://www.atlanticcouncil.org/wp-content/uploads/2018/12/Permanent-Deterrence-Enhancements-to-the-US-Military-Presence-in-North-Central-Eur ope.pdf.

14. Douglas Lute and Nicholas Burns, *NATO at Seventy: An Alliance in Crisis* (Cambridge, MA: Belfer Center for Science and International Affairs, Harvard Kennedy School, 2019).

15. Tom Rostoks, "Managing Deterrence and Escalation on NATO's Eastern Flank," in *Towards #NATO2020: The Regional Perspective of the Baltic States and Poland*, ed. Māris Andžāns and Mārtiņš Vargulis (Riga: Latvian Institute of International Affairs, 2020), 12–13.

16. Osman Bojang and John Jacobs, "Denial or Punishment? Perspectives on the Deterrence Strategy behind NATO's eFP in Lithuania," *Atlantisch Perspectief* 43, no. 3 (2019): 19–20.

17. Jörg Noll, Osman Bojang, and Sebastiaan Rietjens, "Deterrence by Punishment or Denial? The eFP Case," In *NL Arms Netherlands Annual Review of Military Studies 2020: Deterrence in the 21st Century—Insights from Theory and Practice*, ed. Frans Osinga and Tim Sweijs (The Hague: T.M.C. Asser Press, 2021), 109–110.

18. A tabletop exercise is desk-based rather than in the field, with realistic conditions in terms of the deployment of personnel, equipment, and military assets.

19. Robert Czulda, "Enhanced Forward Presence: Evolution, Meaning and the End Game," in *NATO at 70: Outline of the Alliance Today and Tomorrow*, ed. Róbert Ondrejcsák and Tyler H. Lippert (Bratislava, Slovakia: Strategic Policy Institute, 2019), 35–37, https://stratpol.sk/wp-content/uploads/2019/12/panorama_2019_eb ook.pdf#page=27.

20. Group interview with the senior national representatives of eFP Battlegroup Lithuania (Rukla, Lithuania).

21. Jüri Luik and Henrik Praks, *Boosting the Deterrent Effect of Allied Enhanced Forward Presence* (Tallinn, Estonia: International Centre for Defence and Security, 2017), 8, https://icds.ee/wp-content/uploads/2017/ICDS_Policy_Paper_Boosting_the_Det errent_Effect_of_Allied_eFP.pdf.

22. Stockholm International Peace Research Institute, "World Military Spending Rises to Almost \$2 Trillion in 2020," April 26, 2021, https://www.sipri.org/media/press-rele ase/2021/world-military-spending-rises-almost-2-trillion-2020.

23. NATO, *The Secretary General's Annual Report: 2020* (Brussels: NATO, 2020), 48, https://www.nato.int/nato_static_fl2014/assets/pdf/2021/3/pdf/sgar20-en.pdf.

24. Koniuk, "How Could the Baltic States," 44.

25. Vladimir Putin, "Address," in *NATO–Russia Council: Rome Summit 2002* (Brussels: NATO Office of Information and Press, 2002), 18, https://www.nato.int/docu/comm/2002/0205-rome/rome-eng.pdf.

26. Jens Ringsmose and Stenn Rynning, "Now for the Hard Part: NATO's Strategic Adaptation to Russia," *Survival* 59, no. 3 (2017): 129–146.

27. Standing Committee on National Defence, *Canada and NATO: An Alliance Forged in Strength and Reliability* (Ottawa: Standing Committee on National Defence, 2018), https://www.ourcommons.ca/DocumentViewer/en/42-1/NDDN/report-10/page-63#_ftnref193.

28. Margarita Šešelgytė, "Lithuania as Host Nation," in *Lessons from the Enhanced Forward Presence, 2017–2020*, ed. Alexander Lanoszka, Christian Leuprecht, and Alexander Moens (Rome: NATO Defense College, 2020), 76, 78.

29. NATO Force Integration Unit–Lithuania, NATO Deterrence and Stability in the Baltic Region, PowerPoint presentation prepared for the European Business Network, September 27, 2018, 16.

30. "Enemy Armies with Black Mirrors: NATO and Phone Hacking," *The Economist*, May 22, 2021, 44.

31. "Enemy Armies with Black Mirrors," 44.

32. Nolan Peterson, "US Fighter Pilots on the Front Lines of Russia's Spy Games," *The Daily Signal*, March 15, 2018, https://www.dailysignal.com/2018/03/15/us-fighter-pilots-front-lines-russias-spy-games/.

33. Chris Wattie, "Bringing a Knife to a Gunfight: Canadian Strategic Communications and Information Operations in Latvia, Operation *Reassurance* 2019–2020," *Canadian Military Journal* 21, no. 1 (2020): 56.

34. Luik and Praks, *Boosting the Deterrent Effect*.

35. Interview with eFP Task Force Latvia deputy commander (Riga, Latvia).

36. The Canadian-led battlegroup is located in Adazi, which was the only choice in terms of military installations that could accommodate a brigade. The site is also convenient because it is close to Riga, the capital, and to an air force base and has ample space for training activities, including shooting ranges.

37. Interview with eFP Task Force Latvia deputy commander (Riga, Latvia); see also Bojang and Jacobs, "Denial or Punishment?," 18.

38. Breedlove and Vershbow, *Permanent Deterrence*, 3; Noll, Bojang, and Rietjens, "Deterrence by Punishment or Denial?," 124.

39. Luik and Praks, *Boosting the Deterrent Effect*, 9.

40. CDR Eric Lemonnier, Lt. Col. Francisco Gonzalez de Canales, and CDR Alessandro Toni, "Enhanced Forward Presence (EFP): From July 2016 to 2019, the NATO Response to the Evolving Security Environment in Eastern Europe," *Northern Star* (March 2019): 8. Additionally, Allied Joint Forces Command Brunssum would have a role, alongside Multinational Division North East and Multinational Corps North East, to coordinate activities across air, land, and maritime assets.

41. Group interview with NATO military officials at SHAPE (Mons, Belgium).

42. Breedlove and Vershbow, *Permanent Deterrence*, 2.

43. Luik and Praks, *Boosting the Deterrent Effect*, 11.

44. NATO. Action Plan for the Implementation of the NATO/EAPC Policy on Women, Peace and Security 2021–2025. Last updated October 21, 2021c. https://www.nato.int/cps/en/natohq/official_texts_187485.htm.

45. NATO, *Action Plan*.

46. NATO, *Action Plan*, 1, 4.

47. NATO, "Food for Thought Paper: Gender Perspective in the Future of the Alliance," Annex A to IMSM-0521-2021.

48. Some information is made available by the framework nations through the Communications and Information Systems, where capabilities are inputted and there is reporting on all of the activities conducted. This reporting can help detect problems, and there is some coordination between Brunssum and SHAPE stakeholders, though this is a minimal coordination requirement by NATO standards.

49. eFP Battlegroup Latvia gender perspectives placemat, July–December 2018.

50. Battlegroup Standard Operating Procedure 109.

51. Battlegroup Standard Operating Procedure 109.

52. Wattie, "Bringing a Knife to a Gunfight," 55.

53. Steve MacBeth, keynote speech at the Glendon International Symposium on Latvia, "NATO and Latvia Military Relations," Toronto, Canada, March 29, 2019. See also Koniuk, "How Could the Baltic States," 43–44.

54. Liis Mure, "NATO's eFP in the Baltic Region," Danish Institute for International Studies, filmed April 3, 2018, YouTube video, 2:48–19:16, https://www.youtube.com/watch?v=Ea_OAKgydas&ab_channel=DIISpublish.

55. Lara Martinho, *NATO Exercises—Evolution and Lessons Learned* (Brussels: NATO Parliamentary Assembly, 2019), 2, 8, https://www.nato-pa.int/download-file?filen ame=sites/default/files/2019-08/137%20DSCFC%2019%20E-%20NATO%20EX ERCISES%20EVOLUTION%20AND%20LESSONS%20%20LEARNED%20 (EC%20Final%20Rapporteured).pdf.

56. Interview with eFP Battlegroup Lithuania public affairs officer (PAO; Rukla, Lithuania).

57. At the time of my visit, exercise Tomahawk Rising was an example of how geographically dispersed the CAF-led battlegroup activities were.

58. Interview with eFP BG Commander, Ādaži, Latvia.

59. Tactical orders, Tomahawk Smash.

60. eFP Battlegroup Latvia Rotational Order 1802, HQ eFP Battlegroup Latvia, 3350-1 (S5), June 1, 18. See also Bojang and Jacobs, "Denial or Punishment?," 18.

61. eFP Battlegroup Latvia gender perspectives placemat, 2018.

62. Interview with former Task Force Latvia GENAD (Skype).

63. Group interview with enlisted members of the Lithuania battlegroup (Rukla, Lithuania).

64. Interview with NFIU military officers (Vilnius, Lithuania).

65. NATO Force Integration Unit—Lithuania, "NATO Deterrence and Stability in the Baltic Region" (presentation delivered to the European Business Network, September 27, 2018).

66. NATO Force Integration Unit—Lithuania, "NATO Deterrence and Stability," 4–5.

67. NATO Force Integration Unit—Lithuania, "NATO Deterrence and Stability."

68. NATO Force Integration Unit—Lithuania, "NATO Deterrence and Stability," 14. See also Vytenis Miliušas and Viktor Denisenko, "Strategic Communication of NATO Enhanced Forward Presence Battle Group in Lithuania by Assessment of the Parties Involved in the Process," *Lithuanian Annual Strategic Review* 18, no. 1 (2020): 80–85, https://doi.org/10.47459/lasr.2020.18.4.

69. Interview with eFP Battlegroup Lithuania PAO (Rukla, Lithuania).

70. Interviews with eFP Battlegroup Lithuania PAO and chief of information operations (Rukla, Lithuania).

71. Interviews with eFP Battlegroup Lithuania PAO and chief of information operations (Rukla, Lithuania).

72. Kalev Stoicescu and Pauli Järvenpää, *Contemporary Deterrence: Insights and Lesson from Enhanced Forward Presence* (Tallinn, Estonia: International Centre for Defence and Security, 2019), 12–13, https://icds.ee/wp-content/uploads/2019/01/ICDS_Report_Contemporary_Deterrence_Stoicescu_J%C3%A4rv enp%C3%A4%C3%A4_January_2019.pdf.

73. Noll, Bojang, and Rietjens, "Deterrence by Punishment or Denial?," 120–124.

74. While the GENAD position was being filled, a captain at the battlegroup level was working with the Canadian Joint Operations Command GENAD to make sure that the task of incorporating a gender perspective had some continuity.

75. Group interview with enlisted members of the eFP Lithuania Battlegroup (Rukla, Lithuania).

76. Group interview with enlisted members of the eFP Lithuania Battlegroup (Rukla, Lithuania).

77. *Task Force Latvia* refers to the permanent Canadian military presence in Riga, which is different from the CAF battlegroup contingent that is located in Adazi and rotates every six months. At the time of my visit, Task Force Latvia reported to the Canadian Joint Operations Command, and the force generation process was owned by the army. The task force can be said to have an operational role, while the battlegroup's is tactical.

78. Interview with former Task Force Latvia GENAD (Skype).

79. Eric Neumayer and Thomas Plümper, "The Gendered Nature of Natural Disasters: The Impact of Catastrophic Events on the Gender Gap in Life Expectancy, 1981–2002," *Annals of the Association of American Geographers* 97, no. 3 (2007): 551–556.

80. Interoperability can be understood not just in the technical sense but also in reference to military personnel policies. See Carreiras, *Gender and the Military*, 74.

81. Interview with former Task Force Latvia GENAD (Skype).

82. Interview with former Task Force Latvia GENAD (Skype).

83. This is also mentioned in other studies. See, for example, Hurley, "The 'Genderman.'"

84. Interview with former Task Force Latvia GENAD (Skype).

85. David A. Shlapak and Michael W. Johnson, *Reinforcing Deterrence on NATO's Eastern Flank: Wargaming the Defense of the Baltics* (Santa Monica, CA: RAND Corporation, 2016), https://www.rand.org/content/dam/rand/pubs/research_reports/RR1200/RR1253/RAND_RR1253.pdf.

Chapter 6

1. Group interview with civilian and military officials from JFC-Naples (Naples, Italy).
2. Florence Gaub, *Building a New Military? The NATO Training Mission–Iraq* (Rome: NATO Defence College, 2011), 1–2, http://www.jstor.org/stable/resrep10393; Rick Lynch and Phillip D. Janzen, *NATO Training Mission–Iraq: Looking to the Future* (Washington, DC: Institute for National Strategic Studies, 2006), 29–30, https://apps.dtic.mil/sti/pdfs/ADA521751.pdf; Renee de Nevers, "NATO's International Security Role in the Terrorist Era," *International Security* 31, no. 4 (Spring 2007): 34, https://doi.org/10.1162/isec.2007.31.4.34; Hakan Akbulut, ed., *NATO, Cooperative Security, and the Middle East—Status and Prospects* (Vienna: Austrian Institute for International Affairs, 2016), 6, https://www.ssoar.info/ssoar/bitstream/handle/document/59224/?sequence=3; Alejandro Serrano Martínez, "NATO's Level of Ambition in Light of the Current Strategic Context" (master's thesis, School of Advanced Military Studies, 2012), ii, 3, https://apps.dtic.mil/sti/pdfs/ADA566624.pdf.
   Serrano Martínez, "NATO's Level of Ambition," 27.
3. Florence Gaub, *Against All Odds: Relation Between NATO and the MENA Region* (Carlisle Barracks, PA: Strategic Studies Institute, 2012), 13, https://apps.dtic.mil/sti/pdfs/ADA565516.pdf.
4. Lara Martinho, *NATO's Defence and Related Security Capacity Building (DCB) Initiative: Draft Report* (Brussels: NATO Parliamentary Assembly, 2020), 1, https://www.nato-pa.int/download-file?filename=sites/default/files/2020-06/031%20DS CFC%2020%20E%20-%20NATO%20DCB%20Initiative.pdf<.
5. NATO, "Brussels Summit Declaration."
6. In addition to US-led and NATO efforts, there is a UN mission, the UN Assistance Mission for Iraq, which has operated since 2003. It assisted during the drafting of the constitution, has overseen elections, provides mediation support, and coordinates humanitarian efforts, following the mandate set out in UN Security Council Resolution (UNSCR) 1500 (2003) and UNSCR 1770 (2007). There is also the limited-term EU Advisory Mission in Iraq, which provides assistance in the area of civilian security sector reform at the request of the Iraqi government. It works primarily with the Office of the National Security Advisor and the Ministry of the Interior to manage security sector reform with the ultimate aim of stabilizing the country and preventing the resumption of conflict.
7. The United States has the biggest footprint in terms of troop presence (and supporting staff). At the time of my visit, the United States had about 5,200 troops in theater, which was consistent with previous years.
8. Group interview with civilian and military officials from JFC-Naples (Naples, Italy).
9. NATO, *Action Plan*.
10. Niels Schafranek, *NATO and EU Training Missions in Iraq—An Opportunity to Enhance Cooperation* (Rome: NATO Defence College, 2019), 2.
11. Interview with NMI commander (Baghdad, Iraq).
12. Interview with NMI commander (Baghdad, Iraq).

13. Kevin Koehler, *Projecting Stability in Practice? NATO's New Training Mission in Iraq* (Rome: NATO Defense College, 2018), 1–2.

14. With a helicopter capability thrown into the mix, Canada was the first among allies to bid for command of NMI. Turkey may have had the largest footprint in terms of troops on the ground, but Canada's additional helicopter detachment made the difference. It should be noted here too that Turkey being a neighboring country might not have the same "honest broker" authority, which may have also played into the decision-making process that earned Canada the command role.

15. Interview with NMI commander (Baghdad, Iraq).

16. Interview with NMI commander (Baghdad, Iraq).

17. Interview with NMI commander (Baghdad, Iraq). The cultural advisor was one such position. NATO had not thought of it, but the commander could request it and make adjustments to the number and types of positions for NMI.

18. Interview with NMI chief planner (Baghdad, Iraq).

19. Interview with NMI chief planner (Baghdad, Iraq).

20. Interview with NMI chief planner (Baghdad, Iraq).

21. Group interview with civilian and military officials from JFC-Naples (Naples, Italy).

22. It is also the first mission of its kind in that it is an integrated mission across different NATO institutions and command, with NATO HQ, the International Staff, the International Military Staff, Allied Command Operations, and Allied Command Transformation all playing some role.

23. Interview with NMI military advisor #1 (Baghdad, Iraq).

24. Interview with NMI military advisor #1 (Baghdad, Iraq).

25. Interview with NMI military advisor #1 (Baghdad, Iraq).

26. Interview with NMI military advisor #2 (Baghdad, Iraq).

27. Group interview with civilian and military officials from JFC-Naples (Naples, Italy).

28. Interview with NMI military advisory #3 (Baghdad, Iraq).

29. Interview with NMI military advisory #2 (Baghdad, Iraq).

30. Interview with NMI military advisory #2 (Baghdad, Iraq).

31. Interview with NMI military advisory #2 (Baghdad, Iraq).

32. Interview with NMI military advisor #2 (Baghdad, Iraq).

33. Interview with NMI military trainer (Baghdad, Iraq).

34. Interview with NMI ETAT head (Baghdad, Iraq).

35. Group interview with civilian and military officials from JFC-Naples (Naples, Italy).

36. Interview with NMI commander (Baghdad, Iraq).

37. Interview with NMI trainer (Baghdad, Iraq).

38. Interview with NMI trainer (Baghdad, Iraq).

39. Interview with ETAT officer (Baghdad, Iraq).

40. Interview with NMI GENAD (Baghdad, Iraq).

41. Interview with head of ETAT (Baghdad, Iraq).

42. Interview with head of ETAT (Baghdad, Iraq).

43. Interview with GENAD at JFC-Naples (Naples, Italy).

44. Interview with GENAD at JFC-Naples (Naples, Italy).

45. Interview with NMI J3 (Baghdad, Iraq).

46. Interview with three members of FPU (Baghdad, Iraq).
47. Interview with three members of FPU (Baghdad, Iraq).
48. Interview with three members of FPU (Baghdad, Iraq).
49. Interview with NMI head of special program (Baghdad, Iraq).
50. Interview with NMI SSR coordinator (Baghdad, Iraq).
51. Interview with deputy commander, JFC-Naples (Naples, Italy).
52. Interview with deputy commander, JFC-Naples (Naples, Italy).
53. Interview with the NMI GENAD (Baghdad, Iraq).
54. Interview with the NMI GENAD (Baghdad, Iraq).
55. Interview with the NMI GENAD (Baghdad, Iraq).
56. Interview with the NMI GENAD (Baghdad, Iraq).
57. Interview with the NMI GENAD (by phone, pre-fieldwork).
58. Interview with the NMI GENAD (by phone, pre-fieldwork).
59. All staff were mandated to take ADL 169—Improving Operational Effectiveness by Integrating Gender Perspective; ADL 171—Gender Focal Point.
60. For NMI, this means the NATO Bi-Strategic Command Directive 040-001, the JFCNP/Plans/J5/FL/18-00291 Op Order 11210, NMI Op Order 001, and NMI standard operating procedure 111—Inclusive Security and Gender Affairs.
61. NATO, *NMI GENAD Monthly Report*, January 31, 2019 (NATO Unclassified).
62. Interview with NMI GENAD (Baghdad, Iraq).
63. Interview with NMI GENAD (Baghdad, Iraq).
64. Interview with NMI GENAD (Baghdad, Iraq).
65. Interview with CJTF-OIR GENAD #2 (Baghdad, Iraq).
66. Interview with NMI GENAD (Baghdad, Iraq).
67. Interview with CJTF-OIR GENAD #1 (Baghdad, Iraq).
68. Lucy Ferguson, "'This Is Our Gender Person': The Messy Business of Working as a Gender Expert in International Development," *International Feminist Journal of Politics* 17 (2015): 383–386, https://www.tandfonline.com/doi/full/10.1080/14616 742.2014.918787?casa_token=K55uBTYu_bgAAAAA%3AP5Nk0tc4xoIGN5Gsdgb OVXYP50ROJc6A7nt5LQqO903jRnDlgSRLd8Exh0DCsydxakg9DEDOAxYjg-s.
69. Interview with CJTF-OIR GENAD #2 (Baghdad, Iraq).
70. Interview with NMI LEGAD (Baghdad, Iraq).
71. Interview with NMI LEGAD (Baghdad, Iraq).
72. Group interview with civilian and military officials from JFC-Naples (Naples, Italy).
73. Group interview with civilian and military officials from JFC-Naples (Naples, Italy).
74. Group interview with civilian and military officials from JFC-Naples (Naples, Italy).
75. Interview with CIG advisor (Baghdad, Iraq).
76. Interview with CIG advisor (Baghdad, Iraq).
77. David Rock and Heidi Grant, "Why Diverse Teams Are Smarter," *Harvard Business Review*, November 4, 2016, https://hbr.org/2016/11/why-diverse-teams-are-smarter.
78. Interview with two NMI PAOs (Baghdad, Iraq).
79. Interview with two NMI PAOs (Baghdad, Iraq).
80. Interview with two NMI PAOs (Baghdad, Iraq).
81. Interview with NMI J1 (Baghdad, Iraq).

82. Interview with NMI J1 (Baghdad, Iraq).

83. NATO, *NMI GENAD Monthly Report*.

84. For an in-depth discussion on resistance tied to the force generation process, see Meaghan Shoemaker, "Are Her Boots on the Ground? Women's Deployment on NATO-led Operations," Ph.D. Dissertation (Kingston: Queen's University, 2021).

85. On UN representation targets, see United Nations Department of Peace Operations, *Uniformed Gender Parity Strategy 2018–2028* (New York: United Nations), 1–11, https://peacekeeping.un.org/sites/default/files/uniformed-gender-parity-2018-2028.pdf.

86. Interview with NMI commander (Baghdad, Iraq).

87. For a brief overview of the mission see NATO, Public Diplomacy Division—Press & Media Section, "NATO in Iraq," fact sheet (October 2018), available on the JFC Naples website: https://jfcnaples.nato.int/nmi.

88. Magdalena Howland, "Harnessing the Power of Women in NATO: An Intersectional Feminist Perspective of UNSCR 1325," in *Women, Peace and Transforming Security: Visions of the Future of Women, Peace and Security for NATO* (Brussels: Office of the NATO Secretary General's Special Representative for Women, Peace and Security, 2020), 19, https://www.nato.int/nato_static_fl2014/assets/pdf/2020/10/pdf/201110-wps-essay-transforming-security-e.pdf.

89. Angeline Lewis, "WPS, Gender and Foreign Military Interveners: Experience from Iraq and Afghanistan," in *Rethinking Transitional Gender Justice: Transformative Approaches in Post-Conflict Settings*, ed. Rita Shackel and Lucy Fiske (Cham, Switzerland: Palgrave Macmillan, 2019), 122, https://genderandsecurity.org/sites/default/files/Shackel_Fiske_-_Rethinkg_Transitnal_G_Justice.pdf#page=136.

90. Valeria Vilardo and Sara Bittar, *Gender Profile—Iraq: A Situation Analysis on Gender Equality and Women's Empowerment in Iraq* (Oxford: Oxfam International, 2018), 21.

91. Vilardo and Bittar, *Gender Profile—Iraq*, 36.

92. Sexual violence also occurred against men and members of the LGBTQ community, though stigma and feelings of shame are so high that disclosing/reporting and/or accessing support services are rare.

Chapter 7

1. Consistent with findings in previous studies, like Bastick and Duncanson, "Agents of Change?," 563, 565.

2. Isaksson, "Integrating Gender Perspectives at NATO," 235.

3. Bastick and Duncanson, "Agents of Change?," 554.

4. United Nations, "System-wide Strategy on Gender Parity," n.d., ; Government of Canada, "Elsie Initiative for Women in Peace Operations," last modified July 20, 2021, .

5. von Hlatky, "Gender and Peacekeeping."

6. Duncanson, "Forces for Good?," 3.

7. Egnell and Alam, *Women and Gender Perspectives*.

8. Robert Egnell, Petter Hojem, and Hannes Berts, *Implementing a Gender Perspective in Military Organisations and Operations: The Swedish Armed Forces Model* (Uppsala, Sweden: Uppsala University, Department of Peace and Conflict Research, 2012).

9. Kronsell, *Gender, Sex, and the Postnational Defense*, 140.

10. Enloe, *Globalization and Militarization*, 172.

11. Kronsell, *Gender, Sex, and the Postnational Defense*, 11, 139.

12. Carreiras, *Gender and the Military*, 72.

13. Obradovic, *Gender Integration in NATO Military Forces*.

14. Isaksson, "Integrating Gender Perspectives at NATO," 236.

15. Martin Van Creveld, *The Culture of War* (New York: Ballantine Books, 2008), 409.

16. Egnell and Alam, *Women and Gender Perspectives*, 11.

17. Jacqui True, "Mainstreaming Gender in Global Public Policy," *International Feminist Journal of Politics* 5, no. 3 (2003): 321–344.

18. Isaksson, "Integrating Gender Perspectives at NATO," 241.

19. von Hlatky, "Building a Feminist Alliance."

20. von Hlatky, "Building a Feminist Alliance."

21. Duncanson, *Gender and Peacebuilding*; Dara Kay Cohen and Ragnhild Nordås, "Sexual Violence in Armed Conflict: Introducing the SVAC Dataset, 1989–2009," *Journal of Peace Research* 51, no. 3 (2014): 418–428.

22. "Why Nations That Fail Women Fail," *The Economist*, September 11, 2021, .

23. Claire Duncanson, "Mainstreaming Gender in UN Security Policy: A Path to Political Transformation?," in *Global Governance: Feminist Perspectives*, ed. Shirin Rai and Georgina Waylen (Basingstoke, UK: Palgrave Macmillan, 2008), 185–206.

24. For an assessment of Canada on WPS, see Stéfanie von Hlatky, "The Gender Perspective and Canada's Armed Forces: Internal and External Dimensions of Military Culture," in *Women and Gender Perspectives in the Military*, ed. Robert Egnell and Mayesha Alam (Washington, DC: Georgetown University Press, 2019), 73–86.

25. Egnell and Alam, *Women and Gender Perspectives*, 1–21, 253–270.

26. As Obradovic notes in *Gender Integration in NATO Military Forces*, NATO is better positioned to pressure states through its accession process (p. 148) or, I would add, through its partnership process. There are fewer levers to influence NATO allies.

27. Ferguson, "'This Is Our Gender Person,'" 381.

28. Bastick and Duncanson, "Agents of Change?," 562.

Bibliography

Acharya, Amitav. "How Ideas Spread: Whose Norms Matter? Norm Localization and Institutional Change in Asian Regionalism." *International Organization* 58, no. 2 (April 2004): 239–275.

Ackerly, Brooke A., Maria Stern, and Jacqui True. "Feminist Methodologies for International Relations." In *Feminist Methodologies for International Relations*, edited by Brooke A. Ackerly, Maria Stern, and Jacqui True, 1–16. New York: Cambridge University Press, 2006.

Adler, Emmanuel. "The Spread of Security Communities: Communities of Practice, Self-Restraint, and NATO's Post–Cold War Transformation." *European Journal of International Relations* 14, no. 2 (2008): 195–230.

Aggestam, Karin, and Annika Bergman-Rosamond. "Swedish Feminist Foreign Policy in the Making: Ethics, Politics, and Gender." *Ethics & International Affairs* 30, no. 3 (2016): 323–330. https://www.cambridge.org/core/journals/ethics-and-international-affairs/article/swedish-feminist-foreign-policy-in-the-making-ethics-politics-and-gender/FEE6103E38181D831DA1BEBE8861C289.

Aggestam, Karin, Annika Bergman Rosamond, and Annica Kronsell. "Theorising Feminist Foreign Policy." *International Relations* 33 (2018): 23–39.

Akbulut, Hakan, ed. *NATO, Cooperative Security, and the Middle East—Status and Prospects*. Vienna: Austrian Institute for International Affairs, 2016. https://www.ssoar.info/ssoar/bitstream/handle/document/59224/?sequence=3.

Allied Command Operations. *Gender Functional Planning Guide*. Mons, Belgium: Allied Command Operations, 2015. https://www.forsvarsmakten.se/siteassets/english/swedint/engelska/swedint/courses/genad/07-aco-gender-functional-planning-guide.pdf.

Ansorg, Nadine, and Toni Haastrup. "Gender and the EU's Support for Security Sector Reform in Fragile Contexts." *Journal of Common Market Studies* 56 (2018): 1127–1143.

Appiagyi-Atua, Kwadwo. "United Nations Security Council 1325 on Women, Peace, and Security—Is It Binding?" *The Human Rights Brief* 18, no. 3 (2011): 2–6.

Aroussi, Sahla. "Women, Peace and Security and the DRC: Time to Rethink Sexual Violence as Gender-Based Violence." *Politics & Gender* 13, no. 3 (September 2017): 488–515.

Auerswald, David P., and Stephen M. Saideman. *NATO in Afghanistan: Fighting Together, Fighting Alone*. Princeton, NJ: Princeton University Press, 2014.

Australian Government. *Pathway to Change—Evolving Defence Culture*. Canberra: Department of Defence. Accessed September 26, 2019. https://www.defence.gov.au/about/reviews-inquiries/pathway-change-evolving-defence-culture.

Avant, Deborah D. *Political Institutions and Military Change: Lessons from Peripheral Wars*. Ithaca, NY: Cornell University Press, 1994.

Avila, Lt. Col. Miguel Angel Martinez. "NATO and Gender: What Does Gender Mean in the Operational Level." *Northern Star*, March 2019. https://open.cmi.no/cmi-xmlui/bitstream/handle/11250/2474930/Seeking%20out%20their%20Afghan%20sisters%3a%20Female%20Engagement%20Teams%20in%20Afghanistan?sequence=1&isAllowed=y

Azarbaijani-Moghaddam, Sippi. "Seeking Out Their Afghan Sisters: Female Engagement Teams in Afghanistan." CMI Working Paper 1, Chr. Michelsen Institute, Bergen, Norway, March 2014. http://hdl.handle.net/11250/2474930.

Baldwin, Clive. "Implementation through Cooperation? Human Rights Officers and the Military in Kosovo, 1999–2002." *International Peacekeeping* 13, no. 4 (2006): 489–501.

Baruah, Bipasha. "Short-Sighted Commitments on Women in Peacekeeping." *Policy Options*, November 23, 2017. https://policyoptions.irpp.org/magazines/november-2017/short-sighted-commitments-on-women-in-peacekeeping/.

Bastick, Megan, and Claire Duncanson. "Agents of Change? Gender Advisor in NATO Militaries." *International Peacekeeping* 25, no. 4 (August 2018): 554–577.

Basu, Soumita. "Gender as National Interest at the UN Security Council." *International Affairs* 92, no. 2 (March 2016): 255–273.

Baylis, John, James J. Wirtz, and Colin S. Gray. *Strategy in the Contemporary World: An Introduction*. Oxford: Oxford University Press, 2016.

Belkin, Aaron. *Bring Me Men: Military Masculinity and the Benign Façade of American Empire, 1898–2001*. New York: Columbia University Press, 2012.

Belkin, Aaron. "Combat Exclusion RIP. Will Patriarchy's Demise Follow." *Critical Studies on Security* 1, no. 2 (August 2013): 249–250.

Bergman, Mindy E., Regina Day Langhout, Patrick A. Palmieri, Lilia M. Cortina, and Louise F. Fitzgerald. "The (Un)Reasonableness of Reporting: Antecedents and Consequences of Reporting Sexual Harassment." *Journal of Applied Psychology* 87, no. 2 (2002): 230–242.

Bloom, Mia. "Female Suicide Bombers: A Global Trend." *Daedalus* 136, no. 1 (Winter 2007): 94–102.

Bojang, Osman, and John Jacobs. "Denial or Punishment? Perspectives on the Deterrence Strategy behind NATO's eFP in Lithuania." *Atlantisch Perspectief* 43, no. 3 (2019): 16–20.

Boyd, Rosalind, ed. *The Search for Lasting Peace: Critical Perspectives on Gender-Responsive Human Security*. Burlington, VT: Ashgate, 2014.

Brackett, Marc A., Susan E. Rivers, Sarah Shiffman, Nicole Lerner, and Peter Salovey. "Relating Emotional Abilities to Social Functioning: A Comparison of Self-Report and Performance Measures of Emotional Intelligence." *Journal of Personality and Social Psychology* 91, no. 4 (2006): 780–795.

Breedlove, Philip, and Alexander Vershbow. *Permanent Deterrence: Enhancements to US Military Presence in North Central Europe*. Washington, DC: Atlantic Council, 2018. https://www.atlanticcouncil.org/wp-content/uploads/2018/12/Permanent-Deterre nce-Enhancements-to-the-US-Military-Presence-in-North-Central-Europe.pdf.

Bridges, Donna, and Debbie Horsfall. "Increasing Operational Effectiveness in UN Peacekeeping: Toward a Gender-Balanced Force." *Armed Forces & Society* 36, no. 1 (2009): 120–130.

Brooks, Abigail. "Feminist Standpoint Epistemology." In *Feminist Research Practice*, edited by Sharlene Hesse Biber and Patricia Lena Leavy, 53–82. Thousand Oaks, CA: Sage Publications, 2007. https://us.sagepub.com/sites/default/files/upm-binaries/12936_C hapter3.pdf.

Brosig, Malte. "The Interplay of International Institutions in Kosovo between Convergence, Confusing and Niche Capabilities." *European Security* 20, no. 2 (June 2011): 185–204.

Brownson, Connie. "The Battle for Equivalency: Female US Marines Discuss Sexuality, Physical Fitness, and Military Leadership." *Armed Forces & Society* 40, no. 4 (2014): 765–788.

Calgar, Gülay. "Gender Mainstreaming." *Politics & Gender* 9, no. 3 (September 2013): 336–344.

Carey, Henry. "'Women and Peace and Security': The Politics of Implementing Gender Sensitivity Norms in Peacekeeping." *International Peacekeeping* 8, no. 2 (2001): 49–68.

Carreiras, Helena. *Gender and the Military: Women in the Armed Forces of Western Democracies.* London and New York: Routledge, 2006.

Center for Army Lessons Learned. *Commander's Guide to Female Engagement Teams.* Fort Leavenworth, KS: Center for Army Lessons Learned, 2011. Accessed September 25, 2018. https://www.globalsecurity.org/military/library/report/call/call_11-38_v3.pdf.

Checkel, Jeffrey T. "International Institutions and Socialization in Europe: Introduction and Framework." *International Organization* 59, no. 4 (October 2005): 801–826.

Cockburn, Cynthia. "Gender Relations as Causal in Militarization and War." *International Feminist Journal of Politics* 12, no. 2 (June 2010): 139–152.

Cockburn, Cynthia. "Snagged on the Contradiction: NATO, UNSC Resolution 1325, and Feminist Responses." Paper presented at the Annual Meeting of No to War—No to NATO, Dublin, Ireland, April 2011. https://no-to-nato.net/wp-content/uploads/2013/03/NATO13251.pdf.

Cohen, Dara Kay, and Ragnhild Nordås. "Sexual Violence in Armed Conflict: Introducing the SVAC Dataset, 1989–2009." *Journal of Peace Research* 51, no. 3 (2014): 418–428.

Cohn, Carol. "Mainstreaming Gender in UN Security Policy: A Path to Political Transformation?" In *Global Governance: Feminist Perspectives*, edited by Shirin M. Rai and Georgina Waylen, 185–206. Basingstoke, UK: Palgrave Macmillan, 2008.

Cohn, Carol, Helen Kinsella, and Sheri Gibbings. "Women, Peace and Security Resolution 1325." *International Feminist Journal of Politics* 6, no. 1 (January 2004): 130–140. https://doi.org/10.1080/1461674032000165969.

Côté, Isabelle, and Limingcui Emma Huang. "Where Are the Daughters? Examining the Effects of Gendered Migration on the Dynamics of 'Sons of the Soil' Conflict." *Studies in Conflict & Terrorism* 43, no. 10 (2018): 837–853.

Czulda, Robert. "Enhanced Forward Presence: Evolution, Meaning and the End Game." In *NATO at 70: Outline of the Alliance Today and Tomorrow*, edited by Róbert Ondrejcsák and Tyler H. Lippert, 26–45. Bratislava, Slovakia: Strategic Policy Institute, 2019. https://stratpol.sk/wp-content/uploads/2019/12/panorama_2019_ebook.pdf#page=27.

De Jonge Oudraat, Chantel. "The WPS Agenda and Strategy for the Twenty-First Century." In *The Oxford Handbook of Women, Peace, and Security*, edited by Sara E. Davies and Jacqui True, 840–849. New York: Oxford University Press, 2019.

de Nevers, Renee. "NATO's International Security Role in the Terrorist Era." *International Security* 31, no. 4 (Spring 2007): 34–66. https://doi.org/10.1162/isec.2007.31.4.34.

DeRosa, John. *Strategic Defense Review of the Republic of Kosovo.* Kosovo: GAP Institute, 2013. https://www.institutigap.org/documents/81456_SDR.pdf.

Deschamps, Marie. *External Review into Sexual Misconduct and Sexual Harassment in the Canadian Armed Forces.* Ottawa: External Review Authority, 2015. https://www.canada.ca/en/department-national-defence/corporate/reports-publications/sexual-misbehaviour/external-review-2015.html.

Dharmapuri, Sahana. "Just Add Women and Stir?" *Parameters* 41, no. 1 (Spring 2011): 56–70. http://www.peacewomen.org/sites/default/files/1325-1820-partpp_justaddwomenandstir_gender_peaceprocesses__parametersquarterly_2011_0.pdf.

Dobbins, Frank, Beth Simmons, and Geoffrey Garrett. "The Global Diffusion of Public Policies: Social Construction, Coercion, Competition, or Learning?" *Annual Review of Sociology* 33, no. 1 (2007): 449–472.

Duncanson, Claire. "Mainstreaming Gender in UN Security Policy: A Path to Political Transformation?" In *Global Governance: Feminist Perspectives*, edited by Shirin Rai and Georgina Waylen, 185–206. Basingstoke, UK: Palgrave Macmillan, 2008.

Duncanson, Claire. "Forces for Good? Narratives of Military Masculinity in Peacekeeping Operations." *International Feminist Journal of Politics* 11, no. 1 (March 2009): 63–80.

Duncanson, Claire. *Forces for Good? Military Masculinities and Peacebuilding in Afghanistan and Iraq.* New York: Palgrave Macmillan, 2013.

Duncanson, Claire. *Gender and Peacebuilding.* Cambridge: Polity, 2016.

Duncanson, Claire. "Beyond Liberal vs Liberating: Women's Economic Empowerment in the United Nations' Women, Peace and Security Agenda." *International Feminist Journal of Politics* 21, no. 1 (2019): 111–130.

Duncanson, Claire, and Rachel Woodward. "Regendering the Military: Theorizing Women's Military Participation." *Security Dialogue* 47, no. 1 (December 2015): 3–21.

Duriesmith, David, and Sara Meger. "Returning to the Root: Radical Feminist Thought and Feminist Theories of International Relations." *Review of International Studies* 46 (2020): 357–366. https://www.cambridge.org/core/journals/review-of-international-studies/article/returning-to-the-root-radical-feminist-thought-and-feminist-theories-of-international-relations/89763892A2973CE63AE77E1B17767EB9.

Eagly, Alice H., and Linda L. Carli. *Through the Labyrinth: The Truth about How Women Become Leaders.* Boston: Harvard Business School Press, 2007.

Egnell, Robert. "Gender Perspectives and Military Effectiveness: Implementing UNSCR 1325 and the National Action Plan on Women Peace and Security." *Prism: A Journal of the Center for Complex Operations* 6, no. 1 (2016): 72–89.

Egnell, Robert, and Mayesha Alam, eds. *Women and Gender Perspectives in the Military.* Washington, DC: Georgetown University Press, 2019.

Egnell, Robert, Petter Hojem, and Hannes Berts. *Implementing a Gender Perspective in Military Organisations and Operations: The Swedish Armed Forces Model.* Uppsala, Sweden: Uppsala University, Department of Peace and Conflict Research, 2012.

Eichler, Maya. "Militarized Masculinities in International Relations." *Brown Journal of World Affairs* 21, no. 1 (Fall/Winter 2014): 81–93.

Ejdus, Filip, and Marko Kovačević. "Penetration, Overlay, Governmentality: The Evolving Role of NATO in the Western Balkan Security Dynamics." *Journal of Intervention and Statebuilding* 13, no. 5 (October 2019): 566–580.

"Enemy Armies with Black Mirrors: NATO and Phone Hacking." *The Economist*, May 22, 2021. https://www.economist.com/europe/2021/05/22/nato-increasingly-sees-its-soldiers-phones-as-a-liability

Enloe, Cynthia. *Does Khaki Become You?* London: Pluto, 1983.

Enloe, Cynthia. *Maneuvers: The International Politics of Militarizing Women's Lives.* Los Angeles: University of California Press, 2000.

Enloe, Cynthia. *Globalization and Militarization: Feminists Make the Link.* London: Rowman & Littlefield, 2016.

European Union. *Final Report on Gender Work inside EUFOR RD Congo.* Potsdam: EU Operation Headquarters, 2006.

European Union. *Comprehensive Approach to the EU Implementation of the United Nations Security Council Resolutions 1325 and 1820 on Women, Peace and Security.* Brussels: Council of the European Union, 2008.

Farnsworth, Nicole, ed. *1325 Facts & Fables.* Prishtina, Kosovo: The Kosova Women's Network, 2011. https://womensnetwork.org/wpcontent/uploads/2018/10/201301 20165559661.pdf. https://womensnetwork.org/publications/1325-facts-and-fables/

Feaver, Peter. "The Civil–Military Problematique: Huntington, Janowitz, and the Question of Civilian Control." *Armed Forces & Society* 32, no. 2 (January 1996): 149–178.

Feaver, Peter. *Armed Servants.* Cambridge, MA: Harvard University Press, 2003.

Ferguson, Lucy. "'This Is Our Gender Person': The Messy Business of Working as a Gender Expert in International Development." *International Feminist Journal of Politics* 17 (2015): 380–397. https://www.tandfonline.com/doi/full/10.1080/14616742.2014.918 787?casa_token=K55uBTYu_bgAAAAA%3AP5Nk0tc4xoIGN5GsdgbOVXYP50ROJ c6A7nt5LQqO903jRnDlgSRLd8Exh0DCsydxakg9DEDOAxYjg-s

Finnemore, Martha, and Kathryn Sikkink. "International Norm Dynamics and Political Change." *International Organization* 52, no. 4 (1998): 887–917.

Fox, Morgan. "How Will Women, Peace, and Security Fit into NATO's Next Strategic Concept?" *Contact Report,* August 13, 2021. https://medium.com/centre-for-intern ational-and-defence-policy/how-will-women-peace-and-security-fit-into-natos- next-strategic-concept-810a648bff98.

Francke, Linda Bird. *Ground Zero: The Gender Wars in the Military.* New York: Simon & Schuster, 1997.

Fujii, Lee Ann. *Interviewing in Social Science Research: A Relational Approach.* New York: Routledge, 2018.

Fullmer, Nyssa, Stephanie Lipson Mizrahi, and Elizabeth Tomsich. "The Lethality of Female Suicide Bombers." *Women and Criminal Justice* 29, nos. 4–5 (2019): 266–282.

Gailmard, Sean. "Accountability and Principal-Agent Theory." In *The Oxford Handbook of Public Accountability,* edited by Mark Bovens, Robert E. Goodin, and Thomas Schillemans, 90–105. Oxford: Oxford University Press, 2014.

Gaub, Florence. *Building a New Military? The NATO Training Mission–Iraq.* Rome: NATO Defence College, 2011. http://www.jstor.org/stable/resrep10393.

Gaub, Florence. *Against All Odds: Relations between NATO and the MENA Region.* Carlisle Barracks, PA: Strategic Studies Institute, 2012. https://apps.dtic.mil/sti/pdfs/ ADA565516.pdf.

Giegerich, Bastian, and Stéfanie von Hlatky. "Experiences May Vary: NATO and Cultural Interoperability in Afghanistan." *Armed Forces & Society* 46, no. 3 (2019): 495–516.

Goldstein, Andrea N. "'Why Are You Trying to Destroy the Last Good Thing Men Have?' Understanding Resistance to Women in Combat Jobs." *International Feminist Journal of Politics* 20, no. 3 (July 2018): 385–404.

Goldstein, Joshua. *War and Gender: How Gender Shapes the War System and Vice Versa.* Cambridge: Cambridge University Press, 2001.

Goldstein, Joshua S., Jon C. Pevehouse, and Sandra Whitworth. *International Relations.* 2nd ed. Toronto: Pearson/Longman, 2008. https://www.amazon.ca/International- Relations-Third-Canadian-3rd/dp/0321714504

Government of Canada. "Elsie Initiative for Women in Peace Operations." Last modified June 22, 2022. https://www.international.gc.ca/world-monde/issues_development- enjeux_developpement/gender_equality-egalite_des_genres/elsie_initiative-initiativ e_elsie.aspx?lang=eng.

Government Offices of Sweden. "Feminist Foreign Policy." Accessed January 23, 2016. https://www.government.se/government-policy/feminist-foreign-policy/.

Government of the Republic of Kosovo. *Draft Law on Kosovo Security Force.* Kosovo: Government of the Republic of Kosovo, 2018. https://www.kuvendikosoves.org/eng/draft-laws-and-laws/.

Græger, Nina. "European Security as Practice: EU–NATO Communities of Practice in the Making?" *European Security* 25, no. 4 (2016): 478–501.

Guerrina, Roberta, and Katherine A. M. Wright. "Gendering Normative Power Europe: Lessons of the Women, Peace and Security Agenda." *International Affairs* 92, no. 2 (March 2016): 293–312.

Haas, Ernest B. *When Knowledge Is Power: Three Models of Change in International Organizations.* Berkeley: University of California Press, 1990.

Hall, Judith A. "Women's and Men's Nonverbal Communication: Similarities, Differences, Stereotypes, and Origins." In *The SAGE Handbook of Nonverbal Communication,* edited by Valerie Manusov and Miles L. Patterson, 201–218. Thousand Oaks, CA: Sage, 2006.

Hammar, Li, and Annika Berg, eds. *Whose Security? Practical Examples of Gender Perspectives in Military Operations.* Stockholm: Nordic Centre for Gender in Military Operations, Swedish Armed Forces, 2015. https://www.forsvarsmakten.se/siteassets/english/swedint/engelska/swedint/nordic-centre-for-gender-in-military-operations/whose-security-2015-low-resolution.pdf.

Harding, Tyra A. "Women in Combat Roles: Case Study of Female Engagement Teams." Master's thesis, US Army War College, 2012.

Hardt, Heidi, and Stéfanie von Hlatky. "NATO's About Face: Adaptation to Gender Mainstreaming in an Alliance Setting." *Journal of Global and Security Studies* 5, no. 1 (2020): 136–159.

Hauane, Katrine. "Deterrence Strategy in a Hybrid Threat Landscape: An Analysis of NATO's Deterrence Strategy in Estonia, Latvia, and Lithuania Concerning Russia's Hybrid Threats and the Concept of Cross-Domain Deterrence." Master's thesis, University of Oslo, 2020. https://www.duo.uio.no/bitstream/handle/10852/80080/5/K--Hauane--STV4992.pdf.

Henry, Marsha. "Problematizing Military Masculinity, Intersectionality and Male Vulnerability in Feminist Critical Military Studies." *Critical Military Studies* 3, no. 2 (2017): 182–199.

Herbert, Melissa S. *Camouflage Isn't Only for Combat: Gender, Sexuality, and Women in the Military.* New York and London: New York University Press, 1998.

Higate, Paul, and Marsha Henry. "Engendering (In)security in Peace Support Operations." *Security Dialogue* 35, no. 4 (December 2004): 481–498.

Hill, Felicity, Mikele Aboitiz, and Sara Poehlman-Doumbouya. "Nongovernmental Organizations' Role in the Buildup and Implementation of Security Council 1325." *Signs: Journal of Women in Culture and Society* 28, no. 4 (2003): 1255–1269. https://doi.org/10.1086/368321.

von Hlatky, Stéfanie. "The Gender Turn in Canadian Military Interventions." In *Canada among Nations,* edited by Fen Oler Hampson and Stephen M. Saideman, 161–176. Waterloo: Centre for International Governance Innovation, 2015.

von Hlatky, Stéfanie. "Gender and Peacekeeping." *Policy Options,* November 8, 2017. http://policyoptions.irpp.org/magazines/november-2017/gender-and-peacekeeping/.

von Hlatky, Stéfanie. "The Gender Perspective and Canada's Armed Forces: Internal and External Dimensions of Military Culture." In *Women and Gender Perspectives in the Military*, edited by Robert Egnell and Mayesha Alam, 73–86. Washington, DC: Georgetown University Press, 2019.

von Hlatky, Stéfanie. "Building a Feminist Alliance." *Open Canada*, November 18, 2020. https://opencanada.org/building-a-feminist-alliance/.

Holliday, Janet R. "Female Engagement Teams: The Need to Standardize Training and Employment." *Military Review* 92, no. 2 (2012): 90–94.

Holvikivi, Aiko, and Audrey Reeves. "Women, Peace and Security after Europe's 'Refugee Crisis.'" *European Journal of International Security* 5, no. 2 (June 2020): 135–154. https://doi.org/10.1017/eis.2020.1.

Howland, Magdalena. "Harnessing the Power of Women in NATO: An Intersectional Feminist Perspective of UNSCR 1325." In *Women, Peace and Transforming Security: Visions of the Future of Women, Peace and Security for NATO*, 19–21. Brussels: Office of the NATO Secretary General's Special Representative for Women, Peace and Security, 2020. https://www.nato.int/nato_static_fl2014/assets/pdf/2020/10/pdf/201110-wps-essay-transforming-security-e.pdf.

Hudson, Heidi. "Gender and the Globalization of Violence: The Treacherous Terrain of Privatised Peacekeeping." *Agenda: Empowering Women for Gender Equity* 18, no. 59 (January 2004): 42–55.

Hudson, Natalie. "The Challenges of Monitoring and Analyzing WPS for Scholars." In *The Oxford Handbook of Women, Peace, and Security*, edited Sara E. Davies and Jacqui True, 850–862. Oxford: Oxford University Press. 2019.

Hudson, Valerie M., Mary Caprioli, Bonnie Ballif-Spanvill, Rose McDermott, and Chad F. Emmett. "The Heart of the Matter: The Security of Women and the Security of States." *International Security* 33, no. 3 (Winter 2008/2009): 7–45.

Hurley, Matthew. "The 'Genderman': (Re)negotiating Militarized Masculinities When 'Doing Gender' at NATO." *Critical Military Studies* 4, no. 1 (January 2018a): 72–91.

Hurley, Matthew. "Watermelons and Weddings: Making Women, Peace and Security 'Relevant' at NATO through (Re)telling Stories of Success." *Global Society* 32, no. 4 (October 2018b): 436–456.

Ilies, Remus, Nancy Hauserman, Susan Schwochau, and John Stibal. "Reported Incidence Rates of Work-Related Sexual Harassment in the United States: Using Meta-analysis to Explain Reported Rate Disparities." *Personnel Psychology* 56, no. 3 (2003): 607–631.

Irby, Ida. "'FET' to Fight: Female Engagement Team Makes History." US Army, April 18, 2013. https://www.army.mil/article/101111/fet_to_fight_female_engagement_team_makes_history.

Isaksson, Charlotte. "Integrating Gender Perspectives at NATO: Two Steps Forward, One Step Back." In *Women and Gender Perspectives in the Military: An International Comparison*, edited by Robert Egnell and Mayesha Alam, 225–252. Washington, DC: Georgetown University Press, 2019.

Jarvis, Christina S. *The Male Body at War: American Masculinity during World War II.* DeKalb: Northern Illinois University Press, 2004.

JFC-Naples. "KFOR Troops Showcase Support of Women, Peace and Security Initiatives." NATO, 2017. https://jfcnaples.nato.int/newsroom/news/2016/kfor-troops-showcase-support-of-women--peace-and-security-initiatives.

Joint Intelligence. *Joint Publication 2-0.* Washington, DC: Joint Chiefs of Staff, 2013. https://www.jcs.mil/Portals/36/Documents/Doctrine/pubs/jp2_0.pdf.

Jones, Sophia. "The Dangers of Forcing Gender Equality in Afghanistan." *New York Times*, November 21, 2017. https://www.nytimes.com/2017/11/21/opinion/women-afghanis tan-equality.html.

Karim, Sabrina, and Kyle Beardsley. "Gender, Peace, and Security: Implementing UN Security Council Resolution 1325." In *A Systematic Understanding of Gender, Peace, and Security: Implementing UNSC 1325*, edited by Ismene Gizelis and Louise Olsson, 62–95. London: Routledge, 2015.

Kennedy-Pipe, Caroline. "Liberal Feminists, Militaries and War." In *The Palgrave International Handbook of Gender and the Military*, edited by Rachel Woodward and Claire Duncanson, 23–37. London: Palgrave Macmillan, 2017.

Kenney, Keirsten H. "Gender Advisors in NATO: Should the U.S. Military Follow Suit?" *Military Law Review* 224 (2016): 1052–1072.

Keohane, Robert O. "International Relations Theory: Contributions of a Feminist Standpoint." *Millennium* 18, no. 2 (June 1989): 245–253.

King, Anthony. "The Female Combat Soldier." *European Journal of International Relations* 22, no. 1 (2016): 122–143.

Kingsley, Patrick, and Kenneth P. Vogel. "Pushing for Serbia–Kosovo Peace Deal, U.S. Roils Allies." *New York Times*, June 20, 2020. https://www.nytimes.com/2020/06/20/world/europe/serbia-kosovo-peace-elections.html?auth=login-email&login=email.

Kirby, Paul, and Laura J. Shepherd. "Reintroducing Women, Peace and Security." *International Affairs* 92, no. 2 (March 2016a): 249–254. https://doi.org/10.1111/1468-2346.12550.

Kirby, Paul, and Laura J. Shepherd. "The Futures Past of the Women, Peace and Security Agenda." *International Affairs* 92, no. 2 (March 2016b): 373–392.

Klossek, Lara, and Elisabeth Johansson-Nogués. "The Female 'Boot on the Ground': Indian Ambivalence over Gender Mainstreaming in UN Peacekeeping Operations." *International Peacekeeping* 4 (2021): 527–552. https://www.tandfonline.com/doi/pdf/10.1080/13533312.2021.1880899?needAccess=true.

Klot, Jennifer F. "UN Security Council Resolution 1325: A Feminist Transformative Agenda." In *The Oxford Handbook of Transnational Feminist Movements*, edited by Rawwida Baksh and Wendy Harcourt, 723–745. New York: Oxford University Press, 2015.

Koehler, Kevin. *Projecting Stability in Practice? NATO's New Training Mission in Iraq.* Rome: NATO Defense College, 2018. https://www.ndc.nato.int/news/news.php?icode=1216.

Kolenda, Christopher D. *The Counterinsurgency Challenge: A Parable of Leadership and Decision-Making in Modern Conflict.* Mechanicsburg, PA: Stackpole Books, 2012.

Koniuk, Adam. "How Could the Baltic States Better Cooperate to Improve Their Capabilities and Facilitate the Extended Deterrence?" *Security Forum*, (2018): 37–46. https://wsb.edu.pl/files/pages/634/security_forum_02_20183.pdf

Kopsa, K. "Gendering Crisis Management: Examining the Role of Gender in the Report of the Parliamentary Committee on Crisis Management." Bachelor's thesis, Malmö University, 2021.

Kreft, Anne-Kathrin. "The Gender Mainstreaming Gap: Security Council Resolution 1325 and UN Peacekeeping Mandates." *International Peacekeeping* 24 (2017): 132–158. https://www.tandfonline.com/doi/pdf/10.1080/13533312.2016.1195267?needAcc ess=true.

Kronsell, Annica. "Gendered Practices in Institutions of Hegemonic Masculinity." *International Feminist Journal of Politics* 7, no. 2 (June 2005): 280–298.

Kronsell, Annica. *Gender, Sex, and the Postnational Defense: Militarism and Peacekeeping.* New York: Oxford University Press, 2012.

Kruijver, Kimberley, and Visar Xhambazi. *Kosovo's NATO Future: How to Square the Circle?* The Hague: Clingendael (Netherlands Institute of International Relations), 2020. https://www.clingendael.org/sites/default/files/2020-12/Kosovos_NATO_fut ure_Correct.pdf.

Lackenbauer, Helene, and Richard Langlais, eds. *Review of the Practical Implications of UNSCR 1325 for the Conduct of NATO-Led Operations and Missions.* Stockholm: Swedish Defence Research Agency, 2013. https://www.nato.int/nato_sta tic/assets/pdf/pdf_2013_10/20131021_131023-UNSCR1325-review-final.pdf.

Latvian Public Broadcasting. "Namejs 2018 Military Exercise Underway." August 20, 2018. https://eng.lsm.lv/article/society/defense/namejs-2018-military-exercise-under way.a289322/.

Lemmon, Gayle Tzemach. *Ashley's War: The Untold Story of a Team of Women Soldiers on the Special Ops Battlefield.* New York: Harper Collins, 2015.

Lemonnier, CDR Eric, Lt. Col. Francisco Gonzalez de Canales, and CDR Alessandro Toni. "Enhanced Forward Presence (EFP): From July 2016 to 2019, the NATO Response to the Evolving Security Environment in Eastern Europe." *Northern Star*, March 2019.

Leuprecht, Christian, Joel Sokolsky, and Jayson Derow. *On the Baltic Watch: The Past, Present and Future of Canada's Commitment to NATO's Enhanced Forward Presence in Latvia.* Ottawa: Macdonald-Laurier Institute, 2018. https://macdonaldlaurier.ca/files/ pdf/20180327_MLI_LATVIA_WebF.pdf.

Levy, Jacob. "Learning and Foreign Policy: Sweeping a Conceptual Minefield." *International Organization* 48, no. 2 (Spring 1994): 279–312.

Lewis, Angeline. "WPS, Gender and Foreign Military Interveners: Experience from Iraq and Afghanistan." In *Rethinking Transitional Gender Justice: Transformative Approaches in Post-Conflict Settings,* edited by Rita Shackel and Lucy Fiske, 121–139. Cham, Switzerland: Palgrave Macmillan, 2019. https://genderandsecurity.org/sites/ default/files/Shackel_Fiske_-_Rethinkg_Transitnal_G_Justice.pdf#page=136.

Liljegren, Agnes. "A Double Occupation: The Struggle within the Struggle." Bachelor's thesis, Lund University, 2020. http://lup.lub.lu.se/luur/download?func=downloadF ile&recordOId=9033851&fileOId=9036737.

Luik, Jüri, and Henrik Praks. *Boosting the Deterrent Effect of Allied Enhanced Forward Presence.* Tallinn, Estonia: International Centre for Defence and Security, 2017. https:// icds.ee/wp-content/uploads/2017/ICDS_Policy_Paper_Boosting_the_Deterrent_E ffect_of_Allied_eFP.pdf.

Lute, Douglas, and Nicholas Burns. *NATO at Seventy: An Alliance in Crisis.* Cambridge, MA: Belfer Center for Science and International Affairs, Harvard Kennedy School, 2019.

Lynch, Rick, and Phillip D. Janzen. *NATO Training Mission–Iraq: Looking to the Future.* Washington, DC: Institute for National Strategic Studies, 2006. https://apps.dtic.mil/ sti/pdfs/ADA521751.pdf.

MacBeth, Steve. Keynote speech at the Glendon International Symposium on Latvia, "NATO and Latvia Military Relations." March 29, 2019. Toronto, Canada,

MacKenzie Institute. "NATO and Russia: Towards a New Cold War." July 31, 2019. https:// mackenzieinstitute.com/2019/07/nato-and-russia-towards-a-new-cold-war-3/.

MacKenzie, Megan. "True Grit: The Myths and Realities of Women in Combat." *Foreign Affairs*, August 12, 2015a. https://www.foreignaffairs.com/articles/2015-08-12/true-grit.

MacKenzie, Megan. *Beyond the Band of Brothers: The US Military and the Myth That Women Can't Fight*. Cambridge: Cambridge University Press, 2015b.

MacKenzie, Megan, and Nicole Wegner, eds. *Feminist Solutions for Ending War*. London: Pluto Press, 2021.

Martin de Almagro, Maria. "Producing Participants: Gender, Race, Class, and Women, Peace and Security." *Global Society* 32, no. 4 (October 2018): 395–414.

Martinho, Lara. *NATO Exercises—Evolution and Lessons Learned*. Brussels: NATO Parliamentary Assembly, 2019, https://www.nato-pa.int/download-file?filename=sites/default/files/2019-08/137%20DSCFC%2019%20E-%20NATO%20EXERCISES%20EVOLUTION%20AND%20LESSONS%20%20LEARNED%20(EC%20Final%20Rapporteured).pdf.

Martinho, Lara. *NATO's Defence and Related Security Capacity Building (DCB) Initiative: Draft Report*. Brussels: NATO Parliamentary Assembly, 2020. https://www.nato-pa.int/download-file?filename=sites/default/files/2020-06/031%20DSCFC%2020%20E%20-%20NATO%20DCB%20Initiative.pdf.

McLagan, Meg, and Daria Sommers, dirs. *Lioness*. Aired November 13, 2008, on PBS. https://www.pbs.org/independentlens/documentaries/lioness/.

Mehlman, Maxwell J. "Captain America and Iron Man: Biological, Genetic and Psychological Enhancement and the Warrior Ethos." In *Routledge Handbook of Military Ethics*, edited by George Lucas, 406–420. New York: Routledge, 2015.

Miliušas, Vytenis, and Viktor Denisenko. "Strategic Communication of NATO Enhanced Forward Presence Battle Group in Lithuania by Assessment of the Parties Involved in the Process." *Lithuanian Annual Strategic Review* 18, no. 1 (2020): 67–98. https://doi.org/10.47459/lasr.2020.18.4.

Mure, Liis. "NATO's eFP in the Baltic Region." Danish Institute for International Studies. Filmed April 3, 2018. YouTube video, 2:03:49. https://www.youtube.com/watch?v=Ea_OAKgydas&ab_channel=DIISpublish.

Myrttinen, Henri, Lana Khattab, and Jana Naujoks. "Re-thinking Hegemonic Masculinities in Conflict-Affected Contexts." *Critical Military Studies* 3, no. 2 (May 2017): 103–119. https://doi.org/10.1080/23337486.2016.1262658.

Naidu, Maheshvari. "Wrestling with Standpoint Theory . . . Some Thoughts on Standpoint and African Feminism." *Agenda* 83 (2010): 25–30. https://www.tandfonline.com/doi/abs/10.1080/10130950.2010.9676289?casa_token=YR_cQv6xl6MAAAAA:E85HTbqIU5w-ZSNA_UU0Zk607JdGv4PG1LmzjAAJX9NC1n19Dzvih221qwOOk4q4Ptbq5yrvcfDn.

Nalty, Bernard. *Strength for the Fight: A History of Black Americans in the Military*. New York: Free Press, 1986.

NATO. "Resolution 1244 (1999): Adopted by the Security Council at its 4011th Meeting on 10 June 1999." Basic Documents. Updated June 30, 1999. https://www.nato.int/kosovo/docu/u990610a.htm.

NATO. *Strategic Concept for the Defence and Security of the Member of the North Atlantic Treaty Organization*. Lisbon: NATO, 2010. https://www.nato.int/lisbon2010/strategic-concept-2010-eng.pdf.

NATO. *Comprehensive Operational Planning Directive*. Mons, Belgium: Allied Command Operations, 2013. https://www.forsvarsmakten.se/siteassets/english/swedint/engel ska/swedint/courses/nato-copc/07-ch-4-op-v2.0-04-oct-13.pdf.

NATO. *NATO Operations Assessment Handbook*. Brussels, NATO, 2015.

NATO. *NATO Bi-Strategic Command Directive 040-001, Integrating UNSCR 1325 and Gender Perspective into the NATO Command Structure*. Mons, Belgium: SHAPE, 2017. https://www.act.nato.int/images/stories/structure/genderadvisor/nu0761.pdf.

NATO. "Brussels Summit Declaration: Issued by the Heads of State and Government Participating in the Meeting of the North Atlantic Council in Brussels 11–12 July 2018." Last updated August 30, 2018a. https://www.nato.int/cps/en/natohq/official_texts_156 624.htm.

NATO. "Mission." JFC Naples. Accessed September 4, 2018b. https://jfcnaples.nato.int/ kfor/about-us/welcome-to-kfor/mission.

NATO. *The Secretary General's Annual Report 2018*. Brussels: NATO, 2019a. https://www. nato.int/nato_static_fl2014/assets/pdf/pdf_publications/20190315_sgar2018-en.pdf.

NATO. "North Atlantic Treaty: Washington D.C.—4 April 1949." Last updated April 10, 2019b. https://www.nato.int/cps/en/natolive/official_texts_17120.htm.

NATO. *Diversity and Inclusion Annual Report 2019*. Brussels: NATO, 2019c. https://www. nato.int/nato_static_fl2014/assets/pdf/2021/2/pdf/2019-annual-diversity_inclusion_ report.pdf.

NATO. "Views from the Field: Interview with Major-General Jennie Carignan, Commander NATO Mission Iraq, and Major-General Michele Risi, Commander NATO's Mission in Kosovo." In *The Women, Peace and Security Agenda Continues to Have the Power to Transform. We Must Persist in Our Determination to Create Lasting Change*. Brussels: NATO, 2020a. https://www.nato.int/nato_static_fl2014/assets/pdf/ 2020/11/pdf/2011-WPS-Newsletter-Autumn-ENGLISH.pdf.

NATO. "NATO's Role in Kosovo." Last updated November 16, 2020b. https://www.nato. int/cps/en/natolive/topics_48818.htm.

NATO. *The Secretary General's Annual Report: 2020*. Brussels: NATO, 2020c. https://www. nato.int/nato_static_fl2014/assets/pdf/2021/3/pdf/sgar20-en.pdf

NATO. "The NATO Policy on Preventing and Responding to Sexual Exploitation and Abuse." Last updated April 21, 2021a. https://www.nato.int/cps/en/natohq/official_t exts_173038.htm.

NATO. "NATO Policy on Preventing and Responding to Conflict-Related Sexual Violence." Last updated May 31, 2021b. https://www.nato.int/cps/en/natohq/official_ texts_184570.htm.

NATO. *Action Plan for the Implementation of the NATO/EAPC Policy on Women, Peace and Security 2021–2025*. Last updated October 21, 2021c. https://www.nato.int/cps/en/ natohq/official_texts_187485.htm?selectedLocale=en.

NATO. "NATO's Enhanced Forward Presence." March 2021d. https://www.nato.int/nat o_static_fl2014/assets/pdf/2021/3/pdf/2103-factsheet_efp_en.pdf.

NATO. "Brussels Summit Communiqué: Issued by the Heads of State and Government Participating in the Meeting of the North Atlantic Council in Brussels 14 June 2021." Last updated June 24, 2021e. https://www.nato.int/cps/en/natohq/news_185000.htm.

NATO. "Food for Thought Paper: Gender Perspective in the Future of the Alliance." Annex A to IMSM-0521-2021.

NATO. "Madrid Summit Communiqué: Issued by the Heads of State and Governments Participating in the Meeting of the North Atlantic Council in Madrid 29 June 2022." 2022a. https://www.nato.int/cps/en/natohq/official_texts_196951.htm

NATO, *NATO's Eastern Flank: Stronger Defence and Deterrence*. Brussels: NATO, 2022b. https://www.nato.int/nato_static_fl2014/assets/pdf/2022/3/pdf/2203-map-det-def-east.pdf.

NATO Allied Command Operations. *Gender Functional Planning Guide*. Brussels: NATO, 2015. https://www.forsvarsmakten.se/siteassets/english/swedint/engelska/swedint/courses/genad/07-aco-gender-functional-planning-guide.pdf.

NATO Committee on Gender Perspectives—Department Head for Gender in Military Operations and Allied Command Transformation. "Gender Perspective in Military Operations: Strategic/Operational Level." PowerPoint presentation. Accessed September 26, 2019.

NATO/Euro-Atlantic Partnership Council. *NATO/EAPC Women, Peace and Security: Policy and Action Plan*. Brussels: NATO, 2018. https://www.nato.int/nato_static_fl2014/assets/pdf/pdf_2018_09/20180920_180920-WPS-Action-Plan-2018.pdf.

NATO/Euro-Atlantic Partnership Council. *Action Plan for the Implementation of the NATO/EAPC Policy on Women, Peace and Security 2021–2025*. Brussels: NATO, October 2021. https://www.nato.int/cps/en/natohq/official_texts_187485.htm.

NATO Force Integration Unit—Lithuania. "NATO Deterrence and Stability in the Baltic Region." Presentation delivered to the European Business Network, September 27, 2018.

NATO School Oberammergau. "Improving Operational Effectiveness by Integrating Gender Perspective." Course Catalogue. Accessed November 4, 2019. https://www.natoschool.nato.int/Academics/Resident-Courses/Course-Catalogue/Course-description?ID=187&TabId=155&ID=178&Legal-Notice&language=en-US.

Neumayer, Eric, and Thomas Plümper. "The Gendered Nature of Natural Disasters: The Impact of Catastrophic Events on the Gender Gap in Life Expectancy, 1981–2002." *Annals of the Association of American Geographers* 97, no. 3 (2007): 551–556.

Newby, Vanessa F., and Clotile Sebag. "Gender Sidestreaming? Analysing Gender Mainstreaming in National Militaries and International Peacekeeping." *European Journal of International Security* 6 (2021): 148–170.

Newton, Jenny. "The Long Road to Gender Integration in the Canadian Armed Forces." *SITREP* 67, no. 3 (May–June 2007): 3–7. https://ufdcimages.uflib.ufl.edu/AA/00/06/79/21/00019/05-2007.pdf.

NMI GENAD Monthly Report. January 31, 2019 (NATO Unclassified).

Noll, Jörg, Osman Bojang, and Sebastiaan Rietjens. "Deterrence by Punishment or Denial? The eFP Case." In *NL Arms Netherlands Annual Review of Military Studies 2020: Deterrence in the 21st Century—Insights from Theory and Practice*, edited by Frans Osinga and Tim Sweijs, 110–126. The Hague: T.M.C. Asser Press, 2021.

Obradovic, Lana. *Gender Integration in NATO Military Forces: Cross-National Analysis*. London and New York: Routledge, 2014.

Office of NATO Secretary General's Special Representative for Women, Peace and Security. *NATO/EAPC Women, Peace and Security: Policy and Action Plan 2018*. Brussels: NATO, 2018. https://www.nato.int/nato_static_fl2014/assets/pdf/pdf_2018_09/20180920_180920-WPS-Action-Plan-2018.pdf.

Office of NATO Secretary General's Special Representative for Women, Peace and Security. *NATO Gender-Inclusive Language Manual*. Brussels: NATO, 2020.

O'Sullivan, Mila. "'Being Strong Enough to Defend Yourself': Untangling the Women, Peace and Security Agenda amidst the Ukrainian Conflict." *International Feminist Journal of Politics* 21, no. 5 (October 2019): 746–767.

Otto, Diane. "Power and Danger: Feminist Engagement with International Law through the UN Security Council." *Australian Feminist Law Journal* 32, no. 1 (June 2010): 97–121.

Parshar, Sawi. "The WPS Agenda: A Postcolonial Critique." In *The Oxford Handbook of Women, Peace, and Security*, edited Sara E. Davies and Jacqui True, 829–839. New York: Oxford University Press, 2019.

Penttinen, Elina. "Harmless Moments in Peace-Keeping: The Politics of Telling Stories That Do Not Fit into Critical Security Studies Narratives." *Critical Studies on Security* 5, no. 2 (May 2017): 131–144.

Perry, Nick. "Australian Troops Unlawfully Killed 39 Afghan Prisoners, Civilians: Report." *Global News*, November 18, 2020. https://globalnews.ca/news/7471687/australia-troops-afghan-prisoners/.

Peterson, Nolan. "US Fighter Pilots on the Front Lines of Russia's Spy Games." *The Daily Signal*, March 15, 2018. https://www.dailysignal.com/2018/03/15/us-fighter-pilots-front-lines-russias-spy-games/.

PfPC SSRWG and EDWG. *Teaching Gender in the Military: A Handbook*. Geneva: DCAF and PfPC, 2016. https://www.dcaf.ch/sites/default/files/publications/documents/DCAF-PfPC-Teaching-Gender-in-the-Military-Handbook.pdf.

Pottinger, Matt, Hali Jilani, and Claire Russo. "Half Hearted: Trying to Win Afghanistan without Afghan Women." *Small Wars Journal*, February 18, 2010. http://smallwarsjournal.com/jrnl/art/trying-to-win-afghanistan-without-afghan-women.

Pratt, Nicola. "Reconceptualizing Gender, Reinscribing Racial–Sexual Boundaries in International Security: The Case of UN Security Council Resolution 1325 on 'Women, Peace and Security.'" *International Studies Quarterly* 57, no. 4 (December 2013): 772–783.

Pratt, Nicola, and Sophie Ritcher-Devroe. "Critically Examining UNSCR 1325 on Women, Peace and Security." *International Feminist Journal of Politics* 13, no. 4 (December 2011): 489–503.

Prescott, Jody M. "NATO Gender Mainstreaming and the Feminist Critique of the Law of Armed Conflict." *Georgetown Journal of Gender and the Law* 14 (2013a): 85–127. https://heinonline.org/HOL/Page?handle=hein.journals/grggenl14&div=6&g_sent=1&casa_token=eRQLMEkmOC0AAAAA:qmMnvnFh02XxzW7UdIQ2KJY_LYnhiNG1jXI-rGNNbza1__IFQLyQlLosRqKYLkr7TVuZp_kr-mU&collection=journals.

Prescott, Jody. "NATO Gender Mainstreaming: A New Approach to War amongst the People?" *RUSI Journal* 158, no. 5 (2013b): 56–62.

Pryor, John, B. "The Psychosocial Impact of Sexual Harassment on Women in the U.S. Military." *Basic and Applied Psychology* 17, no. 4 (1995): 581–603.

Putin, Vladimir. "Address." In *NATO–Russia Council: Rome Summit 2002*, 17–18. Brussels: NATO Office of Information and Press, 2002. https://www.nato.int/docu/comm/2002/0205-rome/rome-eng.pdf.

Reardon, Betty A., and Asha Hans, eds. *The Gender Imperative: Human Security vs. State Security*. London and New York: Routledge, 2010.

Reeves, Audrey. "Feminist Knowledge and Emerging Governmentality in UN Peacekeeping: Patterns of Cooptation and Empowerment." *International Feminist Journal of Politics* 14, no. 3 (2012): 348–369. https://doi.org/10.1080/14616742.2012.659853.

Ricks, Thomas E. "The Military's Purpose Isn't to Break Things and Kill People, but It Should Be." *Foreign Policy*, September 24, 2015. https://foreignpolicy.com/2015/09/24/the-militarys-purpose-isnt-to-break-things-and-kill-people-but-it-should-be/.

Ringsmose, Jens, and Sten Rynning. "Now for the Hard Part: NATO's Strategic Adaptation to Russia." *Survival* 59, no. 3 (2017): 129–146.

Risse, Thomas. "International Norms and Domestic Change: Arguing and Communicative Behavior in the Human Rights Area." *Politics & Society* 27, no. 4 (December 1999): 529–559.

Risse, Thomas, Stephen C. Ropp, and Kathryn Sikkink. *The Power of Human Rights: International Norms and Domestic Change*. Cambridge: Cambridge University Press, 1999.

Rittinger, Eric. "Arming the Other: American Small Wars, Local Proxies, and the Social Construction of the Principal-Agent Problem." *International Studies Quarterly* 61, no. 2 (June 2017): 396–409.

Rock, David, and Heidi Grant. "Why Diverse Teams Are Smarter." *Harvard Business Review*, November 4, 2016. https://hbr.org/2016/11/why-diverse-teams-are-smarter.

Rostoks, Tom. "Managing Deterrence and Escalation on NATO's Eastern Flank." In *Towards #NATO2020: The Regional Perspective of the Baltic States and Poland*, edited by Māris Andžāns and Mārtiņš Vargulis, 12–22. Riga: Latvian Institute of International Affairs, 2020.

Sasson-Levy, Orna, Yagil Levy, and Edna Lomsky-Feder. "Women Breaking the Silence: Military Service, Gender, and Antiwar Protest." *Gender & Society* 25, no. 6 (2011): 740–763.

Schafranek, Niels. *NATO and EU Training Missions in Iraq—An Opportunity to Enhance Cooperation*. Rome: NATO Defense College, 2019.

Serrano Martínez, Alejandro. "NATO's Level of Ambition in Light of the Current Strategic Context." Master's thesis, School of Advanced Military Studies, 2012. https://apps.dtic.mil/sti/pdfs/ADA566624.pdf.

Šešelgytė, Margarita. "Lithuania as Host Nation." In *Lessons from the Enhanced Forward Presence, 2017–2020*, edited by Alexander Lanoszka, Christian Leuprecht, and Alexander Moens, 71–78. Rome: NATO Defense College, 2020.

Shepherd, Laura J. "Sex, Security, and Superhero(in)es: From 1325 to 1820 and Beyond." *International Feminist Journal of Politics* 13, no. 4 (December 2011): 504–521.

Shepherd, Laura J. "Making War Safe for Women? National Action Plans and the Militarisation of the Women Peace and Security Agenda." *International Political Science Review* 37, no. 3 (2016): 324–335.

Shepherd, Laura J. "WPS and Adopted Security Council Resolutions." In *The Oxford Handbook of Women, Peace, and Security*, edited by Sara E. Davies and Jacqui True, 98–109. New York: Oxford University Press, 2019.

Shepherd, Laura J., and Jacqui True. "The Women Peace and Security Agenda and Australian Leadership in the World: From Rhetoric to Commitment." *Australian Journal of International Affairs* 68, no. 3 (May 2014): 257–284.

Shlapak, David A., and Michael W. Johnson. *Reinforcing Deterrence on NATO's Eastern Flank: Wargaming the Defense of the Baltics*. Santa Monica, CA: RAND Corporation, 2016. https://www.rand.org/content/dam/rand/pubs/research_reports/RR1200/RR1253/RAND_RR1253.pdf.

Shoemaker, Meaghan. "Are Her Boots on the Ground? Women's Deployment on NATO-led Operations." Ph.D. Dissertation. Kingston: Queen's University, 2021.

Simić, Olivera. "Does the Presence of Women Really Matter? Towards Combating Male Sexual Violence in Peacekeeping Operations." *International Peacekeeping* 17, no. 2 (2010): 188–199.

Sion, Liora. "Peacekeeping and the Gender Regime: Dutch Female Peacekeepers in Bosnia and Kosovo." *Journal of Contemporary Ethnography* 37, no. 5 (October 2008): 561–585.

Sjoberg, Laura. *Gender and International Security: Feminist Perspectives*. New York: Routledge, 2010.

Sjoberg, Laura. *Gender, War & Conflict*. Cambridge: Polity, 2014.

Sjoberg, Laura. "Seeing Sex, Gender and Sexuality in International Security." *International Journal* 70, no. 3 (2015): 434–453.

Sjoberg, Laura, and Caron E. Gentry. *Mothers, Monsters, Whores: Women's Violence in Global Politics*. London and New York: Zed Books, 2007.

Sjoberg, Laura, and Caron E. Gentry. "Reduced to Bad Sex: Narratives of Violent Women from the Bible to the War on Terror." *International Relations* 22, no. 1 (2008): 5–23.

Skeates, Stuart. "Command Group Corner." *Northern Star*, March 2019.

Special Inspector General for Afghanistan Reconstruction. *Quarterly Report to the United States Congress*. Arlington, VA: SIGAR, 2016. https://sigar.mil/pdf/quarterlyreports/2016-10-30qr.pdf.

Standing Committee on National Defence. *Canada and NATO: An Alliance Forged in Strength and Reliability*. Ottawa: Standing Committee on National Defence, 2018. https://www.ourcommons.ca/DocumentViewer/en/42-1/NDDN/report-10/page-63#_ftnref193.

Stockholm International Peace Research Institute. "World Military Spending Rises to Almost $2 Trillion in 2020." April 26, 2021. https://www.sipri.org/media/press-release/2021/world-military-spending-rises-almost-2-trillion-2020.

Stoicescu, Kalev, and Pauli Järvenpää. *Contemporary Deterrence: Insights and Lesson from Enhanced Forward Presence*. Tallinn, Estonia: International Centre for Defence and Security, 2019. https://icds.ee/wp-content/uploads/2019/01/ICDS_Report_Contempo rary_Deterrence_Stoicescu_J%C3%A4rvenp%C3%A4%C3%A4_January_2019.pdf.

Stoltenberg, Jens. "Digital Dialogue about the Future of Women, Peace and Security at NATO." NATO Zoom webinar. October 15, 2020. https://www.youtube.com/watch?v=3HuHZQBCmM8

Stoltenberg, Jens, and Angelina Jolie. "Why NATO Must Defend Women's Rights." *The Guardian*, December 10, 2017. https://www.theguardian.com/commentisfree/2017/dec/10/why-nato-must-defend-womens-rights.

Swedish Armed Forces. *Whose Security? Practical Examples of Gender Perspectives in Military Operations*. Kungsängen, Sweden: Nordic Centre for Gender in Military Operations, 2015.

Swedish Armed Forces. *Course Catalogue 2016–2017*. Kungsängen, Sweden: Swedish Armed Forces International Centre and Nordic Centre for Gender in Military Operations, 2016.

Tickner, J. Ann. *A Feminist Voyage through International Relations*. New York: Oxford University Press, 2014.

Tiessen, Rebecca. "Gender Essentialism in Canadian Foreign Aid Commitments to Women, Peace, and Security." *International Journal* 70, no. 1 (March 2015): 84–100. https://doi.org/10.1177/0020702014564799.

Titunik, Regina F. "The Myth of the Macho Military." *Polity* 40, no. 2 (April 2008): 137–163.

Traynor, Ian. "Fourteen Dead as Ethnic Violence Sweeps Kosovo." *The Guardian*, March 18, 2004. https://www.theguardian.com/world/2004/mar/18/balkans.

True, Jacqui. "Mainstreaming Gender in Global Public Policy." *International Feminist Journal of Politics* 5, no. 3 (2003): 321–344.

Tryggestad, Torunn L. "Trick or Treat? The UN and Implementation of Security Council Resolution 1325 on Women, Peace, and Security." *Global Governance* 15, no. 4 (2009): 539–557.

United Nations. "Landmark Resolution on Women, Peace and Security." Office of the Special Adviser on Gender Issues and Advancement of Women, 2000. https://www.un.org/womenwatch/osagi/wps/.

United Nations. "System-wide Strategy on Gender Parity." n.d. https://www.un.org/gender/.

United Nations Department of Peace Operations. *Uniformed Gender Parity Strategy 2018–2028*. New York: United Nations, 2018. https://peacekeeping.un.org/sites/defaul/files/uniformed-gender-parity-2018-2028.pdf.

United Nations Peacekeeping. "Women in Peacekeeping." United Nations Department of Peacekeeping. Accessed October 10, 2019. https://peacekeeping.un.org/en/women-peacekeeping.

UN Women. "HeForShe." Accessed January 23, 2016. http://www.heforshe.org/en/our-mission (webpage discontinued).

US Equal Employment Opportunity Commission. "Charges Alleging Sex-Based Harassment (Charges Filed with EEOC) FY 2010—FY 2019." Accessed September 26, 2019. https://www.eeoc.gov/eeoc/statistics/enforcement/sexual_harassment_new.cfm.

Valenius, Johanna. "A Few Kind Women: Gender Essentialism and Nordic Peacekeeping Operations." *International Peacekeeping* 14 (2007): 510–523.

Van Creveld, Martin. *The Culture of War*. New York: Ballantine Books, 2008.

Väyrynen, Tarja. "Gender and UN Peace Operations: The Confines of Modernity." *International Peacekeeping* 11, no. 1 (2004): 125–142.

Vilardo, Valeria, and Sara Bittar. *Gender Profile—Iraq: A Situation Analysis on Gender Equality and Women's Empowerment in Iraq*. Oxford: Oxfam International, 2018.

Wadham, Ben, Donna Bridges, Anuradha Mundkur, and James Connor. "'War-Fighting and Left-Wing Feminist Agendas': Gender and Change in the Australian Defence Force." *Critical Military Studies* 4, no. 3 (2018): 264–280.

Watson, Angus. "Long a Source of National Pride, the Moral Integrity of Australia's Military Is Now at Stake." CNN, November 20, 2020. https://www.cnn.com/2020/11/20/australia/australia-afghanistan-war-crimes-report-analysis-intl-hnk/index.html.

Wattie, Chris. "Bringing a Knife to a Gunfight: Canadian Strategic Communications and Information Operations in Latvia, Operation *Reassurance* 2019–2020." *Canadian Military Journal* 21, no. 1 (2020): 55–62.

Weitz, Rose. "Vulnerable Warriors: Military Women, Military Culture, and Fear of Rape." *Gender Issues* 32, no. 1 (2015): 164–183. https://doi.org/10.1007/s12147-015-9137-2.

Welsh, Sandy. "Gender and Sexual Harassment." *Annual Review of Sociology* 25 (1999): 169–190.

Wenger, Etienne. *Communities of Practice: Learning, Meaning, and Identity*. Cambridge: Cambridge University Press, 1998.

Whitworth, Sandra. *Men, Militarism, and UN Peacekeeping*. Boulder, CO, and London: Lynne Rienner Publishers, 2004.

Whitworth, Sandra. "Militarized Masculinities and the Politics of Peacekeeping." In *Critical Security Studies and World Politics*, edited by Ken Booth, 89–106. Boulder, CO: Lynne Rienner Publishers, 2005.

"Why Nations That Fail Women Fail." *The Economist*, September 11, 2021. https://www. economist.com/leaders/2021/09/11/why-nations-that-fail-women-fail.

Wiener, Antje. *The Invisible Constitution of Politics: Contested Norms and International Encounters*. Cambridge: Cambridge University Press, 2008.

Williams, Holly. "From the Trenches of Russia's Undeclared War on Ukraine, a Warning for America about Putin's Intentions." CBS News, June 15, 2021. https://www.cbsnews. com/news/biden-putin-meeting-russia-intentions-ukraine-war-zelenskyy-cbs/.

Women's International League for Peace & Freedom. "1325 National Action Plans (NAPs)." http://1325naps.peacewomen.org.

Wright, Katharine A. M. "NATO's Adoption of UNSCR 1325 on Women, Peace and Security: Making the Agenda a Reality." *International Political Science Review* 37, no. 3 (2016): 350–361.

Wright, Katherine A. M., Matthew Hurley, and Jesus Ignacio Gil Ruiz. *NATO, Gender and the Military: Women Organising from Within*. New York: Routledge, 2019.

Index